Other Continental Commentaries from Fortress Press

Genesis 1–11
Claus Westermann

Genesis 12–36
Claus Westermann

Genesis 37–50
Claus Westermann

Psalms 1–59
Hans-Joachim Kraus

Psalms 60–150
Hans-Joachim Kraus

Theology of the Psalms
Hans-Joachim Kraus

Isaiah 1–12
Hans Wildberger

Obadiah and Jonah
Hans Walter Wolff

Haggai
Hans Walter Wolff

Micah
Hans Walter Wolff

Matthew 1–7
Ulrich Luz

GALATIANS

DIETER LÜHRMANN

GALATIANS

A Continental Commentary

Translated by

O. C. Dean, Jr.

FORTRESS PRESS
MINNEAPOLIS

To Egon Brandenburger

GALATIANS
A Continental Commentary

First Fortress Press edition 1992

Translated from *Der Brief an die Galater,* second edition, published by Theologischer Verlag Zurich in the Zürcher Bibelkommentare series.

Copyright © 1978, 1988 by Theologischer Verlag Zurich. English translation copyright © 1992 Augsburg Fortress, Publishers, Minneapolis.

Library of Congress Cataloging-in-Publication Data

Lührmann, Dieter.
    [Brief an die Galater. English]
    Galatians: a continental commentary / Dieter Lührmann ;
translated by O.C. Dean, Jr. — 1st Fortress Press ed.
        p.   cm. — (Continental Commentaries)
    Translation of: Der Brief an die Galater.
    Includes index.
    ISBN 0–8006–9618–2 (alk. paper) :
    1. Bible. N.T. Galatians—Commentaries. I. Bible. N.T.
Galatians. English. Revised Standard. 1992. II. Title.
III. Series.
BS2685.3.L8313   1992
227'.4077—dc   92–3070
                                                                                CIP

Manufactured in the U.S.A.   AF 1–9618

96   95   94   93   92   1   2   3   4   5   6   7   8   9   10

Contents

Prefaces   vii

INTRODUCTION   **1**

The Content of the Letter   1
The Beginnings of the Churches in Galatia   2
The Time and Place of Composition   3
The Occasion for the Letter   3
The Significance of the Letter   4
The Interpretation of the Letter   4

COMMENTARY   **7**

The Opening of the Letter (1:1-5)   7
The Occasion for the Letter (1:6-10)   11
The Gospel: Faith or Law? (1:11—5:12)   14
The Thesis (1:11-12)   16
The Way of the Gospel from Damascus
    to Galatia (1:13—2:21)   20
Paul's History before His Arrival in Galatia   20
Paul's Life before His Conversion (1:13-14)   28
Conversion and Initial Missionary Activity
    in Arabia (1:15-17)   29
The First Visit to Jerusalem (1:18-20)   32
Missionary Activity in Syria and Cilicia (1:21-24)   35
The Second Journey to Jerusalem (2:1-10)   37
The Conflict in Antioch (2:11-21)   43
Questions to the Galatians (3:1-5)   51
The Blessing of Abraham and the Curse of the Law (3:6-14)   55
Abraham's Inheritance and the Law (3:15—4:7)   66
The Promise (3:15-18)   68

Contents

The Law (3:19-22)   71
Faith (3:23-29)   74
Abraham's Inheritance (4:1-7)   79
The Conversion of the Galatians (4:8-20)   82
Hagar and Sarah (4:21-31)   88
Freedom from the Law (5:1-12)   94
Life in Freedom (5:13—6:10)   100
Love as the Realization of Freedom (5:13-15)   102
Flesh or Spirit (5:16-24)   106
Life in the Spirit (5:25—6:10)   114
Postscript in Paul's Own Hand (6:11-18)   119

The Galatians' Alternative: Gospel versus Gospel   123
Paul's Career   135
Map   136
Bibliography   137
Index of Biblical References   155
Index of Names and Subjects   159

Preface to the
Fortress Press Edition

The German original of this commentary (1978, 2nd ed. 1988) is part of
the series *Zürcher Bibelkommentare,* which is intended to introduce New
Testament scholarship to readers familiar neither with the technical
terms of exegesis nor with Greek as the language of the New Testament
writings. Thus the interpreter's task is to transfer the highly sophisticated
means of scholarship into suggestions plausible for any interested reader.
I am very glad that the English translation will become part of a series
with comparable aims.

The bibliographic notes give some hints to literature available in
English. Some of those readers may discover that my interpretation is
quite "Lutheran," not least in my understanding of Paul's conception of
faith (on this see my article "Faith (NT)" in the *Anchor Bible Dictionary*).
The German version of this commentary, however, appeared in a pub-
lishing house that is deeply indebted to the Zwinglian heritage, having its
basis in the *Zürcher Bibel,* the frequently revised edition of Zwingli's
translation of the Bible.

I intended to present a theological interpretation of one of the
fundamental documents not only of a specific Lutheran tradition but of
Christianity in general, and at the same time I intended to take seriously
Paul's claim in this very letter that there is no other gospel than the one
whose truth he had defended for the Galatians. Others may thus determine to what degree my interpretation is Lutheran or not.

The first edition of my commentary in German almost coincided
with the appearance of Hans Dieter Betz's great commentary on Galatians in the Hermeneia series (Philadelphia: Fortress, 1979; German
translation, Munich: Kaiser, 1988). At that time I knew Betz's view of
Galatians from some previous articles, especially "The Literary Composition and Function of Paul's Letter to the Galatians" (*New Testament*

Studies 21 [1974/75] 353–79) on Galatians as an "apologetic letter." I did not follow this line, though his commentary gives more evidence, because I still see some difference between rhetorical genres and epistolography. That the debate following Betz's commentary has shown that Galatians may even fit other rhetorical classifications indicates a certain degree of weakness in such a rhetorical approach. Paul writes his other letters according to the structures of the ancient "letter of friendship" (see pp. 11 and 100). Galatians, however, is a notable exception. His connections to the Galatians are no longer those of friendship (see Betz on 4:12–20). Paul seems not to be in an apologetic position but argues quite strongly against those who proclaim another gospel and against his readers who are considering converting to this other gospel, which in his view is not a gospel.

My own proposal for an outline of the letter is not only to take chapters 1 and 2 as autobiographical but to consider the sequence from 1:11 through at least 5:1 as the way of the gospel to the Galatians, from Paul's conversion to his arrival in Galatia. Thus 1:11—5:12 (or 4:31?) can be seen as a unit in which Paul explains to his readers what is the "truth of the gospel." This is followed by 5:13 (or 5:1)—6:10, which is concerned with the question what it is to live according to the Spirit, which the Galatians had received by the gospel and not by the law.

This commentary for readers in the English-speaking world is for those concerned with single pericopes as well as for those who read Galatians as a whole. In interpreting this document, I hope my reading may help others to grasp the message of Paul's letter, one that reflects a crisis not restricted to early Christianity.

Dieter Lührmann

Preface to the
Second German Edition

This commentary has now been continuously sold and read for ten years —read, as I had hoped, not only on specific passages but as a whole. As far as I can see, it has been generally well received. This second edition has given me the opportunity to undertake some changes, which result from more recent scholarship. However, the fundamental intent remains the same, which is not to trace back the contingent aspects of the letter, either historically or psychologically, but to bring the letter to expression within the context of present-day theological discussion.

Inseparably bound up with this commentary are memories of my years in Bethel. There I profited from collegial discussions with Ulrich Luck, Hans Heinrich Schmid, and Fritz Stolz, to whom I extend my thanks, as also to Helmut Krämer for his correction of my translations. It is appropriate that after ten more years of discussion with him, I can renew the dedication of this volume to Egon Brandenburger on the occasion of his sixtieth birthday.

Dieter Lührmann

Preface to the
First German Edition

The writer of a commentary would like to have readers who read through the work from front to back, as they would a normal book. In actual use, however, it often seems that the reader is merely looking for the interpretation of a particular passage. In seeking to meet both needs, repetitions have been unavoidable, and cross-references necessary.

Although the author naturally has to assume responsibility for his book, this commentary would have been unthinkable without the cooperative effort of many people. The dedication to Egon Brandenburger is made in gratitude for many years of discussion about Paul and his theology. Colleagues and friends of recent years—Ulrich Luck, Hans Heinrich Schmid, and Fritz Stolz—will also recognize many a statement that perhaps one of them first formulated in that way.

Finally, I would like to point to Walther Zimmerli's interpretation of the Old Testament stories of Abraham, also appearing in the Zürcher Bibelkommentare. Paul is occupied with the reinterpretation of these old stories in extensive passages in his Letter to the Galatians. How he does this becomes much clearer if one first reads the Abraham story for itself and not just through Paul's interpretation.

Dieter Lührmann

Introduction

The Content of the Letter

Sometimes we may expect to receive a certain letter and yet hesitate to open it when it arrives because we do not know what it will say. Such may have been the situation, sometime during the fifties of the first century, when someone in a village in the middle of Asia Minor received a small packet. It contained a letter from Paul, who had rather reluctantly missionized in that region several years earlier, and it was addressed to the churches that arose at that time. We do not know who first opened the packet, nor do we know how its contents were used; we do not even know exactly where and when Paul wrote it.

One thing that the first reader must have noticed immediately on thumbing through the letter was the change in handwriting. Paul had written the last lines of the letter (6:11-18) with his own hand, briefly summarizing what, in his opinion, was at stake. Then he closed with a blessing, without adding a personal greeting to anyone in Galatia or a greeting from any of those who had been with him in those days in Galatia.

When the reader then perused the letter from the beginning, it was apparent that after Paul's usual epistolary opening (1:1-5) he did not begin by giving thanks but instead immediately took his addressees strongly to task (1:6-10) because they had so quickly fallen away from the gospel that he had proclaimed to them, even though there really was no other gospel. Then Paul gave an account of his journey to them with the gospel (1:11—2:21), becoming more detailed as he began to speak of Jerusalem.

As Paul's report reached the time when he missionized in Galatia, he asked his readers pointed questions (3:1-5) that could only have rhetorical meaning; for Paul the unequivocal answers must come from the gospel. Did the Spirit his readers possess come from works of the law or from the preaching of faith, in which Paul proclaimed to them the crucified One?

The gospel, as the gospel of Christ, is the antithesis of the law, as Paul demonstrated from the law itself through the person of Abraham. The promise to Abraham of an inheritance belongs to those who are of faith; the law, for its part, cannot bring life (3:6—4:7). But, Paul continued, the Galatians have fallen back again; he feared that he labored in vain for them, and he recalled for them the circumstances under which he himself worked with them and how they received him (4:8-20)—he was at a loss to think that all his efforts had been in vain. Then once again in his scriptural interpretation he returned to the theme of Jerusalem (4:21-31) before going into the main point of contention: the question of adopting circumcision (5:1-12).

Freedom (5:1) is the heading for the actual conclusion of the letter (5:13—6:10), in which Paul described the life of the faithful according to the Spirit they possess. Then follows the closing in his own hand (6:11 - 18).

We do not know the reaction of the first reader or the reaction of the churches to whom it was supposed to be read. Did they accept Paul's reproach, or did they feel themselves misunderstood and remain with that "other" gospel, which they perhaps did not consider so fundamentally different from the gospel of Paul? How did matters come to such a pass that Paul found it necessary to write this letter?

The Beginnings of the Churches in Galatia

From the letter itself we learn a little of Paul's history. After long years of activity in and around Antioch, Paul had left this community, perhaps in the year 49. He set out by land straight through Asia Minor in a westward direction, perhaps with the goal of arriving as quickly as possible in Rome, the capital of the empire. On his way he may have stopped in Galatia because of illness (4:13-14) but was able to evangelize there nonetheless, an astonishing feat, even for him.

This Galatia is in the general area of the present Turkish capital of Ankara. It was a rather inhospitable, mountainous region where, centuries before, the Celtic tribes threatening Greece and Asia Minor from the North had been repelled (their name, *Galatians*, certainly has something to do with Gaul or the Celts). That was long ago, and now, after a history full of change, the region formed the central district of a larger Roman province of the same name; Paul had already evangelized a few years earlier in the southern part, in the area of Lycaonia.

When Paul departed from Galatia, he left behind churches with whom he remained in contact and whom he involved in the support for the Jerusalem church agreed upon earlier by Antioch and Jerusalem (1 Cor. 16:1). In the following years Paul worked in cities around the Aegean Sea, in Philippi and Thessalonica in Macedonia, then a year and a half in Corinth, the capital of the Roman province of Achaia, and more than two years in Ephesus, the provincial capital across the sea on the coast of Asia Minor.

Out of these years, perhaps amounting to six or seven, come the Pauline letters of our New Testament, and also in this region the Pauline inheritance was preserved in the following generations. It is doubtful whether during this time, as Luke reports (Acts 18:18-23), Paul made another journey to the East and on the way back to Ephesus also visited the Galatian churches again (see below under 4:13).

In any case, suspicion is raised by the lack of precision in Luke's description of this journey, especially in its formulation, which is repeatedly paralleled by the reports of other journeys. For Luke the reason for this roundabout trip of Paul's may have lain in the need to have Paul also work before Apollos in Ephesus, so that here as elsewhere Paul appears as the first witness to the gospel.

The Time and Place of Composition

At some time during this period of his activity around the Aegean, Paul must have received news of the dangerous developments in the Galatian churches. The most probable time to assume is after the writing of the First Letter to the Corinthians, since Paul still presupposes here that the Galatians will also participate in the planned collection (1 Cor. 16:1), while the Galatians are no longer mentioned in 2 Corinthians 8 and 9 and in Rom. 15:26, but only Macedonians and Achaians.

Thus the Letter to the Galatians must have been written before the letter that Paul wrote to the Christians in Rome, for in that one he reflects again—but without any concrete disagreement—on the basic issues that were raised by the events in Galatia. Thus the time of composition of Galatians must be placed in the period 52 to 56. It was written from Ephesus or Corinth or somewhere on one of Paul's journeys between these two cities.

The Occasion for the Letter

We do not know how Paul learned of the happenings in Galatia. Since he makes no reference to a letter that might have reached him from there, there was probably also no written inquiry from the Galatian churches concerning how they should act. We have no information from any other hand and for the reconstruction of events are dependent solely on Paul's side of the story. This is all the more troublesome in a letter because, unlike in a memorandum or some other more impersonal form, the happenings that interest us do not need to be described by the writer for the addressee: they both know what the issue is.

We can see, nonetheless, that these Gentile Christian churches (cf. 4:8) have in the meantime received other Christian missionaries who, beyond the apparently uncontested act of baptism (cf. 3:27), apparently require circumcision (5:2-12; 6:12-13) and prescribe the observance of days, months, seasons, and years (4:10). At least for Paul this teaching raises the fundamental question of the law, even if the others do not regard it as so fundamental (cf. 5:3). In hardly any other dispute with opponents does he define the alternatives more clearly; he even suspects that the problem lies with witchcraft (cf. 3:1) and puts it all down as a reversion to idolatry (cf. 4:9).

That Paul tells about himself and his experience with the gospel in such long passages, with the declaration that what he writes is true (cf. 1:20), indicates that he must counter false rumors about himself and his gospel. Finally, even on first perusal of the content, one notices how warmly Paul speaks of Jerusalem; apparently some in Galatia had other assessments of the Jerusalem church. Whether we can order all these individual observations into a historically plausible picture of the opponents will be seen at the close of the commentary after detailed interpretation of all the phenomena discussed.

The Significance of the Letter

As already indicated, we do not know whether Paul did justice to what happened in Galatia or how the recipients of the letter reacted. More important, however, than the historical question of the origin of his opponents and the religious-historical classification of their proclamation is the way Paul develops the gospel in this letter. Later collectors of his letters, who—had they wanted—could have made corrections here and there, believed they should forgo that opportunity; they wanted to let Paul continue to speak for himself.

In this collection of Pauline letters, the Letter to the Galatians is the one that most clearly makes the antithesis between law and faith in Christ the standard for Christianity and prepares the way for the Letter to the Romans. Independent of any situation, in Romans Paul can reflect again on this antithesis, occasionally correcting himself in the process; here he includes especially certain themes that scarcely come into view in Galatians: the doctrine of humanity and the related question of sin (Romans 5–8), the question of the positive significance of the law (Romans 7), which he thoroughly disputed in Galatians, and the question of Israel, the originally intended recipient of the promises of the law (Romans 9–11).

In Romans, however, Paul did not relinquish the position he reached in the Letter to the Galatians, for this was taken for granted by him, from Damascus on, in his own turning from the way of the law toward faith in Christ (cf. Gal. 1:11-16). Also, no other extant letter is as biographical as this one; as will be seen, only with its help is it possible to reconstruct broad stretches of Paul's career. One wishes, naturally, that he had told more about his years in the province of Arabia (cf. 1:17) or in Syria and Cilicia (cf. 1:21). The reason why he does not lies in the fact that he is writing all of this not to give information about his life but, through his own biography, to make clear to his readers the gospel and the fundamental alternatives that it poses. What that means may likewise become clearer in a closing summary after detailed interpretation.

The Interpretation of the Letter

When one undertakes a new interpretation of this letter, one should resist the temptation to slip into the role of Paul vis-à-vis one's readers; one should instead stand together with them alongside the original readers. It probably required a great deal of effort for them to understand what Paul intended and especially why he regarded the current situation so much more seriously than they presumably did.

Also, they occasionally may have felt overtaxed by Paul when once again he did not expressly establish certain intellectual presuppositions or when he drew conclusions that went beyond the current situation. Nevertheless, compared with us later readers, they had the advantage of knowing Paul and his gospel personally and likewise the advantage of being able to understand immediately the manifold references to their relatively short yet exciting experience with the gospel.

The early copyists and collectors of Paul's letters felt that this letter went beyond the immediate occasion of its writing in its formulation of basic Christian assertions, and therefore they handed it down from generation to generation. Thus it passed into new situations with new issues and new presuppositions, and yet from time to time it was pushed to the side to stand ready when someone again went to it seeking answers. In this light we must especially keep in mind the significance of the Letter to the Galatians for Luther's understanding of the gospel.

A new interpretation is thus always an attempt at a new appropriation beyond the purely historical reconstruction of the original relations between Paul and the Galatian churches. That appropriation is shaped—certainly more unconsciously than consciously—by the history that has transmitted this letter to us. The interpretations of history, in their strengths as well as in their weaknesses, determine our own approach. Now, as then, a major role is played by the confessional context out of which certain issues are clarified and various assessments of particular relationships are given.

Naturally, this confessional context is also one historically transmitted by contact with Christianity in general, with the Bible, with Paul, and with the Letter to the Galatians in particular. The transmission occurs in preaching and teaching and involves interpretations that have probably been much more effective than those one hears in academic lectures and reads in commentaries. Yet the latter have themselves had a shaping influence on the less controllable kinds of transmission and in their time were at least expressions of certain contemporary expectations, issues, and general convictions.

In the face of such considerations, it will be difficult to find a common, obligatory point of departure for an interpretation. The style of the commentary series in which this interpretation appears has the advantage of letting the author and reader confront the letter itself and not primarily its interpreters. At the same time, however, the danger arises that the interpretation will be identified with the letter itself. At this point it is perhaps helpful to list explicitly six presuppositions that govern the interpretation of Galatians presented below.

1. To begin with, the letter was intended for churches of another time and not directly for us present-day readers. Hence, we cannot in advance exclude the possibility that it will not take up our questions and that for us other texts or groups of texts in the Bible could be more relevant at the moment. Conversely, however, this letter could also possibly steer our current questions in another direction. In any case, a commentary should attempt to trace the questions and answers of that time without forcing the letter to speak directly to today's issues.

2. Beyond the historical situation we must also express clearly what was crucial for Paul, namely, the gospel. An interpretation cannot be content with the goal of either reconstructing events or emphasizing the psychology of Paul, when Paul himself identifies something else as the

subject of his letter. Such an approach goes beyond the method of the commentary and makes an a priori decision about the nature of Pauline theology.

3. Paul founds his gospel on the law and asserts that the Old Testament can be understood correctly only in relation to Christ. This thesis will have to be taken seriously in the interpretation, which therefore will have to consider in some detail Paul's use of the Old Testament if it is to do justice to its objective.

4. If we as readers of today are basically in a position no different from that of the original recipients, then the commentary must also place itself beside the Galatians and pursue the question of how they may have understood what Paul wanted, rather than trying to understand Paul apart from that. To be sure, we know the Galatians less well than we know Paul. Yet throughout the letter he appeals expressly to their judgment. That provides a glimpse of what Paul thinks he can presuppose about them as a basis for his argumentation. For example, it was apparently not the opponents who had first referred to the Old Testament, but Paul had left the Abraham stories with the Galatians as a text from which he confirmed the gospel.

5. In accordance with the history through which this letter has been transmitted to us, the interpretation must take into consideration what associations we make with the great key words of the letter, such as *faith, law, righteousness, freedom*. Many of them may seem to us trite or ambiguous, as does also, perhaps, the greater matter of justification itself. We must first clarify these associations, as well as the causes of the presumed ambiguity, so that we can grasp what Paul himself means by these terms.

6. It is usual for Paul's letters to have the structure of the ancient "friendship letter," but this does not hold for Galatians (see below, pp. 11 and 100); the friendship which once bound Paul and his readers seems to him to have been terminated by reason of their turning away to new teachers (cf. 4:16). One may discern, however, two main parts in the letter: 1:11—5:12 sets forth the fundamental alternative—faith or law—which Paul substantiates first with reference to his own life and then with his interpretation of the Abraham stories; and 5:13—6:10 sets forth the ethical consequences of this alternative. The exposition follows this two-fold division of the letter's contents.

The Opening of the Letter

Text

1:1 Paul an apostle—sent neither by human commission nor from human authorities, but through Jesus Christ and God the Father, who raised him from the dead—

2 and all the members of God's family who are with me, to the churches of Galatia:

3 Grace to you and peace from God our Father and the Lord Jesus Christ,

4 who gave himself for our sins to set us free from the present evil age, according to the will of our God and Father;

5 to whom be the glory forever and ever. Amen.

Form

When one writes a letter, one uses a particular form, whoever the intended recipient may be, and whatever the occasion—the only exceptions are very personal letters. The opening of a letter includes several essential elements: information about the sender and the addressee, the time and place of writing, a salutation to the addressee, and a reference to the occasion for the letter. Similarly, the closing of the letter is made up of certain elements: a greeting, signature, and perhaps postscripts or the mention of enclosures.

In all the letters of Paul the opening is constructed according to the following format:

> sender (often, as here, with mention of others) in the nominative (1:2a)
> addressee in the dative (2b)
> a blessing in a new sentence (3)

This format occurs in its shortest form in 1 Thess. 1:1; the most extended version is Rom. 1:1-7.

Before Paul, this format is to be found neither in Greek nor in eastern letters. While the normal Greek opening of a letter (as seen in the New Testament in Acts 15:23; 23:26; and Jas. 1:1) likewise includes the sender in the nominative and the addressee in the dative, these are not followed by a second sentence, but by an infinitive that can be rendered "greetings."

The verb used here comes from the same stem as the first noun in the Pauline blessing, which is translated "grace." Hence, the Pauline format can be interpreted as a variation of the usual Greek opening. But where does the blessing in the second sentence come from? It is familiar to us as a liturgical formula, often used at the beginning of a sermon. Perhaps it already had a similar function in the early Christian service of worship.

Structure

The simple basic structure of the format is expanded here, as also in other letters, with the following three additions:

1. the apposition of apostle (v. 1)
2. the christological assertion (v. 4)
3. the praise of God (v. 5)

1. **[1:1]** The information about the sender contains an addition in the form "not . . . but . . ."; it explains how Paul understands his function as apostle. He will soon give a very similar explanation in vv. 11-12, related there to the gospel he proclaims. This shows that for Paul, apostle and gospel belong close together and, at the same time, that even in his opening Paul is addressing a controversial theme—not arguing as he does later, but asserting. He is underscoring his independence. His readers in Galatia of course know quite well what reproaches he is responding to. Since we are not in their situation, very little can be said about the nature of these reproaches on the basis of v. 1.

The formulation of the *but* phrase is not an isolated instance but is often found in Paul in this or a similar form (cf., for example, Rom. 4:24). It has the sound of a formula and, in terms of content and composition, provides a common, undisputed basis for writer and reader, which can serve as the groundwork for the following argumentation.

2. **[1:4]** The same is true of the christological assertion, which speaks of the death of Christ and of the meaning of his death for believers. We will often find similar statements throughout the letter. Especially to be noted in v. 4 is the emphasis on the "present evil age" and thus on the opposition between Christ and this world. Here too the readers in Galatia could recognize even at the beginning of the letter a theme that played a role in the disagreement. Once again, for us as later readers, it is not possible to assess accurately the exact aim of this assertion.

3. **[1:5]** The opening of the letter ends with praise of God, which, from a grammatical point of view, could also be for Christ. Since Paul, in adopting Jewish liturgical language, otherwise applies such doxologies only to God, that is probably also the case here. It may not be accidental that the Greek text repeats the word translated in v. 4 as "age" (KJV: "world") and here as "forever and ever" (literally, "into the ages of the ages"). This word, *aiōn,* has both a spatial and a temporal aspect: over the

aeons, and hence also over the present world, stands the honor, the glory of God.

What is surprising about these additions is precisely that they do not open up Paul's personal agenda but introduce further formulaic expressions. Apparently it is important for Paul—through such language and such a conceptual structure, which bind him with his readers—to achieve a common understanding that will make possible an agreement on controversial points. Apart from the "not . . . but . . ." construction, which initially they must take as Paul's thesis, there is nothing here in the opening that his readers could not accept. The difference does not come until later in the letter in the conclusions that are drawn from this common point of departure.

Commentary

[1:2a] Let us now turn to the basic elements of this opening in its particulars, the information about the sender and recipients. As in other letters, Paul names fellow senders, not by name, but as "all the members of God's family who are with me." It is no longer possible for us to determine who was with him at the time of composition of the letter. What he writes with his fellow workers, however, is undisputed, because it concerns the gospel that is the foundation of missionary work in the Pauline churches.

[1:1b] Through the addition in this verse, Paul underscores his self-designation as an apostle, which is also to be found in other letters. For an understanding of *apostle,* we must free ourselves of the normative image of the twelve apostles found in Luke; in Acts 1:21-22 Luke has Peter name the criterion of an apostle: being an eyewitness to the career of Jesus from his baptism by John to his ascension. Paul does not actually meet this criterion, and thus it is only logical that Luke withholds this title from him (except in Acts 14:4, 14). For Paul himself, on the other hand, *apostle* is not so much a title as a functional designation in the sense, say, of a traveling missionary, who can indeed feel that he belongs to a congregation, but whose essential duty is the proclamation of the gospel in mission. For Paul himself this calling is based on his conversion on the road to Damascus, but he does not derive from this event a general norm for the legitimacy of an apostle. When in his letters he has to defend his own claim, he does not do so by appealing to a fixed concept of the office but emphasizes the "truth of the gospel" that he preaches. As the slave of this gospel, he is the representative of the Lord he proclaims.

A real apostle, in distinction to the false apostles (cf. 2 Cor. 11:13), is decided by the relevance of one's proclamation, not by a formal legitimation. Thus an apostle is totally absorbed in the gospel. Although this makes the gospel very personal, as the Letter to the Galatians itself shows, it is at the same time transmittable to others because it rests not just on personal conviction but on the convincing power of its content.

[1:2b] The recipients of the letter are "the churches of Galatia." Missing here are any otherwise possible and usual attributes of honor, the reason for which will soon become clear. The Greek word *ekklēsia,* which was also brought into Latin as a foreign term, is usually translated into English as "church," even when, as here, it refers to individual congregations and not to an abstract entity such as the church at large. In New Testament usage, nonetheless, the individual "church" is the representation of the body of Christ in a particular place.

The word *ekklēsia,* used as the self-designation of the early Christian congregations, also occurs in the sense of a "popular assembly" of the Hellenistic cities. Through the choice of this rather secular term, the churches set themselves apart at the very beginning from both the synagogues of the Jews and the religious gatherings of the Greeks.

Paul writes to several churches about whose beginnings and further connections with him we have information from his letters and from the Acts of the Apostles (see Introduction above). Those preachers of another gospel who came into Galatia found there, in the middle of Asia Minor, an island of Christian churches that they tried to draw into their own missionary work—a process that since then has occurred again and again in many mission fields. An example from the New Testament itself is the missionizing of the disciples of John the Baptist in Ephesus (Acts 19:1-7).

Thus, even in the opening of the letter, there are very particular accents that for us are not as understandable in all their nuances as they were for the original readers. We can recognize, nonetheless, that already at this point Paul is sounding themes from the dispute, and above all that here—in the additions to the usual format for the beginning of a letter and before a word is said in the main body of his letter—Paul is already coming to his subject: the gospel.

The Occasion for the Letter

Text

1:6 I am astonished that you are so quickly deserting the one who called you in the grace of Christ and are turning to a different gospel—

7 not that there is another gospel, but there are some who are confusing you and want to pervert the gospel of Christ.

8 But even if we or an angel from heaven should proclaim to you a gospel contrary to what we proclaimed to you, let that one be accursed!

9 As we have said before, so now I repeat, if anyone proclaims to you a gospel contrary to what you received, let that one be accursed!

10 Am I now seeking human approval, or God's approval? Or am I trying to please people? If I were still pleasing people, I would not be a servant of Christ.

Form

As a rule, one begins a letter by making reference to prior relations with the addressee and, in the process, mentioning the reason for the letter. This normally occurs in the form of a thank you to the addressee, whether in confirmation of a letter received or in thankfulness for the previous history that links the sender and the addressee. Paul too was normally accustomed to opening his letters with thanks, indeed with thanksgiving to God.

Only in exceptional cases will one choose another opening for a letter, whether because there is no previous mutual relationship, or because one does not feel thankful in view of disturbed relations with the addressee. The latter is the case here for Paul: at the moment there is nothing to be thankful for. In turning away to another gospel, the Galatians have surrendered the mutual relationship. Instead of being able to give thanks for their growth in faith, Paul can only be amazed at their rapid falling away.

11

Commentary

[1:6-7] Right at the beginning Paul defines the antithesis very clearly: on the one side, God, Christ, grace, gospel; on the other side, only another gospel—and immediately Paul corrects himself, saying that there can be no other gospel. There can only be those bringing confusion, who want to twist the real gospel. Here we have the first clear indication of the reason for the letter: people have come to Galatia with a gospel different from the one preached by Paul, and they have had quick success among the churches there. Paul can see in them only troublemakers who pervert the gospel, not legitimate witnesses to the one gospel.

[1:8-9] With two solemn curses, however, he excludes completely the possibility of another gospel, even if an angel or Paul himself were to bring it. Such maledictions (cf. 1 Cor. 16:22) call for the ultimate exclusion from salvation. The gospel is the highest court, to which even Paul himself would have to bow, because the apostle is totally absorbed in the gospel. For him the reason for the curse is not that his own gospel is harmed but that the gospel of Christ is and remains the only possible gospel. It is the property of Christ, just as the apostle can be an apostle only as the property of Christ. It is not through the grace of Paul that he has declared himself ready to preach this gospel; rather, the grace of Christ is the content and cause of his preaching.

[1:10] Thus his writing, like his preaching, does not aim at all at pleasing people, but at being a slave of Christ, who is the only content of the gospel. For this very reason Paul also becomes free to polemicize on behalf of the gospel because his own person is totally absorbed in the gospel.

This emotional beginning of the letter may have sounded a little exaggerated to his readers, especially since the suspicion arises that the issue also concerned Paul personally and involved attacks against his character precisely when he identifies himself so strongly with the gospel. Certainly, by disputing the relevance of the gospel preached by Paul, those who bring confusion must have also called his own legitimation into question. Perhaps they also appealed to a higher revelation—for angels apparently play a certain role in the discussion (cf. 3:19)—so that the "angel from heaven" in v. 8 may not be only an invented example but could represent a much more impressive legitimation than the ailing Paul did at the beginning of the churches; yet they received him as an angel (cf. 4:13-14).

Paul, however, sees the matter differently. The dispute is not over his own legitimation but over the legitimacy of the gospel, with which his own stands or falls. But what is the gospel? The Greek *euangelion* has come into English by way of Latin and French as *evangel* (cf. German *Evangelium,* French *évangile*). The more common *gospel* derives from the Old English *godspel* "good talk," and—like the popular phrase *good news*—is based on the etymology of the Greek word. Calling the gospel good news, however, fails to recognize that it is both salvation and disaster, both grace and judgment. To speak only of "good news" removes the harshness and pointedness from the word proclaimed since the Old Testament prophets, whereas Paul can also pronounce the two curses of vv. 8-9 in the name of the gospel and thus voice judgment against those who preach otherwise.

Paul uses the noun both absolutely and more closely defined as the gospel of God or, as here, the gospel of Christ. Until our century the genitive form translated "of Christ" was taken to mean that the gospel referred to is the one that Christ proclaimed. Christianity was rooted in what Jesus himself had said, and theology was thus the development of Jesus' gospel. It seemed at first a purely philological matter when this genitive was redefined as the content of the gospel; that is, the gospel has Christ as its content, not simply as its speaker. Such a new understanding, however, pointed directly to a fundamental revolution in theology as a whole.

Christ (which is also basically a foreign word that has come from the Greek into our language through Latin) is thus for Paul not simply a personal name that is interchangeable with *Jesus;* rather, it still contains the sense of a title as the translation of *Messiah,* or *anointed One.* Hence *Jesus Christ* means Jesus, the eschatological King send by God. For Paul this title is closely linked with assertions about Jesus' death and resurrection: Jesus is Messiah as the one who died and was resurrected by God. This is what Paul, in 1 Cor. 15:1-4, designates as the content of the gospel and of faith, and this content must also be kept in mind wherever Paul speaks of the gospel of Christ or the gospel of God as the author of this salvation event, as well as where he uses the word absolutely.

The gospel of Christ is accordingly an abbreviation that points to the content of the gospel, which has already been alluded to in Paul's additions to the opening (vv. 1b, 4). Thus the gospel, which in his view is perverted by the troublemakers in Galatia, is the proclamation that God has created salvation in the event of Jesus' death and resurrection—abbreviated with the title *Christ*—and nowhere else. For Paul this understanding has consequences in regard to the law and circumcision, which he will then discuss in the following chapters. For him these consequences are already included in the content of the gospel, and those who turn away from the gospel exclude themselves from salvation. Paul reduces the whole dispute with his opponents in Galatia to this core. Right at the beginning he states the alternatives as clearly as possible. He then substantiates these alternatives in the main part of the letter, since the gospel has, for Paul, its own logic: it is not ecstatic babbling or the charismatic execution of maledictory gestures. The foundation of his argumentation is primarily the content of the gospel, the Christology. Subordinated to it are the Scriptures (for him, only the Old Testament) and the history of the gospel in Paul's own history from his conversion before Damascus to his activity in Galatia.

The Gospel:
Faith or Law?

Introduction

The main body of the Letter to the Galatians consists of two parts. The first extends from 1:11 through 5:12 and contains the gospel that Paul preached, which for him is the only gospel. The second, shorter part (5:13—6:10) sets the standards for a life lived in accordance with the Spirit given to Christians. Then follows the closing in Paul's own hand (6:11-18).

Such a two-part division—briefly stated, into doctrine and ethics —is also found in other Pauline letters, most clearly in the Letter to the Romans. The usual division of the Letter to the Galatians, however, is into three parts: 1:11 to 2:21, 3:1 to 4:31 or 5:12, and 5:1 or 5:13 to 6:10. (We may overlook the matter of the beginning of the ethical section, which is variously placed at 5:1 or 5:13.) In apparent support of a three-part division is the fact that Paul argues biographically in 1:11—2:21 but doctrinally starting at 3:1.

The problem with such a division, however, is that Paul's theme in 1:11—2:21 is the same as that of chapters 3 and 4, namely, the question of the relationship between law and gospel. Moreover, there is another connection: after Paul closes the first part with the conflict in Antioch in 2:11-21, in 3:1 he reminds the Galatians of his activity among them— biographically the first important stop after his departure from Antioch. Both thematically and biographically, therefore, there is complete unity in the whole complex of 1:11 to 5:12.

Furthermore, toward the end of the doctrinal part, Paul returns to themes from the beginning of the letter: 4:12-20 points beyond 3:1-5 to 1:6-10; 4:21-31 takes up again, in a different way, the important theme of Jerusalem in 1:11—2:21; with the themes of freedom and love, 5:1-12 achieves, on the one hand, the transition to the ethical part, but like 1:6-10, on the other hand, it gives a direct polemic against the troublemakers

14

in Galatia. In a three-way division these three passages in 4:12 to 5:12 appear to be isolated addenda, but in a two-way division they can be explained as the rounding off of the whole discussion through a return to the beginning.

In 1:6-10 the way has already been prepared for the theme of the first and larger part, 1:11—5:12; namely, the gospel of Christ. The alternative named there—gospel of Christ or some other gospel—now becomes the alternative between faith and law. It is taken up first in 1:11—2:21 in the reproduction of Paul's speech in Antioch, and then it is substantiated from the law itself in chapters 3 and 4. The rather biographical passage 1:11—2:21 is completely subordinated to this theme, for, as we have already seen, the apostle is totally absorbed in the gospel, and thus his biography becomes the way of the gospel.

The Thesis

Text

1:11 For I want you to know, brothers and sisters, that the gospel that was proclaimed by me is not of human origin;

12 for I did not receive it from a human source, nor was I taught it, but I received it through a revelation of Jesus Christ.

Form

At the beginning of the very large first section, Paul places a thesis that he introduces with a solemn-sounding "I want you to know" (cf. 1 Cor. 15:1). Here again he uses the rhetorical device not . . . but . . . , which we encountered in v. 1; there it was related to his function as apostle; here, to the gospel that he preaches. We have already seen, however, how closely the two are related for Paul.

Commentary

[1:11] First, the negation in this verse is similar to v. 1. Compare "neither by human commission nor from human authorities" (v. 1) with "not of human origin" (literally, "not according to man").

[1:12a] In this verse, with the verbs *receive* (which in Greek has the precise sense of "adopt as tradition") and *was taught,* we have two specifications of what Paul means by a "human" gospel. Here, however, his readers had to pay attention, for right at the beginning Paul is rejecting two ways in which the gospel could be completely legitimized and in the history of the church has actually been legitimized: tradition and teaching. What Paul lacks is precisely such demonstrable authority. (How different it was later when the church fathers asserted the propriety of the rules of faith vis-à-vis heretics by referring to genuine tradition and teaching going back to the origins!)

The structure of this sentence suggests that Paul formulated it against his opponents, yet here again we are not in the position of the original readers, who could immediately tell what significance this thesis

16

had. If the opponents there somehow linked the Jewish law with the preaching of Christ, as the following chapters make probable, they could base their "other gospel" on the tradition and teaching of the law—this connection will also play a role in the interpretation of the Jerusalem theme. Paul, however, rejects from the start such a guarantee of his gospel, yet in 1 Cor. 15:1ff. he puts heavy stress on the traditional nature of his gospel.

[1:12b] Opposing this negation is the phrase "through a revelation of Jesus Christ." The usual explanation goes that in this way Paul presents himself as immediately called by God and not, like others, dependent on tradition and teaching. But does not such an interpretation echo too much the modern ideal of the independent personality towering above contemporaries? The difficulties of this explanation are also seen as soon as one asks, Who, then, could have made against Paul the presupposed accusation of dependence? It was certainly not representatives of the law, who would regard tradition and teaching as positive entities and not describe them as "according to man."

Nevertheless, to infer the opposite—that the opponents in no way were representatives of the law but appeared themselves with the claim of an immediate calling by God—would be to draw the wrong conclusion. Then Paul's argumentation would reduce itself, in effect, to a simple "me too." Such a claim, moreover, would be poorly substantiated in what follows; for Paul mentions his calling only very briefly in v. 16, without describing details of the circumstances or naming witnesses to the event. The train of thought of the whole passage leads not to the reception of the gospel but to the presentation of its content as the antithesis of law and faith in 2:15-21.

Hence, Paul's thesis is to be interpreted not apologetically ("me too") but polemically ("I, in contrast to the others"). Also polemical is his evaluation of tradition and teaching as only "according to man," not according to God. We may conclude, then, that the reproach Paul goes into here is that, unlike his opponents, who have tradition and teaching behind them, he can demonstrate no legitimation for his gospel. This reproach would result from the opponents' linking of the gospel with the law. Paul, by contrast, does not let tradition and teaching draw him away from the one and only content of the gospel, which in v. 7 he abbreviates as *Christ.*

Paul's gospel came through a "revelation of Jesus Christ." *Revelation* in our language is associated especially with the concept of vision as the possible supernatural experience of particular people. In this sense Paul also uses the noun in the plural in 2 Cor. 12:1 alongside of *visions.* Beyond this, however, there is another usage in the New Testament and in Jewish literature: in apocalyptic writings the verb can designate the boundary between this world and the coming new world, as well as the anticipatory disclosure of this new world now in the present world through an apocalyptic seer.

Yet the verb is never used reflexively in the sense "reveal oneself." Hence, in v. 12 the reading "through Jesus Christ revealing himself to me" is excluded. How the genitive "of Jesus Christ" is to be understood is seen in v. 16, which gives the content of the revelation: God's action was "to reveal his Son to me." If we consider here also what for Paul was the titular sense of *Christ,* the result is an apocalyptic interpretation of *revelation* in v. 12: this Jesus, the crucified and resurrected One, is the Messiah, who will bring in the new world; he is the eschatological King.

Apocalypticism expected this turn of the ages in the future. For Paul, however—because of the event of the death and resurrection of Jesus, which is abbreviated with the term *Christ*—the boundary between the old and the new world is marked. Later in the letter (cf. 3:23), employing the same concept of revelation, he will point to the boundary between law and faith. For Paul this boundary also means a break with tradition in regard to the law and thus a break with tradition and teaching.

Biographically he made the break with tradition at his conversion near Damascus, as the following vv. 13-16 will show. But his designating his conversion here as a "revelation of Jesus Christ" is more than just applying to this event a term—*revelation* in the sense of "vision"—which was already available for such experiences. From his standpoint, rather, the terse formulation contains a very pregnant interpretation of the event in the sense of a break with the law.

In Paul's opinion, it is a question here of final validity, of the anticipation of the new world of the future, and this points back to the expansion of the letter's opening in v. 4. Tradition and teaching, and even the law, have come to an end. They can no longer serve to legitimate the gospel, for in the gospel God himself has acted to legitimate himself. Thus even here, right at the beginning of this seemingly so thoroughly biographical section, the apostle is totally absorbed in the gospel. This reading of Paul's initial thesis gives a certain direction to the interpretation of the whole letter and therefore must receive additional support. There is no question that here Paul is speaking of his conversion on the way to Damascus, which also in 1 Cor. 9:1 and 15:8 he can characterize completely in perceptual terms as a vision of Christ.

This account also corresponds to the three reports of Paul's conversion in the Acts of the Apostles: 9:1-19a, a report of the narrator of Acts, and 22:3-16 and 26:9-20, first-person reports in the mouth of Paul. The commission to missionize among the Gentiles, which Paul himself in Gal. 1:16 links directly with the conversion, is completely missing from the first text, which describes the Damascus experience merely as the overpowering of an angry persecutor: only Ananias (and thus the reader) gets an indication at this point (Acts 9:15). In the second text the commission occurs after the conversion through a vision in the Jerusalem temple (Acts 22:17-21); not until the third report is it already a part of the vision on the way to Damascus (26:16-18).

These differences are to be ascribed to the literary purpose of Luke, who intensifies the last text by having Paul himself look back at his total activity. In Luke's presentation Paul preaches first to Jews in Damascus (9:20, 22), to Greek-speaking Jews in Jerusalem (9:29), to Jews and Gentiles in Antioch (11:26) as well as at the beginning of the so-called first missionary journey, before he devotes himself at last in 13:46 to the Gentiles during this journey.

Finally, beyond 1 Cor. 9:1; 15:8; and our present text, Phil. 3:4-11 is the only passage in which Paul himself speaks of his conversion, and it is remarkable how seldom he does so on the whole. In Philippians, however, the visionary element is completely missing. Paul speaks first of his impeccable Jewish heritage and life style and then of the radical break that caused him to give it all up without mentioning the Damascus experience at all. Here also we encounter the conception of faith and righteousness that defines the Letter to the Galatians. Thus this personal explanation of the event by Paul himself can support our interpretation of Gal. 1:11-12.

Accordingly, vv. 11-12, like v. 16, contain more than a reference to the vision of Christ on the road to Damascus that caused Paul to abandon his former way. Here in his terse thesis he is already pointing to the antithesis of law and faith, without using these terms, but rather tradition and teaching on the one side, and on the other the revelation of Jesus Christ as the content of the gospel and of faith.

In the following verses Paul presents this antithesis in his own biography. Thus at the very beginning of this biographical passage we get an early indication of the themes first of 2:15-21 and then especially of chapters 3 and 4. The biographical information is the vehicle for presenting these themes, which govern what Paul mentions only briefly in the following verses and what he describes in detail.

For Paul it is thus not merely a question of proving the divine origin of his gospel by means of his biography—a case not really made by the presentation in 1:13—2:21. Rather, the gospel itself is at stake, not just its origin. Also controversial is the consequence that Paul draws from this gospel: justification is by faith alone. Even in the biographical part of his letter, Paul is already placing everything under this dominant theme and not merely defending here his own direct relationship with God.

Theology for Paul is not a retreat into his own religious experiences, which could perhaps establish his authority, but as such would not be transmittable. Theology, rather, is the unfolding of the content of the gospel, which has eschatological meaning for his own existence, as his interpretation of the Damascus experience as a "revelation of Jesus Christ" shows. The gospel can also acquire such meaning for others, because its convincing power lies not in the personality of the preacher but in its content, which brings salvation.

The Way of the Gospel
from Damascus to Galatia

Analysis

In developing the thesis in vv. 11-12, Paul proceeds first by describing his experience with the gospel from his conversion on the way to Damascus until his activity in Galatia. The goal of the section lies, as already indicated, in 2:15-21, where Paul affirms the consequence of the gospel as justification by faith alone, without the law.

Paul presents his story in such a way that at no time and in no situation—certainly not in Jerusalem—is there ever for him any other gospel than the one that he proclaimed to the Galatians; he has never left the "truth of the gospel" (2:5, 14). It is clear that he must correct other assertions about his life, otherwise he would have no need to declare that the situation was exactly as he reports it (1:20). Again we are not in the position of the original readers, who knew what Paul was struggling against. Because with them he could make this presupposition, there was no need on his part to cite the hostile slander. Thus here too we have no direct indication of what the troublemakers alleged against Paul and what they themselves preached.

With this most comprehensive autobiographical passage in all of Paul's letters, we have the possibility of comparing it with Luke's presentation of the same period in the Acts of the Apostles. We divide the interpretation of the passage into two parts, first to clarify what Paul reports, which will reveal several problems in the comparison between Paul and Luke, and then to ask why Paul presents his story in this way.

Paul's History before His Arrival in Galatia

Neither author, Luke or Paul himself, writes as a historian in the modern sense; both consciously follow instead a certain intention in their presentations. Luke wants to trace the path of the gospel from Jerusalem through Samaria, Syria, Asia Minor, and Greece to Rome (cf. Acts 1:8).

The bearers of this gospel are first the "twelve apostles," among whom Peter especially stands out, and then later Paul by himself. The path of this gospel is presented as continuous rapid expansion.

From a distance of one or two generations from the events, Luke writes at a time when there is no longer a church in Jerusalem and the city itself has been destroyed by the Romans, and also at a time when Christianity has long since established itself as an independent entity that is no longer a part of Judaism. He knows what the final outcome was of everything he reports and thus pursues its development retrospectively.

Paul, in contrast, stands in the middle of this history itself, whose outcome is still unknown. He writes what he writes so that he might help Gentile Christianity (which in Luke's time has long since prevailed) achieve its autonomy. He is a part of this history that Luke is later able to present objectively with historical distance.

Paul is a firsthand witness, not, like Luke, a witness only from hearsay. In his accounts, he is compelled to be exact (cf. his remark in 1:20), so that in case of doubt, preference is to be given to him and not to Luke. This does not mean that Luke's presentation is worthless, for we find there a great deal of information that Paul does not feel he needs to give his readers, either because it is known to them or because it is not relevant to the situation. At the same time, however, we must always ask whether Luke is actually dealing with genuine information or has only filled in gaps in his tradition with the help of speculations about how it might have been.

Paul's Life before His Conversion

(1:13-14). Paul gives no details of his life before his conversion either here or in any of his other letters. We read only that he could boast the purest Jewish ancestry (Phil. 3:5; 2 Cor. 11:22), that he belonged to the party of the Pharisees (Phil. 3:5), and above all that he persecuted the church (Phil. 3:6; 1 Cor. 15:9).

Luke also paints the same picture but gives some biographical details. Paul was born in Tarsus, a provincial city in Cilicia in southern Asia Minor (Acts 21:39; 22:3; cf. 23:34), and had Roman citizenship (16:37; 22:28). He grew up, however, in Jerusalem and was educated there as a Pharisee (22:3). Even if his being a pupil of the famous Jewish theologian Gamaliel (22:3; cf. 5:34) may be legendary, his education in Jerusalem is supported by the fact that we know nothing of Pharisees outside of Palestine, and thus one had to go to the homeland if one wanted to pursue such a course.

Pharisaic theologians also had to practice a trade, and Paul's was that of a tentmaker (Acts 18:3) or perhaps leatherworker. That skill gave him great mobility, since he was not bound to a particular place, and later also made possible his extensive missionary journeys, during which he could provide for his own living expenses.

Luke also calls Paul a persecutor of Christians (Acts 22:4; 26:9). That he was such in Jerusalem, however, is probably excluded by Gal. 1:22, for then he could hardly have been "unknown by sight" to the churches in Judea, which includes Jerusalem. Nevertheless, Luke has him in Jerusalem, participating at the stoning of Stephen and persecuting the Jerusalem church (Acts 7:58; 8:3; 22:4; 26:10), and then he is sent to

Damascus for the same purpose by the Jerusalem authorities (9:2; 22:5; 26:10-12). It is preferable to assume that after his education in Jerusalem Paul worked with the Jewish congregation in Damascus and persecuted the Christian church there. At this time he may already have been active as a missionary to the Gentiles—but for Judaism.

Belonging to the Pharisees obligated Paul to be zealous for the law, with all of its consequences. In order to comprehend what the Pharisees really wanted, we must free ourselves of the caricature of the "hypocritical" Pharisee who *is* not, and *does* not, what he pretends. The Pharisees had pledged themselves to be zealous for the law, which meant total commitment of their very lives to God himself and to the law because the law alone promised to give life. In view of this personal background, we will see what freedom from the law meant for Paul.

His persecution of Christians must have affected above all those Christian groups who, in the name of Jesus, took a critical stand toward the law. We will soon see how—with or without Paul's help—such a group around Stephen in Jerusalem was persecuted and driven out.

Conversion and Initial Missionary Activity in Arabia

(1:15-17). As we have seen, conversion for Paul meant a complete break with his past. He does not describe it here in any detail. That it took place in or near Damascus can be inferred only from v. 17, where he speaks of a return to Damascus. Right after his conversion he went to "Arabia," that is, the semiautonomous kingdom of the Nabataeans, which was under nominal Roman control. This is the region of modern Jordan, reaching in the north to the city limits of Damascus. It was a sparsely settled borderland on the edge of the desert, from which caravans came from the East and moved on to the Mediterranean. The region had a number of Hellenistic cities, including the predecessor of today's Jordanian capital, Amman.

The phrase "after three years" in v. 18 tells how long Paul was active there. With such indications of time, partial years always count as whole ones; thus we must reckon with a period of two years and some months. Since in v. 16 Paul names preaching among the Gentiles as the purpose of his conversion, v. 17 implicitly includes a mission at that time to the Gentiles in Arabia.

In 2 Cor. 11:32-33 Paul mentions escaping Damascus by being lowered from the wall in a basket because the Nabataean king Aretas (d. 40 C.E.) wanted to seize him. Apparently things became too warm for him there, and he left Damascus in the direction of Jerusalem.

Luke, however, asserts what Paul expressly denies in v. 17, namely, that he went directly from Damascus to Jerusalem (Acts 9:26). Luke also mentions the flight in a basket over the city wall (9:25), but here it is the Jews who lie in wait for him, not the king.

The First Visit to Jerusalem

(1:18-20). According to Paul's own presentation, on the first visit to Jerusalem, which lasted only fifteen days, he saw none of the apostles except Peter and also Jesus' brother James, who was not one of the apostles; to the church he remained unknown (v. 22). Was there a desire in Jerusalem not to create a stir with so prominent a renegade?

By contrast, according to Luke, Barnabas, a respected member of the Jerusalem church (cf. Acts 4:36-37), brings Paul to the apostles (9:27). He then preaches in Jerusalem among Greek-speaking Jews (9:29), must therefore flee again, and goes via Caesarea, the harbor city on the Mediterranean, into his homeland, to Tarsus in Cilicia, where he apparently remains for some time (9:30).

Missionary Activity in Syria and Cilicia

(1:21-24). According to Paul's own presentation, he goes into the provinces of Syria and Cilicia, the land around the cities of Antioch and Tarsus. That he made a name for himself as a missionary there is shown by the reaction of the churches in Judea, cited by him in 1:22-24. He does not say how and where he missionized, although it involved a lengthy period of time.

The next indication of time, the "fourteen years" of 2:1 (that is, thirteen years and some months) could mean beginning after the last mention of time in 1:18, so that the mission there involved the whole time of over thirteen years. More likely, it includes the earlier period, so that Paul is summarizing perhaps eleven years in the one terse sentence of 1:21.

Luke has Barnabas, who already knew Paul in Jerusalem and in the meantime worked in Antioch, bring Paul from Tarsus back to Antioch (Acts 11:25-26). The church there had arisen after the persecution of part of the Jerusalem church, in which, according to Luke, Paul had also participated at the stoning of Stephen (6:8-15; 7:54—8:3).

In the interest of harmony within early Christianity, Luke's presentation in Acts 6:1-6 conceals deeper differences within the Jerusalem church between one group, to which Peter and James belonged, and another around Stephen, which apparently consisted primarily of Greek-speaking Jews. Only the second group suffered the aforementioned persecution, because it had set itself more radically against the law (cf. 6:14), and the survivors left Jerusalem, while the members of the first group remained for the time being unmolested.

According to Acts 11:20, in Antioch a group of the scattered Jews for the first time also preached to Gentiles, resulting in the first congregation of Jewish and Gentile Christians. Here also, according to Luke, the group designation *Christians* (11:26) was first applied to them, because even for outsiders they were now clearly different from Jews. The church at Antioch was the right place for a man like Paul, who indeed already understood his conversion as a commission to the Gentile mission and had himself radically broken with his Jewish past.

On Paul's missionary activity during this time, Luke first mentions a year of common effort with Barnabas in Antioch (11:26) and then especially a journey that took him, together with Barnabas and at first also John Mark, from Antioch through Cyprus to Pamphylia and Lycaonia, that is, through the province of Lycia in the southernmost part of the province of Galatia (Acts 13–14). On this trip Paul took the final step toward the mission to the Gentiles (13:46).

The mention of "Syria and Cilicia" in Gal. 1:21 covers his activity in Antioch, the capital of the province of Syria, and in Tarsus, his native city in Cilicia, but not most of the stops on this journey, which led a little beyond this territory to Cyprus and into the province of Galatia. Later, however, Luke presupposes in Acts 15:23, 41 that there are churches (only?) in this area. Did he lump everything together in these two geographic areas?

The first fundamental contradiction between Paul and Luke, however, appears at another point. Although in his own presentation Paul was not in Jerusalem during this whole period, according to Acts 11:30 he traveled there from Antioch together with Barnabas and remained there during a renewed persecution that this time also involved Peter; after its fortunate end, Paul returned to Antioch (12:25) along with Barnabas and John Mark (Barnabas's cousin, according to Col. 4:10). The occasion for this journey, as Luke reports it, is the bringing of a gift from the Antiochene church to Jerusalem, which was faced with the prophecy of a great famine (Acts 11:28-29).

Apparently Luke utilizes here in the wrong place information about an offering from the Antiochene church. Since Paul could not have passed over such a trip in his account, in which the Jerusalem journey in particular played an important role, we must regard it as unhistorical. The purpose of the Lukan presentation is to have the persecution of Christians by the Jews—introduced by Paul in 13:46 as the reason for the mission to the Gentiles—now be experienced by him from the standpoint of the victims and no longer from that of the persecutors.

The Second Journey to Jerusalem

(2:1-10). Paul himself does not mention a journey to Jerusalem again until a later time, and this journey corresponds to Acts 15:1-35, not 11:30. He is a member of a delegation that also includes Barnabas and the uncircumcised Gentile Christian Titus, who, incidentally, is mentioned in Acts neither here nor elsewhere. In the Pauline letters, however, Titus appears also later as an important coworker of Paul.

In his person Titus incorporates the theme of the encounter with those in Jerusalem, namely, the question whether Christians like him must have themselves circumcised and thus subject themselves to the Jewish law for the sake of Christ. The result of the negotiations held with James, Peter, and John is the full equality of Jewish and Gentile Christianity.

Furthermore, they agree on material support from the Antiochene church for those in Jerusalem, to which reference is made in the remark, "They asked only one thing, that we remember the poor" (v. 10). Although at first glance Paul formulates this rather vaguely for us later readers, it presupposes that his original readers knew what was meant. In fact, we learn from 1 Cor. 16:1 that the Galatians are to participate in a collection for Jerusalem organized by Paul, as are the Corinthians and the Macedonian churches (cf. 2 Corinthians 8–9 and Rom. 15:26).

In Luke also, Barnabas and Paul as well as others (Acts 15:2) go to Jerusalem; Titus is not named. The occasion here is a quarrel in the Antiochene church over the issue of circumcision, provoked by Christians from Judea (15:1).

From the beginning the delegation from Antioch is in a different situation in Luke: they are supposed to seek a decision in Jerusalem (15:2) but can only make a report (15:4, 12), and those who actually act are the Jerusalemites. Their assembly (15:22), on the basis of the votes of Peter and James, decides on a letter that reduces the law to certain minimal commandments, does not make circumcision obligatory, but still does not basically give up the law in the mission to the Gentiles (15:23-29).

Gentile Christianity, as represented in his time by Luke himself, is here finally legitimized in a harmonious development out of Jewish Christianity, with the latter's express approval. In Paul's time, however, the two still stand beside each other—in Galatia even against each other—and it has not yet been decided to whom the future belongs.

Luke makes no mention of the offering for the Jerusalem church. Nevertheless, information about it is hidden first in the aforementioned journey of Acts 11:27-30 and then in 21:24, 26, where on his last trip to Jerusalem Paul has a sum of money at his disposal for the redemption of people who had subjected themselves to a vow.

The Conflict in Antioch

(2:11-21). Out of the Jerusalem agreement came the conflict between Paul and Peter in Antioch, which may have happened not very long afterward. Peter had accepted the lifting of the differences between Jewish and Gentile Christians by ignoring the precepts of the law concerning table fellowship and sitting down to eat with uncircumcised Christians. Then, however, Peter and also Barnabas had again held to the law after some of James's people from Jerusalem had spoken to them about it. Paul therefore took them to task. How the quarrel came out, he does not say and did not need to say, because his readers knew the outcome.

Luke also reports something about a quarrel in Antioch, a much more innocuous one, to be sure (Acts 15:36-39). Between Paul and Barnabas there is a difference of opinion as to whether John Mark, who left them in the lurch on the earlier joint missionary journey (13:13), should be taken along on an inspection tour through the new churches, in order to spread the decrees from Jerusalem.

Since they cannot agree, they separate; Barnabas and John Mark go to Cyprus (15:39), while Paul, now together with Silas, the Silvanus of his letters, goes to the churches in Syria and Cilicia established on the first journey in Asia Minor. On the way they are joined by Timothy, one of Paul's most important coworkers in the following years, a half-Jew whom Paul, according to Luke's presentation, has circumcised (16:3)—scarcely an imaginable action for Paul if one considers his totally different attitude in regard to Titus in Gal. 2:3.

They enter new territory in Galatia, where they do not missionize at all, according to Luke (Acts 16:6), although the same Luke in 18:23 takes it for granted that afterward there were churches there. Luke wants to have Paul reach Europe as soon as possible because that was the will of the Holy Spirit. This means tacitly, however, that out of an undertaking that Luke portrays as an inspection tour came the separation from Antioch and the beginning of Paul's independent missionary work apart from Antioch.

Thus we can probably conclude that the conflict in Antioch, whose cause and course we really know only from Paul, was a loss for him.

Together with Titus and Silas/Silvanus, he left Antioch in order to go west. Perhaps at that time he already had Rome as his destination, which he would have quickly reached from Macedonia over the Via Egnatia, the shortest route, had he not turned away from Thessalonica by way of Berea toward the south in the direction of Athens and Corinth.

Presumably occurring at this time was the expulsion of Jews from the city of Rome (cf. Acts 18:2), probably because of disagreements among the Jews there about the proclamation of Christ. Thus for the time being, Paul had to give up his goal of going to Rome (cf. Rom. 1:13; 15:22), especially since recently in Philippi he had also fallen for the first time into conflict with the Roman authorities (Acts 16:19-40). He was detained earlier, however, in Galatia. Concerning his missionary activity there under adverse circumstances, he speaks right away in Gal. 3:1 and then again in 4:13-15.

For the following period we have no similar sequential report from Paul himself. From here on, Luke tells only the story of Paul as bearer of the gospel to Greece and Rome. Into Luke's presentation of Paul's later career we can incorporate the isolated biographical notes in Paul's letters; in this process, of course, Luke's work must occasionally be corrected, for example, in the journey in Acts 18:18-23. This later history of Paul has in part already been presented in the Introduction (see above, p. 2).

Arranging the dates of the Pauline biography given in his letters, as well as in the Acts of the Apostles, produces the chronology of Paul's career that is presented on page 135 below. The approximate ordering of the years in our chronology is derived from the time in office of Proconsul Gallio, who is mentioned in Acts 18:12 and who resided in Corinth, the capital of the province of Achaia. On the basis of an inscription found in Delphi, his tenure is set between 51 and 52 C.E. From Paul's stay in Corinth, one can then reckon backward and forward with the information given by Paul and Luke. Also appended to the commentary is a map on which the reader may find the names of cities and territories mentioned in the book. This should help one keep in mind the great distances involved in the individual journeys.

With the help of comparison with the Acts of the Apostles, we have thus far examined the course of history in Gal. 1:13—2:21, but not why Paul tells this history to the Galatians and what emphases he makes in his story. Before that is attempted in a second pass through the text, let us again summarize the historical information:

1:13-14. Paul was a Jew and belonged to the strict order of the Pharisees. He persecuted the church and especially the part that was critical of the law.

1:15-17. After his conversion Paul carried on Gentile missionary work for more than two years in the kingdom of the Nabataeans (Arabia).

1:18-20. After his return to Damascus he had to leave the city in haste and went for the first time to Jerusalem, where he remained only briefly and met only Peter and James.

1:21-24. Then, based in Antioch, he evangelized about eleven years in Syria and Cilicia and apparently became famous as far as Judea.

2:1-10. On Paul's second trip to Jerusalem, this time together with Barnabas and Titus under a commission from the church in Antioch, the equality of Jewish and Gentile Christians was recognized, and material support of the Jerusalem church by the Antiochene church was agreed upon.

2:11-21. Then in Antioch this recognition was called into question again by the Jerusalemites. Peter and Barnabas went over to that side; with Titus and Silvanus, Paul left Antioch, later adding Timothy. Their aim was mission work farther to the west, perhaps even in Rome. In any case, they wanted independence from Antioch.

3:1. A stay in Galatia because of illness (cf. 4:13-15) led to the beginning of churches there, which were perhaps the first purely Gentile Christian congregations.

Paul's Life
before His Conversion

Text

1:13 You have heard, no doubt, of my earlier life in Judaism. I was violently persecuting the church of God and was trying to destroy it.

14 I advanced in Judaism beyond many among my own people of the same age, for I was far more zealous for the traditions of my ancestors.

Commentary

In contrast to the variety of biographical information that could have been amassed as an initial overview at this point, Paul reduces his presentation here to his persecution of the church during the period before his conversion. The reason for this persecution was his zeal for his ancestral traditions. The word *zealous* is meant as a very positive trait here, without the negative connotation of excessive sectarian enthusiasm, especially in regard to dedication to religious convictions. The persecution of the church was an expression of zeal, and here too Paul excelled over his peers.

There may be two reasons for Paul's speaking of the "traditions of my ancestors." First, this identifies him as a Pharisee, for the Pharisees held that the will of God included the traditions of both the oral and the written law, going beyond the fathers back to Moses himself. Second, here for Paul is an antithesis to his gospel, which according to v. 12 does not rest on tradition.

Thus Paul knows what he is talking about when in what follows he warns the Galatians against adopting the law. As ancestral tradition "according to man," the qualifications of the law are different from those of the gospel that he proclaims. He needs only to remind his readers of all this, because they have already heard it earlier.

Conversion and Initial
Missionary Activity in Arabia

Text

1:15 But when God, who had set me apart before I was born and called
me through his grace, was pleased

16 to reveal his Son to me, so that I might proclaim him among the
Gentiles, I did not confer with any human being,

17 nor did I go up to Jerusalem to those who were already apostles
before me, but I went away at once into Arabia, and afterwards I
returned to Damascus.

Commentary

The contrast with Paul's previous life under the law is indicated by the
phrases *Son [of God]* and *preaching [the gospel] among the Gentiles.* They
already point to what will be reduced later in the letter to the alternative
between the law and faith in Christ. His conversion includes at the same
time his calling as a missionary. Again, however, the apostle himself is
totally absorbed in the gospel, for he mentions what happened to him at
Damascus only in passing and as preparation for stating his goal: "so that
I might proclaim him among the Gentiles." The Greek word translated
here as "proclaim" is the verb related to *euangelion,* "gospel, evangel," a
derivation not reflected here in English because *evangelize* implies a very
particular kind of preaching method.

[1:15] With "before I was born" and "called" come echoes of the calling of
the Old Testament prophets; note especially Jer. 1:5: "I appointed you a
prophet to the nations." Preaching good news is also part of the prophetic
office (cf. Isa. 52:7). Thus the functions of a prophet are transferred to the
apostle. Paul, however, reports no story of his calling in the style of the
callings of the prophets, which might have legitimized him or his gospel.
Just as in v. 12, here he also interprets what has happened to him as a
break between the two worlds, which for him is a break with tradition.

29

The zealot for the law becomes the preacher of the Son of God among the Gentiles.

[1:16] It may not be coincidental that Paul speaks here of Jesus as the "Son [of God]." Later in his Letter to the Romans, he makes a similar connection between the Son of God and the gospel. In Rom. 1:3-4 he cites as the content of the gospel a pre-Pauline christological formula. It speaks of Jesus, who in his earthly existence ("according to the flesh") is descended from David but who, since the resurrection of the dead that begins with his own resurrection, is designated the Son of God in the divine sphere ("according to the Spirit").

As a king from David's lineage, after his enthronement, was considered God's son (cf. Ps. 2:7), so Jesus as the resurrected Lord is now enthroned as King. His resurrection is the beginning of the new age because it is the beginning of the resurrection of the dead expected at the end of the world.

In Rom. 1:9 Paul summarizes this connection again in the phrase "the gospel of his Son" (here too the Son is not the speaker but the content of the gospel—cf. above, p. 12). Then in Rom. 1:17 he names as the content of the gospel the revelation of the righteousness of God through faith, using the same key word *reveal* as here in Gal. 1:16 (cf. 1:12) and later in 3:23.

Thus for Paul there is a connection between this christological title and the question of righteousness, and it is therefore not surprising that he uses it almost exclusively in Galatians and Romans, where justification by faith alone, without the law, is the central theme. This connection was not established first by Paul; it was present before him in the Jewish tradition. It was already an essential function of the king as the son of God to be the guarantor of righteousness, not only in the juristic sense, but also in a more encompassing way as the maintainer of the fruitfulness of the land: in short, the order of the world (cf. Psalm 72).

Son of God, however, can also be the people of Israel as a whole, as well as, increasingly, the individual righteous person who observes the law. As God's child, the righteous one has the promise that in the end he or she will triumph over the unrighteous ones, and they must bow to him.

If in early Christianity Jesus was simply the "Son of God," this phrase implied, for those who knew, that he, as the righteous One, is the righteousness of God (cf. 1 Cor. 1:30; 2 Cor. 5:21). Not until later does the title receive the significance of direct descent from God, which became its essential content through the development of christological dogma in the early church.

Paul uses this title three more times in Galatians: in 2:20 in connection with statements on Jesus' giving of himself in death, and in 4:4, 6 in the statement on the sending of the Son that makes possible the sonship of all believers. Both are also found in other branches of the early Christian tradition. Special with Paul, however, is his understanding the sending of the Son, as well as his giving himself, as the end of the age of the law and the possibility of righteousness outside the law (4:5).

Thus, even by the choice of this title in our passage, Paul points to the opposite of the law: the revelation of the Son is the boundary between law and faith (cf. 3:23), implemented in Paul's life at Damascus by Jesus himself. Hence, it is logical for Paul to preach this message from the beginning to the Gentiles outside the law, not to the Jews. With this title he identified the content of the gospel, which for him included freedom from the law in the confession of the "Son of God"; and this is what he then immediately preached also in Arabia among Gentiles.

[1:17] It is striking, however, that at the beginning of this verse Paul expressly emphasizes that he did not go to Jerusalem to those who were apostles before him. This denial is apparently provoked by the disagreement in Galatia. Again, with *apostles* Paul is not thinking of the "twelve apostles," for this restriction is first made by Luke (see above, p. 9). Certainly, he included Peter, as v. 19 shows, but who else cannot be determined.

It is clear, in any case, that Paul did not seek his legitimation as an apostle through the apostles in Jerusalem. He is indeed an apostle "sent neither by human commission nor from human authorities" (v. 1) and therefore "did not confer with any human being" (v. 16). The only thing that legitimizes him is the gospel itself.

Thus the reproach against which he defends himself cannot be that he is dependent on Jerusalem but, on the contrary, that he lacks genuine legitimation through Jerusalem, which his opponents—rightly or wrongly—asserted for themselves. It is not his independence that he seeks to demonstrate; rather, from the very beginning it is the identity of the gospel, which later he also preached in Galatia.

The First Visit
to Jerusalem

Text

1:18 Then after three years I did go up to Jerusalem to visit Cephas and stayed with him fifteen days;

19 but I did not see any other apostle except James the Lord's brother.

20 In what I am writing to you, before God, I do not lie!

Commentary

[1:18] Paul sought contact with Jerusalem on his own and only after a considerable period of independent missionary activity. He does not give the reason for his departure from Damascus, but it was probably to become acquainted with Peter, who is the only "apostle" he meets. Here also it is not clear who the "apostles" are. Besides Peter, he meets only James, the brother of Jesus, who, however, was not one of the apostles.

He remained there about two weeks; the Greek phrase (literally, "fifteen days") does not mean an exact designation of fifteen times twenty-four hours. It is apparently important to Paul in his presentation that he was already an apostle before he went to Jerusalem, for he had already been active as a missionary to the Gentiles in Arabia for more than two years. He himself attributes to this visit no significance for his own legitimation: for him it is purely a matter of getting acquainted.

Paul speaks of Peter as Cephas here as elsewhere in his letters, with the exception of Gal. 2:7-8, which we consider later. *Kēphas* is the grecized form of the Aramaic word *kepha,* which means "rock." The corresponding Greek word is *petra,* a feminine noun; *petros* was the newly formed masculine counterpart, which passed through the Latinized form *Petrus* to become finally the familiar name *Peter.*

There is no previous evidence of either the Aramaic word *kepha* nor the Greek *petra/petros* as proper names. Hence it is a question of a nickname that was borne by Simon, son of Jonah/John (cf. Matt. 16:17; John 1:41-42; 21:15-17), formerly a fisherman in Capernaum/Galilee. In the well-known passage Matt. 16:17-19, this nickname "rock" is interpreted to mean that Simon is the rock on which the church is built. It does not refer to special character traits of its bearer (firmness, for example, is precisely what Peter did not show at Jesus' passion) but rather to his function in the church. According to 1 Cor. 15:5, Peter was the first witness of the resurrection. .

Why did Paul use the Aramaic and not the Greek form of the name? To Paul, who knew both forms (as 2:7-8 shows) and probably also commanded both languages, the almost titular meaning of the nickname must have been clear even in the Aramaic. The Greek-speaking readers of his letters, however, would immediately perceive the titular character only with *petros,* since *petros,* as indicated, was not a proper name but would be directly associated with *petra* ("rock").

With the word *Kēphas,* however, they could recognize at first merely a foreign personal name. In order to grasp the original titular meaning, they would have needed further linguistic abilities or additional explanations. (Even we can at best only know about the titular sense of *Peter* as the rock; we do not make a direct connection.) Thus Paul apparently uses the Aramaic form of the name intentionally because it does not call immediate attention to a special function of Simon.

[1:19] During Jesus' lifetime James apparently did not belong among his brother's disciples. According to 1 Cor. 15:7, however, he was one of the witnesses to the resurrection, singled out, incidentally, from "the apostles" there as well as here. Afterward he was one of the leaders of the Jerusalem church (cf. Acts 12:17; 15:13; Gal. 2:9) and remained there after Peter had finally left Jerusalem (cf. Gal. 2:12; Acts 21:18). In the year 62 he suffered a martyr's death in Jerusalem, which the historian Josephus reports in his *Antiquities* (20.200).

[1:20] At this point Paul inserts his declaration that he is not lying, which also applies, naturally, to his whole presentation. In particular, however, he apparently has to defend himself against false rumors about his first visit to Jerusalem. Exactly what they were was known to his readers in Galatia, and thus Paul does not need to cite them. In the flow of Paul's writing, he stresses that he was already an apostle beforehand and that this first visit took place on a private level, as it were, and also without any note of discord among the three participants.

For the opponents in Galatia, Jerusalem apparently played a large role, as shown by the fact that in 1:13—2:21 Paul composes an accounting of his relationship to Jerusalem, and as 4:21-31 leads us to suspect. It is thus possible that these adversaries asserted that Paul himself first became an apostle during this visit and that the gospel he preached in Galatia was not his original gospel; rather, he had earlier presented a different, "Jerusalem" gospel that corresponded to theirs, before he then, more recently, deviated from this correct teaching.

This assumption agrees with the phenomena observed up to this point. Paul designates himself as an "apostle—sent neither by human commission nor from human authorities"; that is, he became an apostle, not in Jerusalem through the "apostles before me," but immediately at Damascus. He stresses the identity of his gospel from the very beginning; he has never represented a gospel other than that one, which led from the beginning to his mission to the Gentiles, and that is what he preached in Galatia.

Missionary Activity
in Syria and Cilicia

Text

1:21 Then I went into the regions of Syria and Cilicia,
22 and I was still unknown by sight to the churches of Judea that are in Christ;
23 they only heard it said, "The one who formerly was persecuting us is now proclaiming the faith he once tried to destroy."
24 And they glorified God because of me.

Commentary

[1:21] The relationship to Jerusalem is also the main point of view for Paul's presentation of the following eleven years. First, he states quite briefly that he was in Syria and Cilicia, thereby silently excluding another Jerusalem trip during this period. Such a journey also seems not to have been asserted by anyone in Galatia (only Luke does so), otherwise Paul would expressly deny it.

[1:22-23] More important to him than what he did at that time, however, in view of the Galatian situation, is the reaction of the Jewish churches, including especially the one in Jerusalem. Furthermore, there is no note of discord in his relationship to them; on the contrary, he can report that they are moved to praise God for what he is doing, specifically, the mission to the Gentiles, whose form is of course known to the Galatians. Moreover, the quotation in v. 23 from their own mouths agrees exactly with the way Paul himself understands his previous path: the persecutor (v. 13) became the preacher (v. 16). Thus the Jerusalemites expressly accept what Paul has done and how he understands his mission.

Not until this point in the Letter to the Galatians do we encounter the key word *faith,* which is the content of the proclamation. Whereas v. 16 speaks of proclaiming "his Son," here we have "proclaiming the faith." The emphasis is on *faith,* not on *the:* just as for Paul there is no other gospel beside the gospel whose content is Christ, who is the Son of God, so also there is no faith apart from this content. The antithesis of faith for Paul is unfaith, as opposed, for example, to Christian faith versus Jewish faith as a characterization of his pre-Christian period. Faith for Paul is not an optional formal concept; as faith in Jesus Christ alone, it refers to only one content, which is to be kept in mind both here and in other places where the noun is used absolutely.

The Second Journey
to Jerusalem

Text

2:1 Then after fourteen years I went up again to Jerusalem with Barnabas, taking Titus along with me.

2 I went up in response to a revelation. Then I laid before them (though only in a private meeting with the acknowledged leaders) the gospel that I proclaim among the Gentiles, in order to make sure that I was not running, or had not run, in vain.

3 But even Titus, who was with me, was not compelled to be circumcised, though he was a Greek.

4 But because of false believers secretly brought in, who slipped in to spy on the freedom we have in Christ Jesus, so that they might enslave us—

5 we did not submit to them even for a moment, so that the truth of the gospel might always remain with you.

6 And from those who were supposed to be acknowledged leaders (what they actually were makes no difference to me; God shows no partiality [cf. Deut. 10:17])—those leaders contributed nothing to me.

7 On the contrary, when they saw that I had been entrusted with the gospel for the uncircumcised, just as Peter had been entrusted with the gospel to the circumcised

8 (for he who worked through Peter making him an apostle to the circumcised also worked through me in sending me to the Gentiles),

9 and when James and Cephas and John, who were acknowledged pillars, recognized the grace that had been given to me, they gave to Barnabas and me the right hand of fellowship, agreeing that we should go to the Gentiles and they to the circumcised.

10 They asked only one thing, that we remember the poor, which was actually what I was eager to do.

Analysis

The description of the second journey to Jerusalem is marked by broken off sentences and interjected incidental thoughts. Whereas Luke presents the same event in lively detail (Acts 15:1-35), Paul reduces his report to a very few statements. The picture that emerges is one of two delegations negotiating as equals, the result of which is equal status for the two parties. Striking in Paul's report, moreover, are the somewhat detached statements about those participating on the Jerusalem side (vv. 6, 9) and the emphasis on the "truth of the gospel" in a surprising appeal to his Galatian readers, who at that time could hardly have come under discussion in Jerusalem (v. 5).

Commentary

[2:1] The indication of time in this verse ("after fourteen years"), like the one in 1:18, may be reckoned from Paul's conversion. This would mean that he did not go again to Jerusalem until eleven years later. He himself does not say that he made this trip from Antioch as a member of a delegation from the church there. Here, as in the following sections, he focuses the story on the few people acting in Jerusalem, not on the churches that they represent.

Titus may have been known personally to the Galatians if he was with Paul during his time in Galatia. Barnabas also needs as little introduction as Peter and James earlier in 1:18-19. Apparently, individual churches knew a little about each other. Hence, in 1 Cor. 9:5-6 Paul can also presuppose among the Corinthians knowledge about the "other apostles and the brothers of the Lord and Cephas," as well as Barnabas, although it is unlikely that any of these were ever in Corinth.

[2:2] As occasion for the journey Paul names a "revelation," using the same word as in 1:12, 16. Here too an interpretation as "vision" (cf. 2 Cor. 12:1, 7) is not necessarily required. If one considers how in Acts 15:2 this journey results from a decision of the congregational assembly, then one can also see in the "revelation" of Gal. 2:2 the charisma of revelation that Paul mentions in 1 Cor. 14:6, 26, that is not of an ecstatic nature. Gal. 2:2, combined with 1:12, 16, means that Paul did not decide on his own to go to Jerusalem, any more than his conversion rested on his own decision.

There in Jerusalem Paul lays out the gospel that he is preaching among the Gentiles, the gospel that he also preached in Galatia (1:6-9), as he had preached it from the very beginning in Arabia and in Syria and Cilicia (1:11-12, 16, 23). In his formulation the stress lies not on the concern as to whether his gospel is correct but on the issue of whether his mission work among the Gentiles is perhaps idle activity, which is how it could be viewed if Jerusalem did not accept it as proclamation of the one and only gospel. For Paul there is only this one gospel (1:7, cf. 1 Cor. 15:11), which should be preached to Jews as well as to Gentiles.

[2:3] In Jerusalem Paul meets "the acknowledged leaders," whose names he will cite in v. 9. He spoke with them in a small group, and they indeed accepted the gospel as he had preached it. In a practical test, they did not require the uncircumcised Gentile Christian with Paul to let himself be circumcised. This example would be even more convincing for the Galatians if they had actually known Titus personally, as they knew the circumcised Jewish Christian Paul (cf. Phil. 3:5) and perhaps also Silas/Silvanus (cf. Acts 15:40) and the Gentile Christian Timothy, who was probably not circumcised by Paul—contrary to Luke's presentation (Acts 16:3). If all of these were in Galatia at that time, then they encountered the gospel right from the beginning as a gospel for Jews and Gentiles.

[2:4] Thus the Jerusalem authorities acknowledged at this time that circumcision could be no criterion for being a Christian, and they recognized thereby the gospel that Paul preached among the Gentiles, in which baptism (cf. 3:27), without the addition of circumcision, is the sign of belonging to Christ. At that time in Jerusalem, however, in addition to these authorities, there were others whom Paul can only call "false believers secretly brought in" (v. 4). He says that they want to "enslave us," in contrast to "the freedom we have"—a pair of concepts that appears here for the first time but that later in the letter will be a dominant theme as the antithesis of law and faith (4:21-31; 5:1, 13).

[2:5] Paul did not yield to these false brethren for a moment because for him the truth of the gospel was at stake. "Truth" here is more than simple correctness or truthfulness. It is a question of the content of the gospel, which Paul comprehends in the antithesis of law and faith. Hence it is not possible to bind the gospel with the requirement of circumcision, as this group of Jewish Christians in Jerusalem wanted to do. Since Paul speaks of them as "believers" (literally "brothers")—even if false ones—then it must be a matter of Christians (cf. Acts 15:5: Pharisees who had turned to Christianity).

[2:6] For the situation in Galatia, however, all of this means that those who appeal to Jerusalem on the requirement of circumcision do so mistakenly. They have as authorities only the "false believers secretly brought in," not the real authorities, who agree with Paul and his gospel. These authorities placed no conditions on Paul concerning the mission to the Gentiles. Parenthetically, he limits the significance of these authorities somewhat while referring to a proverbial statement from the Old Testament (cf. Deut. 10:17; Sir. 32:16). For his part he does not want his gospel legitimated by Jerusalem authorities, for it is legitimated by God himself. It is important to Paul to show that Jerusalem cannot be played against him.

[2:7-9] On the contrary, they saw that Paul was entrusted with the gospel for the Gentiles, as Peter was with the gospel for the Jews. In both cases, however, the gospel is the same (cf. 1 Cor. 15:11), and on the unity of the gospel rests the unity of the church; for Peter as well as for Paul, the office of apostle is totally absorbed in the gospel. Only in this passage does Paul use the Greek form *petros*—not the Aramaic *kēphas* that he always uses elsewhere—thus here for once stressing the actual meaning of the nickname (cf. above, pp. 32–33). If Peter is the "rock" of the church, as such he is not over Paul but beside him; the function of both is only their common appointment to mission. The authorities recognize this equality and thus the unity of Jews and Gentiles in the church.

The authorities are now also called by name: James, Peter, and John. Here, compared to the first journey to Jerusalem (1:18-19), we also have John. The author means the disciple of Jesus, the son of Zebedee. According to Mark 3:17, John and his brother James (to be distinguished from Jesus' brother of the same name) bear the nickname "Boanerges," apparently an Aramaic word, which is explained as meaning "Sons of Thunder." In the Synoptic Gospels they, like Peter, are with Jesus on the mount of transfiguration and in Gethsemane. Like the brothers Peter and Andrew, their calling has its own story (Mark 1:19-20), and both pairs of brothers were fishermen in Capernaum. James and John, however, were apparently on a higher level socially, for their father had a fishing boat, on which hired fishermen also worked, while Peter and Andrew threw out their net from the shore.

According to Acts, we find both in Jerusalem, where this James was beheaded during a persecution of the Christians (Acts 12:2); thus at this time he is already dead. The Fourth Gospel, composed by John according to later tradition, nowhere mentions a disciple named John, but perhaps John is the nameless "disciple whom Jesus loved." In the final chapter (John 21:23) an allusion is made to his death at an advanced age. Paul mentions him nowhere else in his letters.

These three—Jesus' brother James, Peter, and John—together bear the honorific name *pillars,* which Paul was not the first to bestow on them. It refers to the supporting function of pillars in a building and hence expresses the function of these three in the church, which can be compared to a temple or a house, whose foundation is Christ (cf. 1 Cor. 3:11, 16). As in the case of the literal sense of Peter's nickname, it is also true here that they have this function, not because of superiority over others, but on the basis of the equality of Jewish and Gentile Christianity that results from the gospel.

[2:9] The outcome of the discussions is a confirmation of the way things had already been: "that we should go to the Gentiles and they to the circumcised." The gospel remains identical, but the responsibility is divided. As simple as this formula sounds, it was difficult to observe. It could function only if the "pillars" remained in Jerusalem and missionized only among the Jews in the homeland, while those in Antioch were accorded their previous missionary territory in Syria and Cilicia, in which they proclaimed the gospel to Jews and Gentiles.

Even at that time, as later in his own mission territory around the Aegean, Paul began with the synagogue (cf. Acts 13:14, 42; 14:1). There he met Jews and those who feared God, that is, uncircumcised Gentiles who held to the law without following through with a complete conversion, and also other interested Gentiles. Out of this mission arose churches of Jewish and Gentile Christians according to the model of Antiochene church, not purely Gentile Christian churches. Thus an ethnic interpretation of the agreement (only Gentile missions for Antioch and Jewish missions for Jerusalem, even in the Diaspora) was not at all practicable.

[2:10] A sign of the unity of Jews and Gentiles in the church is the material care of the Antiochenes for the Jerusalem church. The wording here, to be sure, would not by itself lead us to conclude that the new missionary areas were undertaking such collections. For this conclusion one needs the additional information already utilized in our first look at this passage. This means, however, that Paul is not speaking to the Galatians in regard to something unknown. On the contrary, he is reminding his readers of something that they know. The final clause has exactly this reminding sense: "which was actually what I was eager to do," among other things, by arranging for the collection he had organized for Jerusalem also to be taken among the Galatians (cf. 1 Cor. 16:1). Thus Paul held by this agreement after his separation from Antioch and at the time of his writing is in the process of preparing to take the offering.

The "poor" are the Jerusalem Christians, probably also in the social sense (cf. Rom. 15:26), as citizens of a city that thrives primarily because Jews from all over the world make pilgrimages there. Christians can scarcely still have a part in this business and are therefore dependent on donations, even as Paul himself received them from the church in Philippi for support of his own work (cf. Phil. 4:10-20). Since Old Testament times, "poor" also meant a title of honor for the righteous, and thus here it means not only a poor part of the Jerusalem church in distinction to those who are better off but the church as a whole, which so designates itself.

Also, the word *remember* may not be accidental, for "remember Zion" is an ancient theme (cf. Psalm 137). The delivering of the collection from the Gentile missionary area is thus for Paul something of a pilgrimage of the Gentiles to Zion to bring their gifts. It would be nice if we knew more about the representatives of the churches who accompany Paul on his last Jerusalem journey (cf. Acts 20:4). Then we could answer the question whether Paul intentionally took only Gentile Christians for the delivery of the collection, or whether this delegation itself may have embodied a church of Jews and Gentiles.

Thus even Paul has a definite theology of Zion, but Gal. 4:21-31 will show how much it differs from that propagated by his opponents in Galatia. In any case, the course of the discussions in Jerusalem proves to him that one cannot preach another gospel in the name of Jerusalem, since the Jerusalem authorities have expressly accepted a law-free mission to the Gentiles.

The unity of the church is based on the identity of the gospel. For this very reason, however, it can also find its visible expression in the form of that collection. Furthermore, unity, because it is already given in the gospel, is not something that must be achieved at any price with a compromise. For the sake of the gospel, Paul can defame some Christians as "false believers" (v. 4) and say a curse on those who proclaim another gospel (1:8-9).

In Jerusalem and all the more now in his own new mission area around the Aegean, Paul could have played his trumps: rapidly growing mission areas and no doubt also an economic superiority in the new churches. But he does not do so because what matters is the gospel. What matters is that God is all in all, even in his church of Jewish and Gentile Christians.

Paul maintained this emphasis, in spite of his separation from Antioch, occasioned by Christians from Jerusalem, in spite of proceedings in Galatia where Jerusalem was advanced against him, and although he must in the end fear that Jerusalem will not understand all of this when he arrives with the collection (cf. Rom. 15:31). Freedom from the law brings him precisely to a commitment to Jerusalem. He does not establish his own churches; rather, the newly arisen churches are the representation in each place of the one church that comes from the one gospel.

The Conflict in Antioch

Text

2:11 But when Cephas came to Antioch, I opposed him to his face, because he stood self-condemned;

12 for until certain people came from James, he used to eat with the Gentiles. But after they came, he drew back and kept himself separate for fear of the circumcision faction.

13 And the other Jews joined him in this hypocrisy, so that even Barnabas was led astray by their hypocrisy.

14 But when I saw that they were not acting consistently with the truth of the gospel, I said to Cephas before them all, "If you, though a Jew, live like a Gentile and not like a Jew, how can you compel the Gentiles to live like Jews?"

15 We ourselves are Jews by birth and not Gentile sinners;

16 yet we know that a person is justified not by the works of the law but through faith in Jesus Christ. And we have come to believe in Christ Jesus, so that we might be justified by faith in Christ, and not by doing the works of the law, because no one will be justified by the works of the law.

17 But if, in our effort to be justified in Christ, we ourselves have been found to be sinners, is Christ then a servant of sin? Certainly not!

18 But if I build up again the very things that I once tore down, then I demonstrate that I am a transgressor.

19 For through the law I died to the law, so that I might live to God. I have been crucified with Christ;

20 and it is no longer I who live, but it is Christ who lives in me. And the life I now live in the flesh I live by faith in the Son of God, who loved me and gave himself for me.

21 I do not nullify the grace of God; for if justification (*or:* righteousness) comes through the law, then Christ died for nothing.

Analysis

Paul tells more of his story, but in the end it amounts to a fundamental presentation of the gospel. At this point we no longer know to what extent

43

it is still a report of his speech in Antioch and how much it has become a direct address to the readers in Galatia. The two are closely intertwined.

Commentary

[2:11] The church of Jewish and Gentile Christians in Antioch formed a test case for the Jerusalem agreement. At first Peter also stood the test (Paul does not say why or how he came to Antioch) by concretely achieving mutual recognition through his participation in table fellowship with uncircumcised Gentile Christians. In connection with these meals the Lord's Supper was also celebrated (cf. 1 Cor. 11:17-34).

The unity of the church is realized in table fellowship. Lack of such fellowship is a problem that breaks out repeatedly in the history of the church. In any case, it was practiced at that time in Antioch, in spite of all the purity precepts of the law, which hindered Jewish Christians. Paul, Barnabas, and even Peter, as Jewish Christians, celebrated the common meal with Gentile Christians like Titus.

[2:12-13] This practice was called into question by people who came from James and thus from Jerusalem. Whether they were commissioned for this purpose cannot be learned from the text. In view of the heavy traffic back and forth between the two churches, their appearance in itself is nothing unusual. Out of fear of them, Paul asserts, Peter (and with him the other Jewish Christians, including Barnabas) gave up his previous attitude, and there came a schism in the church, a separation into a Jewish Christian part and a Gentile Christian part.

Concretely we could perhaps imagine that the church could come together in the same room at the same time and celebrate the meal, but still in separated groups at different tables—there are also examples of such division in the history of the church up into recent times. Barnabas likewise observes this separation, which Paul can only call "hypocrisy." In the eyes of the Jewish Christians, it was perhaps only a very pragmatic arrangement that made it possible for the Jerusalemites to take part in the meal and was thus supposed to save the unity of the church. Such compromises, however, are not Paul's thing. For him the "truth of the gospel" is at stake now as it was then in Jerusalem (cf. v. 5), and here too the gospel compels him to polemicize.

[2:14] He takes Peter to task, not the people sent by James, because in Paul's eyes Peter has been proved guilty precisely by this pragmatism, guilty according to the "truth of the gospel." Before the gathered congregation, Paul confronts Peter on the matter. One can scarcely imagine that Peter would have replied nothing, as Paul's account here might suggest, especially since the continuation of the story indicates that Paul, not Peter, is the loser in this conflict. Paul's intention, however, is not to describe objectively a historical process for its own sake but to let the "truth of the gospel" be spoken, and in his opinion the truth was represented at that time in Antioch by himself and not by Peter.

Paul sees in Peter's behavior a basic demand that the Gentile Christians respect the law, which makes table fellowship between Jews and Gentiles impossible, although Peter himself did not hold to it earlier. This means, however, that the law is placed de facto above the gospel, even though there may be no quarrel about the Gentile Christians belonging to Christ. The consequence would have to be that the Gentile Christians should let themselves be circumcised and then commit themselves to the rules of purification in order to reestablish the full unity of the church. But could that conclusion not have seemed extreme to Peter and Barnabas, when they were merely trying to cope with an immediate problem?

The quarrel between Peter and Paul has repeatedly been felt as a problem throughout the history of the church, usually with a tendency to relativize Paul's strong condemnation of Peter. For Luther, here lay proof that Peter's followers, the popes, could also err as he did.

Peter's tracks are lost after this incident; we do not know how long he remained in Antioch or where he missionized in the following years (cf. 1 Cor. 9:5). In any case, when Paul returns to Jerusalem later, Peter is not there. His death as a martyr is indicated in John 21:18-19; according to later sources, he was executed in Rome.

Similarly, we know little about the further development of the Antiochene church. It is unlikely that Paul went back there again a few years later (versus Acts 18:22; cf. above, p. 2). Two or three generations later, the Antiochene bishop Ignatius, while on the way to martyrdom in Rome, wrote letters to churches in Asia Minor, Greece, and Rome that reveal a theology clearly influenced by Pauline doctrine. At the same time they also show signs of the continued development of traditions that were already presupposed by Paul and probably adopted in Antioch.

Paul understands the concrete occasion in Antioch as a question of principle and thus gives his first principled development of the content of the gospel (vv. 15-21). Here we also find the whole relationship of law, faith, and righteousness; until now only the key word *faith* has occurred, in 1:23, but not *law,* although naturally that has often been the topic in the interpretation.

These concepts are still found together in our language, but in only one particular connection: the Protestant doctrine of justification, which has itself been radically called into question. Outside of this, *righteousness* is an ethical value that indicates an ideal not only of the legal system but also of interpersonal relationships in general. Likewise, one naturally encounters *law* in the language of jurisprudence and beyond that in the realm of the sciences, which are about the task of determining the laws of reoccurring courses of events. Not least in the train of the Protestant tradition, however, there is also a strongly critical attitude toward *laws* in general, which can be linked with a negative estimation of, for example, "law and order."

Faith, however, is no longer actually felt to be also a part of legal language, in spite of such expressions as "in faith and trust," "good faith," and "keep faith." Our current linguistic usage of *faith* contains two opposing elements. On the one hand, faith involves the element of absolute conviction, for which one is ready to take responsibility with one's own person. On the other hand, faith is precisely that which one cannot guarantee. The positive opposite concept is then *knowledge.*

In contrast to our associations, nevertheless, we must understand that in Paul's religious and linguistic situation all three concepts are closely united: faith is life according to the law from Sinai, which includes the promise of righteousness for those who hold to it. Righteousness here is in no way only an ethical concept: it reaches into the realm of cosmic order. As we will see, however, Paul takes the law out of this positive context and orients faith no longer toward the law but toward what is abbreviated with the term *Christ* (cf. above, p. 13).

[2:15-16] Paul begins his line of argument by adopting a Jewish prejudice. The self-designation *Jews* is defined in distinction to Gentile "sinners" and thus as something with natural superiority over the latter. Hence, personal identity is gained here through a negative qualification of the "outsiders." All the more surprisingly, however, Paul takes precisely this presupposed superiority and turns it on its head. The negative "sinner" would require the positive "righteous," but instead Paul concludes the opposite: righteousness comes not from the way of the "works of the law," which defines the Jews, but through leaving this way and going over to faith in Christ.

In its new conceptual structure, this idea corresponds exactly to Paul's own interpretation of his conversion in 1:11-16. We saw there how he does not reduce the Damascus event to an individual experience but understands it as a turning from one world to another. Only thus was his experience theologically transmittable; the gospel, not the apostle himself, is the content of his preaching (cf. 2 Cor. 4:5).

Thus righteousness comes from faith in Christ and not from works of the law, for the Scripture itself says that no one shall be justified before God (cf. Ps. 143:2). According to Paul, however, this limitation is true only as long as faith has not yet come (cf. 3:23-24). Hence, it is only logical that he expands the statement taken from Ps. 143:2 with "by the works of the law."

This principle, which Paul will formulate again in quite similar fashion in the Letter to the Romans (cf. Rom. 3:20-22, 28), contains the theological essence of what Paul's own conversion meant to him. Like this experience, it is grounded in Christology, for here too, in giving the content of faith "in Jesus Christ," the titular sense of *Christ* is maintained.

Under *works of the law* are to be understood, first, circumcision, then everything decreed in the law of Sinai. "The law" is the content of the first five books of the Bible, which are understood as the law that Moses received from God himself on Sinai. The Pharisaic tradition from which Paul came includes also the "traditions of my ancestors" (1:14), which claim the same origin. On the whole, it is important that the "five books of Moses" not only contain ethical and cultic commandments but also recount some of God's history with his people and, not least of all, give information in their first chapters on the ordering of the world. The law is thus the documentation of the ethical as well as the natural order of the world.

What the law promises is righteousness and life. Even righteousness here is more than only an ethical category. In order to understand what Paul means by justification, we must free ourselves of the distorted image of a Pharisee as one who is a natural hypocrite, who never does what he expects of others, or who only discusses curious particular requirements of the law. In that case it would actually be only reasonable that Paul would leave the Pharisees. He argues, however, not from mere reasonableness but from very much deeper experiences: meaningful life is promised to those who hold to the law. Because of this promise, Jews have held to the law even when, as in the wars of the Maccabean period, it apparently brought the opposite: death.

When Paul supports his thesis with a formulation from Ps. 143:2, he takes up a line in which the psalms of lament, such as this one, raise the question of the honoring of God's promises. In spite of the law's promises of life, God's righteousness cannot be experienced. In such psalms it is primarily the absence of help with illnesses and enemies that the petitioner laments. It is necessary for God to intervene as proof of his righteousness. The psalms of lament are written precisely to report such an actual intervention of God, and therefore they include an element of praise.

In this complex of the separation of God's promise of life and the seemingly contrary personal experience of humanity, talk of *faith* also has its place in Judaism. It designates the attempt to mediate between what is handed down as creed, what is promised concerning righteousness, and the experience of humanity, in which the creed is not verifiable and the promise seems not to be honored.

In Judaism the law shapes the possibility of this mediation; faith is then the behavior of humanity according to the law, even if holding fast to the law eventuates in martyrdom. At this point, the question of the fulfillability of the law is not a primary question in Judaism, nor does it form the main theme for Paul's reorientation of the relationship of law, faith, and righteousness toward Christology; indeed, in reference to his time before Christ, he can call himself blameless "as to righteousness under the law" (Phil. 3:6), without expressing a doubt as to the basic fulfillability of the law.

Paul now breaks up this close relationship between law, faith, and righteousness and sees the mediation between promise and experience no longer in the law but in the new reference point of faith indicated by "Jesus Christ." Hence, the antithesis of his proclamation of justification is, strictly speaking, not faith versus law, but faith in Jesus Christ versus the law, because the mediation sought in faith no longer lies in the law, but rather in Christ. The real theme of his statements on justification is thus Christology. Against the Jewish perception, "in spite of the law, there is no righteousness," he places "by doing the works of the law . . . no one will be justified." He will offer the exegetical proof for this understanding out of the law itself in 3:6 to 4:7.

Thus, once again we see the central function of Christology and note also that Paul is not just attacking some aberrant developments of a so-called late Judaism, with which he would have an easy time; rather, he is directing questions at the heart of the Old Testament itself. The very "knowledge" of the Jews leads him to this conclusion, which he reached for his own life at Damascus.

[2:17] This raises an objection that Paul presumably heard often from the Jewish side: Is it not precisely the crucial difference between righteousness and sin that is compromised here? Are the Jews, then, not just sinners like the Gentiles? Is Christ just a servant, or agent, of sin, not of righteousness?

[2:18] Paul here denies this objection. Peter was not oversteping the law in Antioch when he at first did not hold to the legal precepts, but only when he then consciously returned to the law and thereby called his previous behavior into question.

[2:19-20] Paul substantiates this conclusion with first-person statements whose subject, however, is not the individual *I* of Paul in contrast to Peter; rather, he lifts up in exemplary form how he understands his conversion. The logic of the assertions does not rest primarily on his individual experience, which at best could be a model but would not be theologically transmittable; it rests on Christology.

The statements on "dying" and "living" indeed have the same structure as the christological assertions that speak of Jesus' death and resurrection: Christ died and lives; "I died . . . so that I might live to God" (cf. also 2 Cor. 13:4; Rom. 6:10). The logic is grounded precisely in Paul's assertion that "I have been crucified with Christ."

The law itself killed this *I* but in the process forfeited its power over the dead (cf. Rom. 7:1-2, 6). In the cross of Christ, the law abolishes itself, as Paul will show in 3:13. The new life of the murdered *I* is now no longer one's own life; it is life for God. And one's own *I* no longer lives: the place of this *I* is taken by Christ. If the theme of righteousness in Judaism can be described as seeking life through the law, then Paul reverses the issue: the law brings to the *I* not the life it promises but death; finding one's identity comes only in what is represented by the term *Christ,* not by way of the law.

This new life, however, is still not a life in the heavenly world but a life "in the flesh," a life that faith has as the transmitter of promise and experience in the Christ event, which is now expressly named again with the title "Son of God" (cf. 1:16) and again in the form of assertions about the death of Christ (cf. 1:4).

This Christology makes it possible for Paul to revolutionize the question of righteousness. To a great extent the law could, of course, integrate the negative experiences of humanity, such as illness and suffering, and even death. Nonetheless, Jesus' death on the cross stood under the curse of the law (cf. 3:13) and was not covered by the law; on the contrary, Christ destroyed the law itself.

[2:21] It was already known in Judaism that righteousness is the grace of God. Hence one could use against Paul the argument that he overlooks this motif. Paul believes, however, that he is the first to let God's grace really come into its own, in that he understands it on the basis of Christ's death, whereas the law cannot give the promised righteousness, and this defect is shown precisely by the death of Christ.

Paul's speech in Antioch contains what is customarily designated as the apostle's "doctrine of justification." For him it is the consequence of Christology and, beyond Christology, also the personal consequence of his conversion at Damascus. The concrete cause of the conflict in Antioch shows that not everyone drew this fundamental conclusion from the one gospel. To be sure, there was a mission to the Gentiles, there were churches with Jewish and Gentile Christians, and the authorities in Jerusalem recognized the missionary activity of Paul as the preaching of the one gospel. And yet on this point he remained alone. A later writer would even attempt, in the name of the Lord's brother James, to carry all of this ad absurdum (cf. Jas. 2:14-26). And yet for Paul this is where the church stands or falls—the church, be it noted, of Jews and Gentiles.

The whole passage beginning with 1:11, which reaches its goal in 2:15-21, presents the history of the gospel from Damascus to Galatia, with the aim of defending it against another gospel, but Paul never cites any particular content of this other gospel. He continually tells his story, however, from the viewpoint of "Jerusalem": a good deal of space is taken by the two visits there, and the descriptions of the periods outside of Jerusalem are focused on his relationship to the church there (cf. 1:17a, 22-24).

Clearly Jerusalem is one theme of the discussion. This does not mean that Paul is concerned only with proof of his own independence from Jerusalem. If he had such a proof in mind, it would not succeed with a presentation that showed him plainly fixed on Jerusalem. We must assume, rather, that the opponents brought Jerusalem into the discussion for themselves and their gospel. According to Paul's intention, however, when he mentions the false believers in Jerusalem (2:4), the Galatians are supposed to think of their new teachers—as Paul's direct address in 2:5 shows—and recognize them as such false believers.

This does not necessarily mean that they were actually sent out from Jerusalem, as perhaps those "from James" were sent to Antioch (2:12). There is, indeed, always the possibility of appearing in the name of a distant metropolis, without being directly legitimized by it. Such a penetration into the purely Gentile Christian churches of Galatia on the part of Jerusalem would also be a clear violation of the spirit and letter of the Jerusalem agreement (cf. 2:9).

Paul exposes such an appeal to Jerusalem as a lie. The gospel he preached was, from the very beginning, in agreement with the gospel of the Jerusalemites and also accepted as such by them. The Jerusalemites, including James, are not missionaries of the law who place the law above the gospel; rather, as Jewish Christians, they allow the law still to have its own validity, without trying to force it on the Gentile Christians. This is seen in their behavior regarding Titus, but it is perhaps also seen precisely in the conflict in Antioch, where Peter and Barnabas are, for Paul, the guilty ones, not the people from James. When the opponents offer their proclamation as pure Jerusalem teaching, they are deceiving the Galatians.

The basis of the argument for Paul is simply the one gospel, not a Jerusalem or a Gentile Christian gospel. Its content is the Christology in the titles *Christ* and *Son of God* or in brief statements on the meaning of Jesus' death. And this one gospel is what Paul preached from the very beginning and also what he represented in critical situations in Jerusalem and Antioch. Because the Christ event itself is the end of the law, the gospel, in Paul's opinion, cannot be the continuation of the Jewish tradition, but only its antithesis. This understanding he presents in his own way, which he logically maintains from the beginning.

For Paul the legitimation of the gospel lies in the content of the proclamation, not in his own conversion. His experience made him a preacher of the gospel but did not create the gospel. As often as Paul comes back to Damascus (1:12, 16; cf. 1:23; 2:7, 16, 19), he does so not for his own benefit but for the sake of the gospel; the apostle is totally absorbed in the gospel. He reduces his own biography to the gospel, not the gospel to his own experience. Likewise, faith is not defined primarily from the standpoint of believers, but by its content, which is identical with the content of the gospel.

Questions to the Galatians

Text

3:1 You foolish Galatians! Who has bewitched you? It was before your eyes that Jesus Christ was publicly exhibited as crucified!

2 The only thing I want to learn from you is this: Did you receive the Spirit by doing the works of the law or by believing what you heard?

3 Are you so foolish? Having started with the Spirit, are you now ending with the flesh?

4 Did you experience so much for nothing?—if it really was for nothing.

5 Well, then, does God supply you with the Spirit and work miracles among you by your doing the works of the law, or by your believing what you heard?

Analysis

Paul could have continued in his report, "And then, after I left Antioch, I came through Cilicia to you in Galatia." But he had already abandoned the report style toward the end of the previous chapter and switched to a fundamental presentation of the gospel. He takes what in 2:15-21 was evidently his earlier speech in Antioch and now reshapes it into questions to the Galatians. He reminds them of the gospel that he preached to them: no other gospel than the one whose path from Damascus to them he described in 1:13—2:21. He asks them questions that they can really answer only his way; otherwise, of course, everything that has happened before would truly be in vain, which he does not believe at all possible.

They know why Paul came to them: for the sake of the truth of the gospel—this he does not need to tell them again. What he tries to convince them with, however, is not simply the memory of his earlier preaching but the gospel itself; not his appearance with them but the crucified Christ, whom he had exhibited before their eyes. Beyond the refutation of the opponents' assertions in reference to Jerusalem, which Paul

51

accomplished in 1:13—2:21, he now begins the proof of the gospel itself, a proof he draws largely from the law itself.

Commentary

[3:1] It is almost as if Paul can explain the Galatians' rapid falling away from the gospel (cf. 1:6) only by saying that witchcraft must have been involved. As in the previous chapters, he gives the content of his earlier preaching again as "Jesus Christ," recalling here too the titular sense of *Christ,* emphasized with the addition here of "as crucified."

Actually, one would have to marvel at this lifting up of the cross, had it not been long ago rendered harmless as only a Christian symbol. When Paul consciously named nothing but the crucified One as the content of his preaching, it constituted a hindrance to his missionary work. The key word *cross* signaled to his listeners first of all that here he was talking about someone whom the Roman authorities had executed, and with this gospel Paul now stepped publicly right into the middle of the eastern half of the Roman Empire.

It is not surprising, then, that the early Christian tradition that Paul adopts prefers to speak more neutrally of the "death" of Christ, without mentioning the particular manner of death. But Paul believes he must insert into this tradition the memory that Jesus did not die just any death, but death on the cross, without noting, say, that this happened unjustly or rested on pure misunderstanding. It must have been a stumbling block to the Jews—indeed, death on the cross stood under the curse of the law (cf. v. 13)—and folly to the Greeks, who could perhaps have pity on someone executed by the Romans but would not expect any wisdom from the event (cf. 1 Cor. 1:23).

To what extent was precisely this crucified Christ—and he alone —"the power of God and the wisdom of God" (1 Cor. 1:24)? The Galatians, in any case, had accepted this proclamation, and through it they had experienced God's power and God's wisdom: his power in the bodily weakness of the apostle (cf. 4:13-14), his wisdom in the folly of the gospel.

[3:2] What they have had since then is the Spirit, and they cannot deny that they received the Spirit earlier by believing—by hearing with faith— and not later when they devoted themselves to "doing the works of the law." With "believing what you heard" Paul picks up what in 1:7 is called the gospel of Christ, in 1:16 proclaiming the Son of God, and in 1:23 proclaiming faith. The key word *gospel,* which ruled over the first two chapters of the letter, is now missing while Paul is busy presenting this gospel itself, which he indeed began already in 2:15-21. Nonetheless, the word itself occurs twice more (cf. 3:8 and 4:13).

The "Spirit" is what matters to the life of the Christian as a whole: not only in regard to ethics (Paul will talk about this under the key word *Spirit* in the final part of the letter, 5:13—6:10), but as an effect that is experienced as quite real, for example, in the miracles Paul refers to in v. 5, in prayer (cf. 4:6), and in the multiplicity of gifts of the Spirit in the church, with which he must deal in 1 Corinthians 12–14. Such possession of the Spirit is linked with baptism (Gal. 3:27), but not exclusively. The Galatians know what Paul is talking about here, the reality of which should actually convince them: the gospel had opened up for them new experiences of meaningful life.

[3:3] Will they also accept it, however, when Paul considers their recent conversion to a different gospel not a further advance but a falling back from the possession of the Spirit? Their new teachers, in any case, could not let that stand, for the law also promised the Spirit and the possibility of leaving the flesh, transferring out of the earthly sphere and participating in the divine. Thus, like the alternative of faith and law itself, this is another alternative that cannot be accepted by Judaism. The law promises this very Spirit, but Paul asserts that to hold to the law means to live in the flesh, just as for him the law, as the "traditions of my ancestors," is only "according to man."

[3:4-5] The opponents promised the Galatians the Spirit as the result of works of the law, and Paul asks them whether the Spirit they have experienced is not enough for them, whether everything had been in vain. He is at a loss (cf. 4:11), and so he repeats then in v. 5 the question he had asked in v. 2, in order to answer it exegetically in the following sections.

The "demonstration of the Spirit and of power" (cf. 1 Cor. 2:4), in recalling what the Galatians possess, is supported argumentatively from the law. The interpretation of the story of Abraham in 3:6—4:7 will show that the Spirit can come only from faith and not from works of the law (3:6-14), that only those who believe are heirs to the promise issued to Abraham, not those living from the law (3:15-29), because through the only Son of God, Christians have become God's children and thus heirs (4:1-7). For the "truth of the gospel," the law itself is called as a witness (cf. Rom. 3:21). Christology and the interpretation of the Old Testament form the two basic elements of Paul's theological reflection.

In the address to the Galatians (vv. 1-5), we have the first concrete indication of the content of the opponents' preaching. In 1:6-11 Paul polemicizes only against "a different gospel"; in 1:11—2:21 "Jerusalem" and "faith versus law" are to be presumed as themes, but they are never expressly cited. Now, however, Paul accosts the Galatians with the thought that their turning to that other "gospel" is a turning to "the works of the law" and that they are thereby going backward along his own path from the law to Christian faith, which he has described to them as the way of the gospel and not just that of some individual named Paul (1:13ff.).

In the following sections Paul questions whether the law can achieve at all what it promises: to give righteousness, life, Spirit, and blessing. He demonstrates that faith in Christ can bring all of this, whereas on the path of the law one always remains in the world of sin, death, flesh, and curse.

Once again, Paul does not make it easy for himself by attacking merely the aberrant developments in Judaism. He begins, rather, at the center of the Old Testament itself with the promise to Abraham (v. 6), the giving of the law at Sinai (v. 19), the law's promise of blessing (vv. 6-14), and the promise to the righteous of becoming God's children (4:1-7), before he comes back to the beginnings of the gospel in Galatia (4:8-20) and again to the two themes of "Jerusalem" and "Abraham" (4:21-31), and before finally in 5:1-12 he goes directly into the demand for circum-cision in Galatia.

For Paul circumcision is one of the "works of the law," and he starts by assuming that the Old Testament is accepted by the Galatians as well as by their new teachers as a basis for argument. Certainly, his argumentation goes beyond the concrete situation, but not so much that he completely fails to address it. Whoever lets himself be circumcised holds to the law, and vice versa—that double implication for Paul was the content of his life and his proclamation before Damascus, and that is also the consequence of the other "gospel" in Galatia, especially since the law was offered not as coercion but as liberation.

The Blessing of Abraham
and the Curse of the Law

Text

3:6 Just as Abraham "believed God, and it was reckoned to him as righteousness,"

7 so, you see, those who believe are the descendants of Abraham.

8 And the scripture, foreseeing that God would justify the Gentiles by faith, declared the gospel beforehand to Abraham, saying, "All the Gentiles shall be blessed in you."

9 For this reason, those who believe are blessed with Abraham who believed.

10 For all who rely on the works of the law are under a curse; for it is written, "Cursed is everyone who does not observe and obey all the things written in the book of the law."

11 Now it is evident that no one is justified before God by the law; for "The one who is righteous will live by faith."

12 But the law does not rest on faith; on the contrary, "Whoever does the works of the law will live by them."

13 Christ redeemed us from the curse of the law by becoming a curse for us—for it is written, "Cursed is everyone who hangs on a tree"—

14 in order that in Christ Jesus the blessing of Abraham might come to the Gentiles, so that we might receive the promise of the Spirit through faith.

Analysis

The aim of this passage is to answer the question in v. 5: the Spirit comes indeed from faith and not from the law (v. 14b). Paul demonstrates this truth through an interpretation of Gen. 15:6. The theme of *Abraham* is not chosen arbitrarily, for whoever in Judaism and early Christianity spoke of faith had to speak of Abraham, of whom the "law" in Gen. 15:6 said that God "reckoned it to him as righteousness." As we shall see, however, the whole tradition of the interpretation of this fundamental text stands against the interpretation that Paul gives it, and the tradition seems not to be purely erroneous but to have support in the text itself. The author who wrote in the name of James also attempts to play off this tradition of interpretation against Paul (Jas. 2:21-24).

Israel called itself "Abraham's children." But Paul questions the right of this appeal to the father Abraham even more fundamentally than John the Baptist had done (cf. Luke 3:8/Matt. 3:9) and calls Abraham the father of believers only, not of those who live by the law.

For the Jewish mission to the Gentiles, however, Abraham was the very model of the one who converted from paganism to the true God and to the law. To this extent Abraham could have also been an attractive preaching theme for the Galatian opponents, an awe-inspiring figure from the distant past whom one could read about in the law and whose significance was that one should hold to his God. Thus Paul was perhaps forced even by the preaching of the opponents in Galatia to address this theme and lay out his own interpretation of Gen. 15:6.

We are admittedly accustomed to reading this fundamental text, Gen. 15:6, on the basis of the Pauline interpretation, and thus it seems only reasonable that Paul should choose this very passage and set it against the linking of faith with law. It looks different, however, when one reads the text for itself and then inquires into its transmission through the Jewish tradition.

The Old Testament text, like its interpreter Paul, is oriented toward the question of righteousness; its form recalls sentences such as Ezek. 18:9: If a person "follows my statutes, and is careful to observe my ordinances, acting faithfully—such a one is righteous; he shall surely live, says the Lord God." Ezekiel 18 compiles a sort of confessional list of things that a righteous person does not do, and one who refrains from these things is granted life. Psalm 24 shows that the form of an originally cultic ritual has apparently been adopted here and continues to be effective, even without the cultic connection.

In Gen. 15:6 believing the Lord, or "faith," takes the place of "follows my statutes, and is careful to observe my ordinances," and then Gen. 26:5 breaks up the short formula "faith" again: there the promise given to Abraham is justified "because Abraham obeyed my voice and kept my charge, my commandments, my statutes, and my laws."

Similar is the text of Hab. 2:4, which Paul cites in v. 11: "The one who is righteous will live by faith" (this follows the Hebrew text; the Septuagint says, "The righteous shall live by my faithfulness"). Here too faith/faithfulness is the encompassing concept for a life in accordance with God's commandment, and the definition of faith from the standpoint of the law is thus maintained even more strongly in Judaism.

The word *faith* does not occur in what are assumed to be early layers in the Old Testament, and Gen. 15:6 is also not to be included in the original source writings of "the five books of Moses." The term *faith* appears when the problem it designates becomes more and more urgent: the problem of the separation of creed and promise from the experience of reality that seems to contradict them (cf. above, p. 47).

This tension, in fact, also defines the whole story of Abraham: the promise of the possession of the land and the blessing of children versus his actual existence as a landless nomad and childless old man. What he relies upon is the promise, and this holding fast to the promise, which cannot be verified in reality, is what is meant by *faith.* In faith he anticipates the promise, just as later a life in accordance with God's life-giving law is asserted as already possible in this world and in spite of this world.

Whoever read the story of Abraham could find in it a little of one's own experience of the tension between promise and reality, but now one could also read in the "law" itself, which tells Abraham's story, that righteousness is pledged to those who hold to the promise given in the law. Faith as the maintenance of this tension then expresses itself in obedience to this law.

Thus the interpretation of Gen. 15:6 on the basis of the law is precisely not a misunderstanding of this text that Paul merely needed to straighten out in order to reemphasize its original sense. On the contrary, he is disavowing something that appears to be a part of Gen. 15:6 itself.

Several representative examples of the history of interpretation of this passage in Judaism can be given, and their number could be multiplied almost at will. Before Paul, however, no one can be found who, like him, interpreted Abraham from the standpoint of the antithesis between law and faith.

> [19] Abraham was the great father of a multitude of nations,
>   and no one has been found like him in glory;
> [20] he kept the law of the Most High,
>   and was taken into covenant with him;
>   he established the covenant in his flesh.
>   and when he was tested he was found faithful.
> [21] Therefore the Lord assured him by an oath
>   that the nations would be blessed through his posterity;
>   that he would multiply him like the dust of the earth,
>   and exalt his posterity like the stars,
>   and cause them to inherit from sea to sea
>   and from the River to the ends of the earth.
>
>   (Sir. 44:19-21)

The book of the Jewish scribe Jesus Ben Sira, known as Sirach or by the later name Ecclesiasticus, was written in the Hebrew language around 200 B.C.E. and later translated by his grandson into Greek. This translation is a part of the Septuagint, as well as the Vulgate, and thus is also in the canon of the Roman Catholic church, although in Protestant Bibles the book belongs to the Apocrypha.

In this adaptation the most important motifs of the Abraham story are repeated: father, people, covenant, circumcision, oath, posterity, blessing, and inheritance. The word rendered "faithful" is the same word that Paul uses in Gal. 3:9 (those who "believe," literally, are "of faith"). Thus the promise applies to Abraham's faith (Gen. 15:6), which he demonstrated under ordeal; the reference here is to the story of the sacrifice of Isaac in Gen. 22:1-19, which ends with the promise renewed (cf. also Jas. 2:21-23).

At the beginning and as a summary of the whole, however, is the statement in Sirach 44 that Abraham observed the law of the Most High. Keeping the law, the covenant agreement with God that was sealed with circumcision, and perseverance in the ordeal as proof of his faith are what made Abraham the model and established the promise of blessing.

⁵⁰Now, my children, show zeal for the law, and give your lives for the covenant of our fathers. ⁵¹Remember the deeds of the fathers, which they did in their generations; and receive great honor and an everlasting name. ⁵²Was not Abraham found faithful when tested, and it was reckoned to him as righteousness? (1 Macc. 2:50-52)

First Maccabees was originally written in Hebrew before 100 B.C.E. Like Sirach, it is also found in the Apocrypha, because it was included in the Septuagint and the Vulgate.

The cited verses are part of a testament that the dying Mattathias left behind for his sons, the "Maccabees." The first two verses contain the admonition to hold oneself completely and totally to the law to the point of giving one's life, to be fervent as Paul was (cf. Gal. 1:14). The promise for such giving is seen in the works of the fathers, the first of whom was Abraham. Here Gen. 15:6 is even more closely linked with the sacrifice of Isaac than in Sirach. Abraham's perseverance, with the resulting recognition by God, is the model of zeal for the law.

The Jewish theologian Philo of Alexandria (about whose dates we know only that at an advanced age he was in Rome in 39–40 C.E.) presents the way of Abraham as the way from the false gods of his homeland Chaldea to the true God and thus as the way of Gentiles who convert to Judaism (cf. his writing "On Abraham," 60–88). Here Abraham is the first proselyte and thus the model for all proselytes.

In Abraham's time the law to which the proselytes committed themselves, including circumcision, had not yet been proclaimed at Sinai; but he knew it already as unwritten law and obeyed it. The relationship between Abraham and the law to be given later is defined in a quite different way by Paul in v. 17!

Even in the New Testament there are other interpretations of Abraham than those that Paul gives here and in Romans 4. As already mentioned, Jas. 2:21-23 harks back to the connection between Gen. 15:6 and the sacrifice of Isaac in order to derive the thesis that works of the law belong quite well to righteousness. In Heb. 11:8-19 Abraham's faith is his unwavering hope in the future promise, yet without any reflection here of the relationship between law and faith in regard to the promise (cf. also Heb. 6:12-20).

Therefore, if Paul intends to assert his antithesis of faith and law, he must justify it through a new interpretation of Gen. 15:6, because what this text seems to suggest is precisely not such an antithesis but rather an intimate connection between faith and law, one that was even intended in the passage's origin. Thus Gen. 15:6 could be held forth to him as a counterargument, as proof of the very thesis of a linkage between faith and law. In any case, Paul could not simply take this passage at face value and use it against the proclamation of the law. For this purpose he needed a convincing new interpretation.

Structure

The course of the argumentation in vv. 6-14 strikes us as very complicated, especially since Paul seems indiscriminately to take Old Testament passages out of their context and apply them just as it suits him. That has brought him the scorn of many Old Testament scholars who believe that in his line of reasoning they can see only caprice. In this connection, one might advance the excuse that Paul had in mind only a contemporary Pharisaic understanding of the law, not what the law was originally. But can we make such a distinction? The exegesis of old writings is always determined in part by the transmission of those texts. And can we exclude the possibility that Paul nevertheless understood the Old Testament better?

The structure of this section can be outlined as follows:

5 Question: Does the Spirit come by doing the works of the law, or by your believing what you heard (i.e., by faith)?
  6 Gen. 15:6 is cited, leading to the thesis that
    7 "those who believe (literally, who are of faith) are the descendants of Abraham."
    Substantiation:
      8 Justification comes from faith.
        8-9 With faith comes blessing (Gen. 12:3; 18:18).
        10 With the law comes the curse (Deut. 27:26).
      11 Justification does not come from the law.
        Righteousness comes not from the law but from faith (Hab. 2:4).
        12 Law and faith are opposites (Lev. 18:5 vs. Hab. 2:4).
      13 Christ's death ends the curse of the law (Deut. 21:23).
    14a Conclusion: Therefore the blessing belongs to the Gentiles.
14b Answer: Therefore the Spirit comes through faith.

The question in v. 5 is answered in v. 14b. The reasons for this rest on the interpretation of Gen. 15:6 asserted in advance as a thesis in v. 7, which is repeated as proved in v. 14a. Verses 8-13 provide the substantiation for the interpretation of Gen. 15:6 given in v. 7. In vv. 8-9 the topic is the blessing that is associated with faith; v. 10 speaks of the curse that belongs to the law. Verses 11-12 demonstrate the antithesis between faith and law, and v. 13 establishes the end of the time of the curse with the death of Jesus on the cross.

We thus have again the same temporal order of law and faith as in Paul's biography in 1:13-16; before the law, however, the gospel was preached "beforehand to Abraham" (3:8):

gospel	law	through Christ	faith
	curse		blessing
	flesh		Spirit

Thus the law falls into the same column with curse, just as it was already linked with the flesh in vv. 2-3, whereas blessing and Spirit alone are to be grouped with the faith made possible by Christ.

Commentary

[3:6] In this verse Paul cites Gen. 15:6 in the form in which the Septuagint offers the text, that is, with the passive voice in order to avoid the divine name: "and it was reckoned to him as righteousness," in contrast to the Hebrew text: "and he reckoned it to him as righteousness." The introductory word should be translated "as" (note KJV: "even as"), not "thus" (RSV); it is probably not the abbreviation of a complete introductory formula, "as it is written," but is supposed to underscore syntactically the connection between faith and righteousness even more strongly than the text does by itself. The "as" does not designate the quantity or quality of Abraham's faith but only stresses the connection between faith and righteousness, from which Paul, against all tradition, infers that for the law, righteousness is excluded (cf. vv. 11-12).

[3:7] Thus Paul chooses for himself a key text of his tradition—perhaps also a key text of his opponents—into which he must go if he wants to speak of faith. He asserts, against all tradition, that it is wrong to lay claim to this text as an association of law and faith; he interprets it in such a way that only "those who believe" are descendants of Abraham, which in this connection also means that those under the law wrongly give themselves this designation.

Here too, under *faith* we must keep in mind the content asserted in 2:16 with "Jesus Christ," in 2:20 with the title "Son of God," and in the statement on the meaning of Jesus' death. In Rom. 4:23-25 Paul expressly establishes the link between the faith of Abraham and the faith of Christians. "Those who believe" are those who have accepted the gospel that has the same content that faith has; they are Jewish and Gentile Christians who do not follow the way of the law.

[3:8-9] Here Paul first establishes this interpretation of Gen. 15:6 positively with the promise of blessing to Abraham. The text to which he refers is a mixture of Gen. 12:3 and 18:18. *Blessing* here is similar in meaning to *righteousness*. The antithesis of blessing and curse is already contained in Gen. 12:3, even if in a somewhat different form: "I will bless those who bless you, and the one who curses you I will curse."

For Paul the argument of these passages lies in the fact that the blessing, even in the Old Testament text itself, is related to "the nations," which naturally means all nations, including Israel, to which Abraham belongs. In other Old Testament texts, however, "the nations" can be precisely the opposite of Israel, the people of God, and then means the Gentiles (cf. 2:15). This is the way Paul understands these passages, and therein lies the logic of his conclusion in v. 9: "those who believe" are the "Gentiles" (cf. 1:16: "that I might proclaim him among the Gentiles"), or conversely, the promise of blessing is for the Gentiles, that is, for all (Jewish and Gentile Christians) who are of faith. Thus up to this point Paul has proven exegetically the binding of blessing to faith.

[3:10] The curse, in contrast, belongs to the law. Paul bases this connection on Deut. 27:26, which stands at the end of a short series of curses in Deut. 27:15-26. In it offenses are named that are not easily discovered and hence are also hard to punish. Therefore, they bear the threat of a self-fulfilling curse. Here, naturally, it is a question of the cursing of those who do not follow these commandments; correspondingly, a blessing is promised to those who keep the commandments. Paul, however, interprets the verse in the opposite way, as is linguistically possible—even if logically difficult—in the Greek text: the very doing of the commandments that are written in this book stands under the curse, and under the curse falls the person who does not hold to these commandments.

The text is located toward the end of "the five books of Moses," so that "the book of the law" means precisely the whole law. One should translate (in contrast to NRSV), "Everyone who does not observe and obey all the things written in the book of the law is cursed to do them." Paul's meaning is: "No one who adheres to all that is written in the book of the law stands under the blessing." Of course, Paul cannot find such a sentence in the law, and therefore he must force his interpretation of Deut. 27:26 against its original meaning.

[3:11-12] Through this association of blessing and faith, curse and law, Paul proves the point that righteousness and faith belong together. He here goes further to the opposite conclusion that righteousness and law consequently have nothing to do with each other. The association of righteousness with faith alone is demonstrated to him by the juxtaposition of Hab. 2:4 and Lev. 18:5. This can have the power of proof only if *live* in the two texts is understood without any emphasis and not taken in the sense of the full promise of life, which would then be given also to the law in Lev. 18:5.

| The righteous person | lives | by faith | (Hab. 2:4) |
| Whoever does the law | lives | by it | (Lev. 18:5) |

Paul concludes that no one can be justified by works of the law, since righteousness, according to Hab. 2:4, is associated only with faith, but not with the doing of the law in Lev. 18:5.

[3:13] How, then, can one ever come to faith, righteousness, blessing, and Spirit? The answer has already been given in the first two chapters of Paul's letter: through that which is designated briefly by *Christ* as the content of the gospel as well as of faith. Here in v. 13, however, it also becomes clear why in v. 1 Paul placed so much emphasis on the manner of execution on the cross: such a death stands under an express curse of the law. For this conclusion Paul cites Deut. 21:23. The text refers to the public display of the body of the executed person, a custom one occasionally still hears about today. In Judaism this passage was related to those who had been crucified, who did not die until on the cross—they were not killed beforehand. The curse associated with the law came to an end, in that the law itself cursed Christ (cf. 2:19).

The motif of redemption (cf. 4:5), which recalls the redemption of slaves, perhaps suggests a later theme of the letter, the antithesis of slavery and freedom, which, like the previous antitheses, Paul will associate with the basic antithesis of law and faith. The death of Christ has its counterpart in the dying of the self through the law; his resurrection, in the new life of Christ in place of the dead self (2:19-20).

[3:14] The first conclusion that Paul draws from all of this (v. 14a) is the confirmation of his interpretation of Gen. 15:6 in v. 7: the blessing of Abraham does indeed belong to the Gentiles, to those who are of faith and not to those who keep the law. From this point there follows as a second conclusion (v. 14b) the correctness of his thesis, already contained in the question of v. 5: the Galatians did indeed receive the Spirit from the preaching of faith, not from the works of the law, because this is the Spirit of the Son of God (cf. 4:6).

Yet what has Paul actually proved here? We have seen how he employs some quotations completely in their original sense but interprets others in a fashion that is at least questionable, and even cites Lev. 18:5 in v. 12 against its real meaning. If his logic were based merely on such poor familiarity with the Old Testament, it would still not be excusable on the grounds that at that time (as today) there were others who were even worse. His argumentation would have been quickly dismissed even then in Galatia; it would not have had to wait for the presuppositions of today's exegesis. The trenchancy of the discussion around Paul then (as today) is explained by Paul's assertion that after Christ there is a new and more appropriate understanding of the Old Testament, and the Galatians and their new teachers had to deal with this assertion.

Let us recall once again the antithesis of *blessing* and *curse*. This comes from the Old Testament itself, but the relationship there is different from that in Paul, as shown in the accompanying table.

Blessing and Curse in the Old Testament and in Paul

Old Testament		Paul	
In the covenant	Outside the covenant and the law	Before	Now
law	—	law	Christ → faith
blessing	curse	curse	Christ → blessing
life	death	death	Christ → life

What in Paul becomes a temporal sequence through Christ operates in the Old Testament as two simultaneous possibilities, whose realization is decided by one's behavior vis-à-vis the law: whoever accepts the life offered in the law, the promise of the covenant, stands under the blessing; whoever rejects the law stands under the curse, under death. Thus Paul tears apart what belongs together in the Old Testament, in which even faith or nonobservance can be inserted into the scheme as the life that, respectively, corresponds or does not correspond to the law and merits the promise of blessing or the threat of curse.

The presupposition of the whole matter in the Old Testament, however, is the covenant as God's action of grace, his promise of life, so that blessing or curse, life or death, actually does not depend on humanity's earning them through works, but on the fact that God himself gives blessing and life. The law is the document of this promise and thus the possibility of maintaining this promise.

In the Old Testament this whole relationship can be seen most clearly in Leviticus 26 and Deuteronomy 28–30. Leviticus 26 is the closing section of an originally independent corpus of the law, the so-called Law of Holiness of Leviticus 17–26: "These are the statutes and ordinances and laws that the Lord established between himself and the people of Israel on Mount Sinai through Moses" (Lev. 26:46). In its present form it clearly presupposes the destruction of Jerusalem in 587 B.C.E. and the deportation of its inhabitants to Babylon (cf. 26:31-33, 44).

The closing section of this corpus of the law begins in 26:1-2 with the repetition of the first commandment as the basic commandment of the law in general. Then in 26:3-13 follows a series of promised blessings if Israel will "follow in my statutes and keep my commandments and observe them faithfully" (26:3): fruitfulness, peace, victories, and God's own presence—in short, everything that is described, for example, in Psalm 72 as "righteousness." Verse 12 cites the covenant formula: "I . . . will be your God, and you shall be my people." The covenant of God will be in effect if both parties behave in accordance with this covenant.

In vv. 14-39, however, a disproportionately longer series announces the curse that will come if Israel does not hold to the law and thus breaks the covenant: diseases, barrenness, war, defeats, and the absence of God—a total catastrophe, in everything the opposite of that hoped-for condition of righteousness. As already mentioned, this series of curses, however, addresses the reality of the exile period and not merely the possibility that is exhibited solely for pedagogical reasons. These curses have been realized: the cities of Israel are trash piles, the land is desolated, and Israel is scattered among the nations (vv. 31-33).

God's history with his people Israel does not have to end here, however. Verses 40-45 show the possibility of a new beginning initiated by God, who will remember his covenant with the fathers, who experienced the blessing. The prerequisite for this is Israel's conversion and renewed dedication to the law. The actual aim of this text is thus not to establish the fulfillment of the curse but to make the ensuing catastrophe comprehensible and to show the way out. The promised blessings of God outlast the curse that has been executed against Israel. The criterion for blessing and curse, including a new time of blessing, is and remains the law. The result is thus three historical periods that are bound together by the law and the covenant:

The time of the fathers	The present	The future
blessing	curse	blessing
the promise of the law ⟶		

Similarly, Deuteronomy 28 was originally the closing section of a corpus of the law that began with Deuteronomy 12. Here too the series of blessings and curses are of disproportionate length. Deut. 28:1-14 likewise describes the blessing as fruitfulness, military success, and covenant with God. Here too, however, the curse is the reality of the present. Israel did not hold to the law and was led into exile (vv. 36, 49-65); indeed, God even revoked part of the promise to Abraham: "Although once you were as numerous as the stars in heaven, you shall be left few in number" (v. 62).

Deut. 29:1 presents a conclusion: "These are the words of the covenant that the Lord commanded Moses to make with the Israelites in the land of Moab, in addition to the covenant that he had made with them at Horeb." In 29:2-29 Moses anticipates the execution of the curse, and with this account the present time of the exile is reached. Not until the next chapter, however, do we have the possibility of a new beginning through renewed dedication to the law, which will have as its consequence the lifting of the curse and the carrying out of the blessing.

Chapters 28–30, however, also come at the close of "the five books of Moses" and thus of the law as a whole. This law tells of the blessing in the time of the fathers, a repeatedly jeopardized blessing, to be sure; yet the reader can pick up from the story of Abraham, as from the fathers in general, what is the point of trusting in the promise of blessing. That is why the law contains so much history, including the history of Israel's lapse in the wilderness and of God's maintaining the promise in spite of everything. At the same time, the law looks forward to Israel's falling away and the resulting realization of the curse in the time of exile and offers anew the blessing for the future.

Thus the sequence of those three sections of promise, curse, and blessing asserted by Paul has its origin here, and that is why the systematic diagrams on pages 62 and 63 correspond so well. For the Jewish tradition these three sections are held together by the covenant and the law itself; Paul, in contrast, associates the times of blessing only with faith, and only the time of the curse with the law. The promise that lies in the covenant is no longer related to the law, which is granted the possibility of effecting blessing. Thus through this new definition Paul fundamentally reinterprets a relationship that is part of the law itself and not just of a later misunderstanding of the law. The basis for this interpretation comes from the ongoing history of dealings with this law. Israel did indeed comply with the exhortation to renewed dedication to the law. It took the law seriously even in daily life, as Paul himself had done in model fashion during his Pharisaic past.

What did not occur, however, was an actual realization of the promised blessing. The deportees were indeed able to return home, and the temple was rebuilt, but what was that measured against the abundance of promised blessings that one read in the law? Furthermore, was Israel not repeatedly under foreign rule? Did it not, moreover, experience sickness, defeat, hunger, and even the absence of God? In the comparison of the promises with the experienced reality, the problem of faith and the reconciliation of experience with the promises and the confession cracked further open—at times so much so that the two were scarcely to be brought into congruence again.

Israel, however, was dependent on the law, which promised to achieve this reconciliation and could give the experience of blessing to those who held to it. This promise was especially reflected in theological wisdom, even to the extent of proposing solutions that, with the help of the law, invalidated the reality of experiences with the real world in favor of newer experiences. Apocalypticism also pushed forward with interpretations of the present as the experience of the curse in spite of the law, because the blessing promised in the law remained further in a future that would realize the promises at the end of this world. This certainty transmitted by the law made it possible to persevere in this world with the help of the law.

Paul now radically changes all of this in a very simple way from the standpoint of Christology. For him the reconciliation between promise and experience, which the law promised but in his opinion did not achieve, lies in this "Christ." In the confession of his death and his resurrection, the most extreme experiences of suffering and dying—indeed, under the curse of death on the cross—are found once again in the confession itself, and the promise of life is realized in his resurrection. Experience is thus no longer the opposite pole from confession but is incorporated into confession itself.

Gal. 2:20 shows how, after the death of the self, which is caused by the law, identification with this Christ makes life possible. For Paul the reason why the blessing failed to come lay in the law itself, because in his opinion it was not capable of accomplishing what it promised. Not until Christ stood under the curse did blessing, righteousness, and life become possible.

Thus the logic of the Pauline argumentation in vv. 6-14 rests on the christological interpretation of a key portion of the Old Testament itself. The question of a relevant interpretation of the Old Testament is thereby handed back to his critics. Certainly, the matter went beyond the current situation in Galatia, but was it therefore necessarily an inappropriate reaction to that situation? At least Paul himself gives an accounting from the law for the foundation of his gospel, as he earlier gave an accounting of the path of the gospel from Damascus to Galatia. In this way the gospel becomes transmittable and does not remain trapped in a purely individual experience, even if it is such a special experience as Paul's conversion.

What was at stake in the relationship between law and faith was also not just the issue of missionary methodology but the interpretation of human experience from the standpoint of the faith; this interpretation, not some methodology, explains the great attraction of Paul's proclamation of the crucified One particularly in the modern metropolises of the Roman Empire. What was offered here was the possibility of finding one's identity through identification with Christ.

If circumcision was a requirement of the other gospel in Galatia, then Abraham (who through circumcision entered into a covenant with God—cf. Gen. 17:10-11), combined with the promise of blessing also and especially for the Gentiles, could be a theme for his opponents' proclamation of that promise. Paul snatches from them this theme that they thought was theirs to bring into battle against him, and he demonstrates that Abraham belongs on the side of faith without the law.

Abraham's Inheritance
and the Law

Analysis

The last clause of the preceding section (v. 14b) contains a new key word, *promise,* which does not appear in the questions of vv. 1-5 or in the interpretation of Gen. 15:6 in 6-14 but which, as the central motif of the Abraham tradition, was already unavoidable in our commentary. That key word now dominates the following section, 3:15—4:7. In 3:6-14 Paul demonstrated from the Scripture itself that the Spirit cannot come from works of the law, but only from faith, and he now proves conversely that the promise given to Abraham is actually realized in faith.

The whole section of 3:15—4:7 is held together by a series of themes from the Abraham tradition:

promise: 3:14, 16-19, 21-22, 29
will/covenant (see under v. 15): 3:15, 17; cf. 4:2
offspring: 3:16, 19, 29
inheritance/heir: 3:18, 29; 4:1, 7
righteousness/justification: 3:21, 24
faith: 3:22-26

If we read again beside this list the text of Sir. 44:19-21 cited above (see p. 57), we see how, in contrast to the Jewish tradition, Paul removes the themes of law and circumcision from the Abraham connection (but cf. Rom. 4:11), disputes the law's right to the promise given to Abraham, and specifically avoids linking the covenant/will with circumcision.

Paul's interpretation of the Abraham tradition serves, furthermore, as proof of the antithesis of faith and law that he asserts. Again it seems possible that his opponents in Galatia based their requirement of circumcision on the promise of Abraham. Thus the issue once again is, Who has the right to appeal to the Old Testament, Paul or his opponents?

In contrast to the previous section, Paul is arguing here, except in

3:16, no longer with individual scriptural passages, but with the Abraham tradition as a whole. The line of reasoning leads up to the assertion in 3:29, which is repeated in 4:7: the people of faith, not the people of the law, are the legitimate heirs of Abraham.

The structure of the whole section results from the series of promise, law, and faith, worked out in vv. 6-14. Paul demonstrates first that the promise cannot become invalid through the law (3:15-18), then that the law is invalidated by faith (3:19-22), that those of faith are the heirs (3:23-29), and finally, summarizing in 4:1-7, that consequently the people of faith have actually entered the inheritance.

The Promise

Text

3:15 Brothers and sisters, I give an example from daily life: once a person's will has been ratified, no one adds to it or annuls it.

16 Now the promises were made to Abraham and to his offspring; it does not say, "And to offsprings," as of many; but it says, "And to your offspring," that is, to one person, who is Christ.

17 My point is this: the law, which came four hundred thirty years later, does not annul a covenant previously ratified by God, so as to nullify the promise.

18 For if the inheritance comes from the law, it no longer comes from the promise; but God granted it to Abraham through the promise.

Commentary

[3:15] Paul begins with an example out of the human sphere. The comparison with the laws of inheritance here and in 4:2 is not as immediately enlightening in English as in Greek, because for us *will* and *covenant* (as well as *testament*) are different words; the different meanings, however, are included in the Greek word used by Paul and employed in the Septuagint to render the Hebrew word that we normally translate "covenant" (cf. also the Old and New "Testaments").

Paul is thus working with the Greek text of the Old Testament, and this text, not the Hebrew one, is also the text the Galatians could read. That covenant with Abraham, however, also had in common with a will the fact that it had significance for following generations. A will cannot be changed in any legal system except, of course, by the one who drew it up.

The Old Testament story of Abraham speaks in two places of a covenant of God with Abraham. In Gen. 15:18, following the Gen. 15:6 passage just interpreted by Paul, that covenant is linked with the promise of land for the generation coming from Egypt, which is supposed to take possession of the territory from the Euphrates to the Nile (and almost did under Solomon). In Gen. 17:1-14, 23-27, God's covenant with Abraham

68

(including the promise of land) is sealed with the circumcision of Abraham and his son Ishmael. Circumcision is the sign of this covenant, and thus later on Abraham also circumcises his heir Isaac on the eighth day after birth (Gen. 21:4).

Paul is evidently referring to the situation in Genesis 15, while the Jewish tradition harks back to Genesis 17, which was perhaps also followed by the opponents in Galatia. Circumcision and the covenant with Abraham belong together here; then, however, the law is also a part of the Abraham story, because circumcision is a part of the law.

[3:16] In Paul's use of the comparison, the will/covenant is replaced by the "promises" as the content of this covenant. Here he quite objectively follows the Old Testament understanding of the covenant, which likewise comprehends it from the standpoint of promise. Now, however, Paul points out that according to the wording of the Old Testament texts, the promises were made to the "offspring" in the singular, not plural. In the Abraham stories the singular means first Isaac (Gen. 12:7; 13:15), but along with him also the numerous descendants who were likewise promised.

This leads to the conclusion that all descendants of Abraham who, like him, are circumcised are heirs of the covenant of Abraham, and *offspring of Abraham* is then also a self-designation of Israel, which named itself after a grandson of Abraham (cf. 2 Cor. 11:22). Paul, however, draws a different conclusion: for him "offspring" is a singular term that he can interpret only as Christ. Here again, *Christ* has the titular sense and thus points to the content of the gospel and of faith. The promise issued to Abraham is first realized in faith in this Christ (cf. Rom. 4:23-25!), and not earlier.

Now, "Abraham's offspring" is, to be sure, no common christological title. At best, Matt. 1:1 could be used to support the idea, but it does not assert descent from Abraham exclusively for Jesus. Thus the logic of the Pauline interpretation of "offspring" as Christ does not come from any usual association, but from the exegesis of Gen. 15:6 developed in vv. 6-14: the blessing of Abraham is transmitted through him who, by abolishing the curse, opens up the possibility of faith and is himself the content of faith.

In the Old Testament context the content of the promise is the son as heir, the abundant progeny coming from him, and the possession of the land of Canaan. Although Abraham lived to see the birth of the heir—who, nevertheless, was soon placed in danger by God's order to sacrifice him (Genesis 22)—he sees no more of his progeny, and in the promised land he himself lives for the rest of his life as a foreigner. In the end, all the land that he possessed was a grave acquired at a horrendous price (Gen. 23:17-18).

Thus for Abraham the promise remained promise. But the Israel that later came out of Egypt had indeed possessed this land, and so the Israel in exile could read these stories as exhortation to hold fast to the old promise, which still had not failed and was still valid. As Israel once came out of Egypt, it could now come back out of Babylon into the promised land. The difficulty of the transmission of the blessing and the promise from one generation to the next, even in the very beginning, is shown by the old stories themselves—most clearly in the story of Jacob and Esau in Genesis 27.

[3:17] Paul now employs this comparison with a human testament to show that the law can effect no change in the promise originally given to believing Abraham. This was actually announced by the law in Deut. 28:62 for the time of the curse, and in 30:5 the promise was renewed in case of a return to the law.

The law, however, was not added until 430 years after God made the covenant with Abraham. Paul certainly did not calculate this number himself but adopted it from Jewish tradition. Indeed, Gen. 15:13 speaks of a 400-year stay in Egypt; Exod. 12:40, of 430 years. In the Septuagint, however, Exod. 12:40 states that Israel was 430 years "in Egypt and Canaan." If one calculates according to the chronological notices found from Gen. 12:4 through Gen. 47:28, that yields a figure of 215, half of 430, for the period from Abraham's arrival in Canaan down to Jacob's resettlement in Egypt. Since, according to Exod. 19:1, Israel reached the wilderness of Sinai three months after the departure from Egypt, the span of time given by Paul corresponds to what can be calculated from Scripture, and indeed again from the Greek translation. We do not know how many years Paul may have assumed for the time from Sinai until his day. His contemporary, the Jewish historian Josephus, says that Moses was born about 2,000 years earlier (*Antiquities* 1.16).

The promise is, in any case, far older than the law. Accordingly, we can indicate a temporal scheme similar to that of the tradition of blessing and curse (see above, p. 63):

Abraham	430 years later	Since Christ
promise	law	faith
blessing	curse	blessing

The fundamental difference between the Jewish tradition and Paul lies in the fact that for Judaism the law combines all three sections. For Judaism, the law was there from the beginning of the world, as well as righteousness, before Moses had known it—how else could they have been righteous? Paul, in contrast, "historicized" the law: he gave it a datable beginning at Sinai and an end with Christ.

Finally, the use of the comparison perhaps also contains the idea that God himself could have changed his "testament"; consequently, the law cannot actually come from God himself at all, as Paul also soon indicates in vv. 19-20. Otherwise the testator could have made completely legitimate subsequent changes in the promise.

[3:18] The conclusion is that promise and law are thus mutually exclusive, as also are faith and law (cf. vv. 22, 29); the inheritance belongs to those who are of faith.

The Law

Text

3:19 Why then the law? It was added because of transgressions, until
the offspring would come to whom the promise had been made;
and it was ordained through angels by a mediator.

20 Now a mediator involves more than one party; but God is one.

21 Is the law then opposed to the promises of God? Certainly not! For
if a law had been given that could make alive, then righteousness
would indeed come through the law.

22 But the scripture has imprisoned all things under the power of sin,
so that what was promised through faith in Jesus Christ might be
given to those who believe.

Commentary

[3:19-20] Following the argumentation up to this point, it is logical to ask,
Why have the law at all? Paul raises this question here and answers it first
with a statement that was also possible in the Jewish tradition: it came in
because of transgressions—not to be overlooked is Paul's disparaging
tone in "it was added" (cf. Rom. 5:20). He will elaborate on this in vv. 21-
22 in a way that is different from the way such a statement could be
intended in the Jewish tradition. Even in v. 19 he indicates the temporal
limitation of the law until the coming of the offspring, that is, according
to v. 16, until the coming of Christ. The law does not outlast the curse.

Paul adopts Jewish traditions all the more in the assertions on the
origin of the law. The Greek version of Deut. 33:2 speaks quite positively
about the participation of an angel in the giving of the law at Sinai (cf.
also Acts 7:53), and *mediator* may be a common honorary title for Moses.
Yet in v. 20 Paul uses these two normally laudatory bits of tradition to
speak against the law. In his opinion it actually goes back only to angels,
for otherwise it would make no sense to speak of a mediator since in the
linguistic usage presupposed here, *mediator* is applied only to groups, not
to individual persons. And not even an angel from heaven could change

the gospel that Paul preached in Galatia (cf. 1:8), any more than the promise given to Abraham. Thus from its origin on, the law is inferior to the promise, which goes back to God himself.

Moses, who is meant here by *mediator,* is encountered in Paul's letters surprisingly seldom in comparison to the significance of the theme of the law. Above all, except in 1 Cor. 9:9 Paul does not employ the usual designation of the law as the "law of Moses"; only three times does Moses appear as the author of a statement of the law (Rom. 9:15; 10:5, 19). In 2 Cor. 3:7-18 there is a discussion of the function of Moses, who belongs on the side of the dispensation of death and has to place a veil over his face, corresponding to the veil that lies over the law, whereas the dispensation of the Spirit opened by Christ brings splendor.

As earlier in the argumentation with the schema of vv. 6-14, now also in the dating of the law in v. 17 and the description of the participation of the angels and of the mediator Moses in the giving of the law, we see how precisely Paul knows the Jewish tradition and the law itself. Because of this familiarity with Jewish law he can initiate his argumentation precisely as a radical reinterpretation of the law and Jewish history.

[3:21] Here and elsewhere, to be sure, Paul avoids the obvious conclusion that the law does not go back to God himself at all. Yet he stops short of this conclusion, only then to make a completely fresh approach to the problem of the function of the law later in his letter to Rome (Romans 5–8). There he also ponders the theme of sin more fundamentally than here. In v. 21 he also wards off rhetorically a conclusion in that direction. Otherwise the law could be accorded its own authority, which ill befits it, and the uniqueness of God would fall into danger. The law, however, also does not have the power to give life, since it produces only the context of the curse; righteousness, blessing, and life are associated only with faith in Christ.

[3:22] According to Jewish tradition the law is there to form a fence around Israel to hold off sin and block the curse. For Paul, however, the context of the curse has its cause not in disobedience of the law but in the law itself, which cannot at all effect righteousness as it claims. Here Paul makes a wholesale reference to "the scripture" without citing individual passages.

The logic of this line of argument lies in the continuation of the earlier antithesis. Since blessing, Spirit, life, and righteousness belong on the side of faith, sin is consequently to be added to the list of curse, flesh, and death. In Rom. 7:7-11 Paul will go even further and say that the law not only does not block sin but even produces it. The promise was superior to the law to the extent that it maintained itself in spite of the context of the curse, until it was redeemed in the offspring Christ, who lifted the curse and opened up the possibility of blessing. Thus the course of the argument in vv. 15-22 demonstrates the already-presented alternative of law and faith. What is new here is that the reinterpretation of the old sequence of promise-curse-blessing in vv. 6-14 is substantiated by the exegesis of the key word *offspring* and by the interpretation of the giving of the law at Sinai.

Even if these exegeses of Old Testament texts may be vulnerable in themselves, their logic, like that of the scriptural interpretation in vv. 6-14, rests on the christological view of Old Testament law-theology, and on the interpretation from the standpoint of Christology of experiences that one has with oneself, with the world, and with God. Paul asserts that the question of the unfulfilled promise will find its answer only here in Christ—in accordance with the titular sense, in the death and resurrection of Jesus—and not in the law. Only by overestimating itself can the law claim to fulfill the divine promises.

Faith

Text

3:23 Now before faith came, we were imprisoned and guarded under the law until faith would be revealed.

24 Therefore the law was our disciplinarian until Christ came, so that we might be justified by faith.

25 But now that faith has come, we are no longer subject to a disciplinarian,

26 for in Christ Jesus you are all children of God through faith.

27 As many of you as were baptized into Christ have clothed yourselves with Christ.

28 There is no longer Jew or Greek, there is no longer slave or free, there is no longer male and female; for all of you are one in Christ Jesus.

29 And if you belong to Christ, then you are Abraham's offspring, heirs according to the promise.

Commentary

[3:23-25] The time of the curse of the law ended with the revelation of faith (v. 23). As in 1:12, 16, *revelation* designates here the separation of two worlds, which for Paul himself had been accomplished at Damascus, but even there he understood it in principle as the final end of the law. The previous time of the law was a time of confinement, of being kept under restraint, for which Paul uses the same word as in v. 22: it was the time of sin, from which the law could not liberate or give righteousness, life, and blessing. Comparison with 1:12, 16 shows that the faith that ended the time of the curse is none other than faith in Jesus Christ (2:16), in the Son of God (2:20). Thus also in v. 24 Christ, the coming offspring (cf. v. 19—again we must keep in mind the titular sense of *Christ*), appears at the same point of transition from the time of the curse to the time of blessing. Here too faith is defined completely by its content. The law was only a "schoolmaster" (KJV) before Christ, not a carefully guiding pedagogue in the modern sense, but comparable to the slave called a *paidagōgos,* who with thrashing and force held the children to the task of learning without being a teacher himself. Justification comes from faith, not from the law (cf. 2:16), and indeed through that which is the content of faith, which here again is given as "Christ." Now that there is such a faith (v. 25), the reign of the law has ended, and righteousness is possible.

[3:26] In substantiating this understanding, Paul now turns to the beginnings of the churches in Galatia. He points out first that all the Galatian Christians are "children of God" through faith. "Child of God," however, is a title for the righteous person (see above, p. 30). Through the phrase "in Christ Jesus" this righteousness of the believer as being a child of God is anchored in the sonship of Jesus (cf. 4:5; 1:16; 2:20). Since the Galatians can call themselves "children of God," they are the righteous— through faith in the Son of God as Paul preached him to them, the Gentiles (cf. 1:16), not through the works of the law, to which they turned later on.

[3:27] This verse offers further substantiation by pointing to baptism as the sign of entrance into the church. Baptism is "clothing oneself with" Christ (cf. Rom. 13:14 and then Eph. 4:24) or the giving up of one's old identity in death with Christ and acquiring a new one in Christ (cf. 2:19-20; Rom. 6:1-11). As natural as baptism is for Paul, he seems to have been just as careful about being too quick to baptize as many as possible.

How proper such care was, was seen in Corinth (cf. 1 Cor. 1:14-17), where parts of the church were more closely related to their respective baptizers than to Christ. Paul understands preaching the gospel as his primary duty; others could then do the baptizing. Even in Galatia Paul seems to presuppose that not all of his readers are baptized. Baptism is, to be sure, the total acceptance of the gospel, the fulfillment of the gospel in one's own existence, but possession of the Spirit and of faith does not ultimately depend on baptism.

[3:28a] Another substantiation follows here with reference to a basic rule of the churches, which originated in the Pauline proclamation. Abolished among them was the difference between Jews and Greeks (actually, the Galatians were neither: to the Jews they were Gentiles, but to the Greeks, barbarians), as well as the differences between slave and free and between men and women. Here enumerated are the differences in humanity that existed by birth in the ancient world; of these, only that between men and women has not become history and still concerns us today. Paul himself, however, could accept Jewish linguistic usage and say in 2:15: "Jews by birth and not Gentile sinners."

What Paul cites here did not remain purely a statement of policy: the people mentioned in Acts as well as in the Pauline letters show that all the named groups were actually represented in the churches of the Pauline mission. There were problems especially in the relationship between Jewish and Gentile Christians, as 2:11-21 emphatically shows; there were also problems in Corinth in regard to the relationship between women and men in the church. Yet, amazingly, we hear nothing about problems between slave and free.

Such problems, however, did not basically call this policy into question; they arose only when it came time to realize the policy. Early Christianity must have been a great power for social integration, which made it attractive for all groups and did not let it become an organization separated according to nationality, class, or sex. And this integrating power lay in the gospel itself, which called such communities to life.

The antitype of the series in v. 28 would be the free Jewish or Greek man who is not a slave, not a woman, and not a Gentile or barbarian. The Pauline principle, however, employs for each apparently inferior part of the paired concepts words that can also be used as a self-designation without denigration: Jews and Greeks, not "Jews by birth and not Gentile sinners" (cf. 2:15), and also not "Greeks and Barbarians" (cf. Rom. 1:14). Likewise, the master and the male are not defined by words that disqualify the slave and the female. One's own identity is not based on supposed superiority over others.

In the Hellenistic cities of the Pauline missionary territory, the old differences had been leveled anyway. Even barbarians could get ahead there. Slaves could assume key positions in their master's administration, and slaves in the household ordinarily had it somewhat better than most free wage earners. Finally, women there were more emancipated than their sisters in purely agrarian areas. These developments certainly form the background of the Christian mission. But at the same time there were also contrary tendencies toward the assertion of traditional privileges, which were found precisely in the context of religious communities.

In 1 Cor. 12:13 Paul writes the same text, but without the male-female pair, for the role of women in the church was precisely what was under dispute in Corinth. As in our text, we encounter the reference to baptism and above all the emphasis on unity. In 1 Cor. 9:19-21 Paul seems to carry the same schema over to his proclamation of the gospel, which indeed produces churches of this type. (From the viewpoint of later churches citing Paul's authority, it is no accident that in Col. 3:11 the Greek comes first, since the relationship between Jews and Greeks is no longer as urgent as it was in the time of Paul.)

What this negatively formulated statement in Gal. 3:28 means positively for the upbuilding of the church is shown by 1 Corinthians 7. The problem that the Corinthians laid before Paul in writing (7:1) concerns various aspects of the relationship between men and women in the church. On the whole, his answer amounts to saying that everything should stay the way it is. Although he himself gives preference to the ascetic life, he recommends that those who are married remain married, and that those who are single remain single. In 1 Cor. 11:3 he presents a christologically based superiority of the man, and in 14:33-36 (if that is not a later addition by another hand) he even orders that women be silent in church.

As substantiation of the rules about the behavior of women, in 1 Cor. 7:17-24 Paul now brings in the other two pairs in the schema of Gal. 3:28: a Jew should remain a Jew and not try through an operation to reverse his circumcision; conversely, a Greek should not have himself circumcised (v. 18). The meaning of the example of the slave in v. 21 is disputed. It corresponds better to the flow of the text, however, to interpret the sentence to mean that Paul urges the slave to forgo freedom, even if offered. In any case, he closes in v. 24 with a repetition of v. 20, that one should remain in one's calling. Also, in Philemon he does not press for a freeing of the slave Onesimus, although he certainly does not rule it out.

Thus, 1 Corinthians 7 offers, so to speak, Paul's authentic commentary on our text. The two conceptual pairs that were undisputed in Corinth, Jew-Greek and slave-free, serve him there to substantiate his answer to the questions of the Corinthians regarding the relationship of men and women. In so doing, he understands the schema of our concepts in an astonishingly conservative fashion precisely as an argument for the status quo. Certainly, this is also related to the fact that he anticipated the imminent end of the world (1 Cor. 7:29), and therefore it was not worth the effort to change this world. The liberation of slaves in itself, however, could even be downright inhumane in its effect if slaves were not given some form of property or capital for establishing their own households. Well-meant appeals do not in themselves create any real changes if their immediate consequences are not thought through, examples of which can be found throughout the history of the church and the world.

Yet explanations of this kind can at best excuse Paul from the standpoint of those who claim to know what Paul "logically" must have said: freedom, emancipation, and so forth. More important, however, is the question, What was it in the missionary situation of early Christianity that made such a program, as the consequence of the gospel of the crucified Christ, and also the resulting churches, so attractive for both Jews and Greeks, slaves and free, men and women? What caused all of them to commit themselves to this gospel and as a consequence to sit down at table with each other?

What the gospel offered was new possibilities of identification (cf. 2:20) that could supersede old, and now questionable, privileges and fixed roles and a new integration of opposites in the face of developments that pointed to disintegration. This meant finding one's identity and integration in the crucified One, where human experiences were not bypassed in favor of harmonizing or dualistic designs, but rather where one rediscovered precisely in a confession of faith one's experiences with oneself, with God, and with the world.

With this, early Christian missions went into competition especially with Judaism, which promised just such reconciliation in the law. Thus Paul also made repeated contact with the synagogue, even if Luke perhaps presents this a little too schematically. Here in the missionary situation offer stood against offer, assertion against assertion, and their power to convince must have been great on both sides. From the standpoint of the law, even Judaism—for which Paul may have worked as a missionary before his conversion—made a certain amount of sense, which the new teachers in Galatia attempted to link with Christology.

Paul, however, thoroughly recast a principle that was also at least a theoretical possibility in Judaism when he abolished the seemingly natural barrier between Jews and Greeks without making it mandatory, as it was in the Jewish mission, that one accept circumcision and thus integration into Judaism.

The interpretation of v. 28a must be deep enough to make plausible the argument that Paul uses here: the experience of the lifting of seemingly natural differences in the church follows from the believer's being a child of God. The unity vis-à-vis the division into opposing groups lies in Christ, the content of the gospel and of faith. Thus the church is the realization of the new world under the conditions of this world. What is said of the self in 2:20 finds here its counterpart in the ecclesiological and social realization of justification by faith alone.

[3:28b-29] Perhaps the "one in Christ" in v. 28b refers back to the "one" offspring Christ (v. 16), for whom the promise is valid. At any rate, v. 29 draws the conclusion that people "of faith" are Abraham's offspring through the one Christ and thus also Abraham's heirs according to the promise. The promise survived the time of the curse of the law but could not be realized by the law itself.

Abraham's Inheritance

Text

4:1 My point is this: heirs, as long as they are minors, are no better than slaves, though they are the owners of all the property;

2 but they remain under guardians and trustees until the date set by the father.

3 So with us; while we were minors, we were enslaved to the elemental spirits of the world.

4 But when the fullness of time had come, God sent his Son, born of a woman, born under the law,

5 in order to redeem those who were under the law, so that we might receive adoption as children.

6 And because you are children, God has sent the Spirit of his Son into our hearts, crying, "Abba! Father!"

7 So you are no longer a slave but a child, and if a child then also an heir, through God.

Commentary

[4:1-2] Paul secures the thesis of 3:29 with yet another opposition of law and faith. In vv. 1-2 he harks back to the example from the law of inheritance used in 3:15-17, again exploiting the association between *covenant* and *testament,* or *will.* There he used it to show the unchangeability of the promise; here, with the end of guardianship anticipated in the will, he describes again the transition from law to faith (cf. also 3:23-25).

The legal order introduced in vv. 1-2 clearly corresponds better to Hellenistic than to Jewish law, but for this very reason it must have had cogency for Galatians living in such an area. Paul presents the situation in which minors have been named by their father to become heirs on a certain date. Until then the estate is administered by guardians and trustees, generally slaves at that time. During this period the heirs have no executive power over themselves or over their future possessions. Thus they are almost in the position of being slaves.

[4:3] Paul does not exploit the comparison in detail, but only to make the point that those who were (like) slaves now, with the coming of their inheritance, receive the rights of children. Instead of "enslaved to the law" in v. 3, we find, surprisingly, "enslaved to the elemental spirits of the universe" (literally, "elements of the world"–KJV), which is then followed up in vv. 4-5 with "under the law." Thus with "elemental spirits" in place of "law," Paul suddenly introduces a concept that he does not need to explain to his readers. They know what he means. It appears again in v. 9, and not until then will it be possible to learn a little more about its meaning.

[4:4] In speaking of "when the fullness of time had come," Paul stays for the time being with the terminology of the laws of inheritance: the "fulness of the time" (KJV) corresponds to the "date set by the father" in v. 2, when the period of minority is over. Intended here is the time of the change from the one world to the other—which Paul calls revelation in 1:12, 16; 3:23—the end of the age of the law and the opening of the age of faith in the Christ event. Thus it is a question of a break between ages, not a fulfillment in the sense of a logical culmination. For Paul, Christ is the end of the law (cf. Rom. 10:4), not the fulfillment of history.

Here the Christ event is presented with the traditional statement of the sending of the Son (cf. Rom. 8:3; John 3:16-17 in contrast to Gal. 1:16; 2:20). It contains the substantiation of the believers' adoption as children (cf. 3:26). The Son became human (cf. Rom. 8:3) by being born of a woman like any other human being (thus Paul says nothing here of a virgin birth), and he was under the law, whose curse he abolished in his death on the cross (cf. 3:13).

[4:5] Here, as in 3:14, come two purpose clauses. The first repeats the assertion of the redemption of a slave from slavery to the law (cf. 3:13); the second, in an allusion to the comparison with the inheritance, names the attainment of adoption as children (cf. 3:26). Together with this adoption, Christians have received the Spirit (cf. 3:2, 5, 14b): no other Spirit than the Spirit of the Son of God. Expressed in different terminology, this means that justification comes by faith, not by works of the law.

[4:6] This Spirit expresses itself in the addressing of God as Father (cf. Wis. 2:16: the righteous man, who is the son of God, calls God his Father). This form of address is first rendered as *Abba* in the Aramaic language and then followed by the translation "Father" (cf. Rom. 8:15; Mark 14:36). This usage points to liturgical language, in which, even into our day, words are adopted from old languages (*amen, hallelujah, hosanna, kyrie eleison*). It is nonetheless astonishing that with the Greek-speaking Galatians Paul can obviously presuppose this prayer address, which he himself may well have introduced to them. Unfortunately, we know almost nothing at all about the liturgical forms of the early Christian churches and just as little about the extent to which Paul may have adopted such forms from his many years of missionary work around Antioch and passed them on to his churches. Besides the *amen* that originates from Jewish liturgical language (cf. 1:5; 6:18), we also find in 1

Cor. 16:22 the Aramaic *maranatha* ("our Lord, come!"), which probably belonged to the liturgy of the Lord's Supper.

Perhaps the prayer address "Abba, Father" refers to the Lord's Prayer, which in Matt. 6:9 begins with "Our Father" and in the more original version in Luke 11:2 contains not the Aramaic *abba* but the Greek vocative "Father." We find no other indication that Paul knew the Lord's Prayer. In our context this prayer address means that the experience of worship becomes a further argument for the assertion that the Spirit is given through faith.

[4:7] This verse draws the conclusion that is already found in 3:29: the heirs are those of faith, not those under the law. With this statement the long line of argumentation that began in 3:6 comes to an end. As a whole it is an interpretation of Gen. 15:6 that corresponds to the interpretation given in 3:7. Abraham's children and thus his heirs are those who are righteous by faith, because the promise of Abraham applies to the one offspring Christ, in whom those who live by faith have become heirs. The age of the curse of the law is over; the age of blessing has dawned, and its signs are Spirit, righteousness, life, and adoption as children—all of which mean more or less the same. None of this is achieved by the law, in spite of being asserted by the law itself and by the new teachers in Galatia. On the contrary, to the law belong only flesh, sin, death, and slavery. The question in 3:5 is finally answered: the Spirit comes from faith, not from the law.

The Conversion
of the Galatians

Text

4:8 Formerly, when you did not know God, you were enslaved to beings that by nature are not gods.

9 Now, however, that you have come to know God, or rather to be known by God, how can you turn back again to the weak and beggarly elemental spirits? How can you want to be enslaved to them again?

10 You are observing special days, and months, and seasons, and years.

11 I am afraid that my work for you may have been wasted.

12 Friends, I beg you, become as I am, for I also have become as you are. You have done me no wrong.

13 You know that it was because of a physical infirmity that I first announced the gospel to you;

14 though my condition put you to the test, you did not scorn or despise me, but welcomed me as an angel of God, as Christ Jesus.

15 What has become of the good will you felt? For I testify that, had it been possible, you would have torn out your eyes and given them to me.

16 Have I now become your enemy by telling you the truth?

17 They make much of you, but for no good purpose; they want to exclude you, so that you may make much of them.

18 It is good to be made much of for a good purpose at all times, and not only when I am present with you.

19 My little children, for whom I am again in the pain of childbirth until Christ is formed in you,

20 I wish I were present with you now and could change my tone, for I am perplexed about you.

Analysis

After the basic presentation of the gospel in 3:6—4:7, Paul now addresses his readers directly and comes back to the situation that is the topic of 1:6-10 and 3:1-5. He reminds the Galatians of their conversion to the gospel and measures against it their new conversion to that other gospel (vv. 8-11); he calls to mind the circumstances under which they once accepted the gospel and contrasts it with their current behavior (vv. 12-20).

Commentary

[4:8-9] The line of argumentation from 3:6 to 4:7 closed with slaves becoming children of God. This change corresponds to what happened to the Galatians at their conversion (vv. 8, 9b). Earlier, when they did not know the true God, they were slaves to gods who by nature could be no gods at all. They were Gentiles, and hence the churches are to be designated Gentile Christian without a Jewish Christian component. Yet they were just as enslaved as those living under the law. Thus there is no difference at this point, any more than there is a difference in Christian churches between Gentile and Jewish Christians.

The qualitative difference between Jews and Gentiles that is asserted from the standpoint of Judaism has already been relativized by Paul in 2:15-16, and in Rom. 3:22-23, in a new context, he reduces the matter to a terse formula: "For there is no distinction, since all [Jews and Gentiles] have sinned and fall short of the glory of God." Sin, to which "the scripture has imprisoned all things" (Gal. 3:22), has become everyone's fate, from which neither the law nor pagan idols can free us.

The disqualification of Gentile gods as "by nature . . . not gods" is a typical motif of Jewish missionary language, as is the expression "Gentiles who do not know God" (cf. for Paul 1 Thess. 4:5). Such missionary language also includes the assertion in v. 9a, "to know God, or rather to be known by God" (cf. 1 Cor. 8:2-3; 13:12), and the technical use of *turn to* in the sense of "convert" in v. 9b (cf. 1 Thess. 1:9b).

For the Galatians, remembrance of their conversion must bring to mind what acquiring such knowledge of God meant to them (cf. 3:1-5). Paul contrasts this gain with the loss that, in his opinion, they have now suffered through their new conversion to "another gospel." It is nothing more than backsliding from what they have already achieved (cf. 3:3-4); fundamentally, it is even backsliding into their earlier paganism, for the word *again* indicates that from the standpoint of the gospel there is absolutely no difference between pagan idolatry, Jewish legalism, and that "other gospel." Here we find again the key term *elemental spirits*, which occurred earlier in v. 3.

Thus there is clearly polemic in the value that Paul places on their reconversion. It is seen especially in the equating of Jewish obedience to the law and pagan idolatry. We know little about pagan religions in Galatia at this time. The presumed reason is quite simply that they were generally not different in character from the normal type of Hellenistic religion: ancient tribal gods—here probably of Celtic origin—who had long been identified with the Greek gods of Olympus, and whose worship was carried out in similar forms everywhere. Worship of "elemental spirits" as such could hardly have been the most important part of the Galatian paganism that Paul names here as the goal of their reconversion.

Thus it would seem more likely to see in the "elements of the world" a part of the "other gospel" and a key word of the new teachers. The Greek term used by Paul is covered by the Latin translation *elementum*, and the English loanword *element* has a semantic range that corresponds approximately to the Greek word: basic matter in the natural sciences, but also in a more general sense (cf. also *elementary*).

The term *elements of the world* calls to mind the theory developed by Empedocles that the world can be reduced to the four basic elements: earth, air, fire, and water. In cosmological terms those are the basic materials of which the world consists, and the human being, as a microcosm, is likewise put together from these basic materials. Mythologically, they may be gods understood as earth, sky, sun, and sea, whose worship is necessary in order to assure the harmony of the cosmos, or as angelic beings in Judaism, which knows no other gods but the one God.

Paul discounts the devotion of the Galatians to the law as idolatry of the same kind. This does not explain, however, why he speaks here especially of the "elements of the world" and not, as elsewhere, simply of impotent idols (cf., for example, 1 Cor. 8:5-6). Does he perhaps tie the law to elements of the world because the new teachers in Galatia themselves asserted at this point a positive connection, which only Paul presents negatively?

There is, in fact, support for this idea. The law given at Sinai was not only a book that contained ethical rules for human interaction. It also defined how cultic matters were to be performed, and one essential function of the cult is to uphold the world order. This world order itself, however, was likewise documented in the law. Whoever read Genesis 1–2, the first chapters of the "law," could learn from it how the world is ordered. Thus the law of Moses contains not only ethics but also cult and cosmology, three things (moral law, ceremonial law, natural law) whose unity was not disrupted until modern times; in Greek as well as Jewish tradition, and later also in medieval Christianity, all three were bound closely together.

In its mission Judaism could not ultimately offer reliable information about the nature of the world and thus interpretation and assurance for the experiences that humans have in the world. *World* here is not yet *nature* in the romantic sense or in the sense of the "natural" sciences, which have taken over this function of assurance and interpretation of the world through the discovery of "natural laws" and which claim to be able to explain where everything comes from and how it all interrelates.

One only needs to transform the four named elements (earth, air, fire, and water) into the hazards that come from them (earthquake, storm, conflagration, and flood), or to describe positively their vital functions concerning the elementary needs of humanity, in order to see how important is the assurance of the maintenance of the cosmos and the functioning of its order. And this is what the law promised to give.

[4:10] Also corresponding to the cosmic dimensions of the law is the enumeration of days, months, seasons, and years, which is oriented toward the course of the year as defined by the heavenly bodies. Their "observation" refers not so much to a cultic observance (although that may be involved) as to an integration of one's whole life into the operation of the world.

In Gen. 1:14 the priestly report of creation speaks of the heavenly bodies, according to which the seasons, days, and years are to be defined; and Philo of Alexandria, in his work entitled "The Creation of the World" (58–61), interprets this in terms of the connection between the stars and the whole life of humanity. Thus, according to Jewish tradition, the law itself gives information on the "operation of the world," which is closely connected with the orbits of heavenly bodies.

The science of their observation is astronomy, whose invention is occasionally traced back to Abraham. Since astronomy and astrology were not separated until recent times, such knowledge of the stars was of vital importance for everyday life.

A connection of the law with the elements of the world and the course of the world that is dependent on the stars is thus thoroughly demonstrable in Judaism and therefore also conceivable in the new teachers in Galatia; we do not need to see foreign influences here. At this very point lay a powerful promotional theme of the Jewish mission for the law vis-à-vis paganism, because elementary questions of humanity were addressed. Not until Paul was this connection with the world denounced as equivalent to idolatry.

[4:11] Paul seems resigned, for he cannot accept that teaching as "gospel." For him the assurance of human experience does not lie in the law or in a law thrust into the realm of cosmology but in the cross of Christ alone (cf. 6:14). Here the uncertain experience that one has with oneself, with God, and with the world comes together with a confession that speaks not least of all about the Father of Jesus Christ as the Creator of heaven and earth. It also includes the promise that life in this world has meaning, that righteousness, blessing, and life in this world are there in the crucified One.

The "Lord's day" (Rev. 1:10) that the Christian church celebrates lies beyond the natural rhythm of the seven days and is an anticipation of the "day of the Lord," the end of all days. As the "first day" of the week (1 Cor. 16:2), it is the eighth day of creation, the beginning of the new creation in the resurrection of Jesus. Hence, Christians are free both from the law and from the threat of the elements of the world, against which the law promised protection. In the cross the cosmos lost some of its autonomy (cf. 6:14); the world is again creation.

The closest parallel to vv. 9-10 in the New Testament, Col. 2:17-23, shows how the further development of such teachings threatened Pauline churches again at a later time. There angels are also mentioned in this connection, and perhaps we may therefore also assume that for the opponents in Galatia there was a connection between the participation of angels in the giving of the law at Sinai, mentioned by Paul in 3:19, and these "elements of the world," as well as the observation of the cosmic rhythm of the year.

[4:12] In any case, Paul fears that his efforts on behalf of the Galatians were in vain (cf. 3:4) and now bids his readers to become as he is, that is, to follow his path from the law to faith (cf. 1:13-16) and not to turn back; for on this path he has become like them: "To those outside the law I became as one outside the law" (1 Cor. 9:21). Unlike the definite situation of disagreement in Corinth (cf. 2 Cor. 7:12), he says that he has suffered no wrong at the hands of the churches; they have treated not him unjustly but themselves and the gospel.

[4:13] Therefore, he reminds them how they had once received him when he preached the gospel to them. The Greek word translated "first" in v. 13 can have the meaning "the first time" as opposed to later times, as well as the meaning "at one time, formerly." If the first sense were intended, however, one would expect Paul to continue, "and also the second time. . . ."

Hence one cannot conclude from this passage alone that Paul was in Galatia at least twice. Thus the only text in Paul's letters that can support the so-called third missionary journey of Acts 18:18-23 proves to be highly insecure (cf. above, pp. 2–3). If Paul had already had this trip behind him, he would probably have also written something about his latest visit to Antioch, which would have occurred in the meantime.

Thus there remain two possibilities: to place the composition of the Letter to the Galatians before the so-called third missionary journey, if one holds it to be historically certain, or to say that this journey is unhistorical. At least v. 13 provides no unambiguous argument that such a journey actually took place.

[4:14-15] As the occasion for his preaching, Paul reminds his readers of his illness, which kept him from immediately traveling further to the west (cf. above, p. 26). He does not need to say what the illness was, because his original readers knew that. Does v. 14 point to offensive external symptoms, or does Paul mean here, in somewhat exaggerated fashion, only a possible, usual reaction to illness in general? Can we infer from v. 15 an eye ailment, or is it merely a matter of a comparison? From 2 Cor. 12:7 we learn that Paul apparently suffered from a chronic illness, but there also it is impossible to arrive at a more exact diagnosis according to the categories of our modern medicine.

[4:16] With his own weakness Paul contrasts what the Galatians have seen in him: an angel of God (cf. 1:8) or even Christ Jesus himself, the content of his gospel. He, too, was the one crucified in weakness who lives in the power of God (cf. 2 Cor. 13:4), like the apostle, who here, as in the letter as a whole, is totally absorbed in the gospel. There is nothing left of all that the Galatians did and were prepared to do. Indeed, Paul even asks himself (v. 16) whether the situation has now reversed itself to the extent that he has become their enemy: he who brought them the "truth of the gospel," which he had once defended for them in Jerusalem (cf. 2:5).

[4:17] He finds fault with his opponents for being zealous only for themselves; they try to isolate the churches. He assumes that their goal is to bind the churches completely to themselves. Whereas Paul subordinates himself to the gospel, he asserts that his opponents are about to put themselves in the place of the gospel.

[4:18-19] According to these verses, zeal in itself is not bad (cf. 1:14); on the contrary, there is a zeal for the good, as the Galatians had earlier concerned themselves about Paul as the representative of the gospel and could continue to do so. He himself feels for his church like a mother in labor (cf. 1 Cor. 4:15; Phlm. 10). Through his pains Christ is to take shape in them anew. Perhaps this image already anticipates the quotation from Isa. 54:1 used in v. 27. The gospel, whose content is Christ, is realized in the church as the body of Christ (cf. 3:28).

[4:20] Paul wishes to be with them in person, instead of dictating a letter. He is perplexed and therefore launches into further exegetical argumentation with the Abraham tradition.

Hagar and Sarah

Text

4:21 Tell me, you who desire to be subject to the law, will you not listen to the law?

22 For it is written that Abraham had two sons, one by a slave woman and the other by a free woman.

23 One, the child of the slave, was born according to the flesh; the other, the child of the free woman, was born through the promise.

24 Now this is an allegory: these women are two covenants. One woman, in fact, is Hagar, from Mount Sinai, bearing children for slavery.

25 Now Hagar is Mount Sinai in Arabia and corresponds to the present Jerusalem, for she is in slavery with her children.

26 But the other woman corresponds to the Jerusalem above; she is free, and she is our mother.

27 For it is written,
"Rejoice, you childless one, you who bear no children,
burst into song and shout, you who endure no birthpangs;
for the children of the desolate woman are more numerous
than the children of the one who is married."

28 Now you, my friends, are children of the promise, like Isaac.

29 But just as at that time the child who was born according to the flesh persecuted the child who was born according to the Spirit, so it is now also.

30 But what does the scripture say? "Drive out the slave and her child; for the child of the slave will not share the inheritance with the child of the free woman."

31 So then, friends, we are children, not of the slave but of the free woman.

Analysis

Paul resorts once again to the Abraham tradition in order to substantiate his alternative of faith and law. With it, however, he now also connects the theme of 1:13—2:21, Jerusalem, and works out the last of the great antitheses of the letter: freedom and slavery.

Commentary

[4:21-22] In v. 21 Paul speaks to his readers about their willingness to give themselves to the law, and he asserts again, as in 3:6—4:7, that the law itself speaks for his alternative of law and faith, which is derived from the gospel, and that he interprets the Old Testament more correctly than the new teachers in Galatia. In v. 22 he harks back to Gen. 16:15-16 and especially to Gen. 21:1-21, without considering the other sons of Abraham by Keturah (cf. Gen. 25:1-2). The readers know that the "two sons" mentioned are Ishmael and Isaac.

[4:23] Paul immediately stresses the difference between the two mothers: the one is a slave (cf. Gen. 16:1), the other a free woman. Here too the readers know the names: Hagar and Sarah. And anyone who comes from the Jewish tradition also knows that Sarah is the mother to whom, through Isaac, Israel can trace back its ancestry. She is the recipient of the promise, which according to the Old Testament text, however, comes in connection with the establishment of the covenant (Gen. 17:15-22), of which circumcision is a part. Therefore, Isaac was born through the promise (Gen. 21:1-7), whereas Ishmael came into the world through natural means (cf. Gen. 16:4, 15-16).

[4:24] Paul now asserts that this story is to be understood allegorically, thus using a method of interpretation that in his day and long afterward was considered a legitimate exegetical method. It was developed by the Greeks in the interpretation of Homer and then applied by Jewish exegesis to the law. Our primary testimony to such allegorical interpretation of the Old Testament is the work of Philo of Alexandria.

The basic assumption is that behind every story another meaningful and "actual" narrative level is to be found, on which one must read the same story again, point for point. The method as such could not have seemed illegitimate to Paul's readers and their new teachers. They would have questioned only the conclusions he reached, and presumably they would have been able to set forth an allegorical interpretation of the same text that was quite contrary to his.

Paul places the story of Hagar/Ishmael and Sarah/Isaac on the level of two covenants, using the same word that in 3:15 is translated "will" (NRSV) or "covenant" (KJV). The "one" covenant with Abraham was already interpreted there as promise, which is not by law but by faith. Paul's direction must be clear to the reader in advance: Sarah and Isaac on the side of the promise and of faith, but the law on the side of Hagar and Ishmael.

Yet such an arrangement is completely contradicted by Jewish exegesis, which carries forward what was already set out in Genesis 17 on the relationship of promise, covenant, and circumcision: not only Ishmael (cf. Gen. 17:23-27) but notably Isaac (cf. Gen. 21:4) and Abraham himself were circumcised. Thus, even more clearly than in 3:6-14 with the interpretation of Gen. 15:6, Paul, on behalf of his thesis of the alternative of faith and law, lays renewed claim here to a connection with the Abraham tradition that his opponents could more likely claim for themselves. In Rom. 4:11 he goes further and even uses Abraham's circumcision as an argument for justification without the law.

Paul's first argument comes from the fact that Ishmael, the son of a slave, was born for slavery. Admittedly, this son was originally supposed to be born as the son of Sarah (cf. Gen. 16:2), and in Gen. 17:23 he is obviously distinct from the slaves. According to Gen. 25:9, he undertakes, together with Isaac, the burial of Abraham and is likewise to become the progenitor of a people, even if not the people of the promise (Gen. 21:12-13). In his argument, however, Paul resorts to the slave law of his time, according to which the children of slaves could only be slaves also.

Since in 4:1-7 Paul has already made the connection between the law and slavery, on this basis he can assert the relationship of Hagar to the covenant of the law established at Sinai. In 3:17 he has already said of this law, which came 430 years later, that it cannot nullify the promise given to Abraham. In 3:19 he declared the law's origin questionable and then labeled it as a means of enslavement (3:24; 4:1-7), an enslavement to which the Galatians now want to commit themselves with their renewed conversion to "another gospel" (4:9).

[4:25] What is actually new in Paul's argument lies in the first clause. The manuscript tradition of the text shows the problems that early copyists and translators had with this argument. Paul's intention here is to equate Hagar with Mount Sinai in Arabia. How does he arrive at this? The reader is first reminded that Paul himself was in Arabia (cf. 1:17) and will therefore credit him with a certain local familiarity.

Arabia is indicated both by the name *Hagar* as well as by the location of Mount Sinai. Hagar is, to be sure, an Egyptian according to Gen. 16:1, but the region that is later accorded to her son Ishmael and his offspring is to be found in Arabia (cf. Gen. 25:6, 18). There one can also find *Hagar* as the name of a locality (cf. 1 Chron. 5:10, 19-20; Ps. 83:6), and this name may be preserved today in the place named *Chegra.*

In the vicinity of this modern city of Chegra, however, to which the Hagar/Ishmael traditions seem to be related, is also the possible location—according to the geographic concepts of the Old Testament—of Mount Sinai, on which Moses received the law. Not until around the fourth century C.E. was it located on the peninsula that is known to us as Sinai. The writers of "the five books of Moses" seem to identify the "reed sea" with the Gulf of Aqaba, not with the Red Sea, and to have imagined Mount Sinai in the mountains that one can find in today's atlases south of the city of Tabūk in extreme northwest Saudi Arabia, where the city of Chegra also lies. The only question is whether the mountains actually bore the name *Hagar* from that city. That, however, is what Paul seems to assert here, for that is where the logic of his argument seems to rest. Paul is apparently referring to information that he acquired during his stay in Arabia (cf. 1:17).

After the rationale for equating Hagar with Mount Sinai, the allegorical explanation now goes further, saying that Hagar therefore corresponds to the present Jerusalem because—and here Paul harks back again to 4:1-7—the present Jerusalem is in slavery just as Hagar and her children were. The logic of this conclusion rests on the fact that the present Jerusalem is under the law. The "present Jerusalem" means the not yet destroyed Jerusalem of Paul's time, where he himself had been at least twice (cf. 1:18; 2:1) and had probably also enjoyed his education in the law.

Thus with "Jerusalem" the Abraham interpretation acquires a theme that in the Old Testament was already suggested in Gen. 14:18-20 but that then lacked the connection with the themes of covenant, promise, faith, and law, which are important for Paul, and also the connection with Sarah and Hagar, Ishmael, or Isaac. Also, Paul does not refer to the story of the meeting of Abraham with the priest-king Melchizedek (cf. Heb. 7:1-10).

Not to be overlooked, however, is the major role played by "Jerusalem" in the discussion on the identity of the gospel in 1:13—2:21 and also in the arrangement of material support from the Gentile churches, which was a result of the Jerusalem negotiations, according to 2:10. The new teachers in Galatia in some way or other presumably based their gospel on "Jerusalem," even if they could hardly be justified in basing it on the "pillars" of the Christian church there.

[4:26] Paul, however, now devalues this present Jerusalem, which he can compare only to the law, in favor of the "Jerusalem above," which is "our" mother, the mother of believers, who is free like Sarah. The concept of a heavenly Jerusalem above has an old tradition in Judaism. Thus, according to the priestly account, Moses had already seen on Sinai the heavenly model for the Jerusalem temple (Exod. 25:9), which thus belongs to the law itself. In the exile period, when the temple of Solomon had been destroyed, Ezekiel 40–48 describes the model of a Jerusalem that exists in heaven and is supposed to provide the pattern for rebuilding the earthly Jerusalem.

During the times when the temple actually stood, Mount Zion was the point of intersection between heaven and earth, with the earthly Jerusalem to a certain degree already a part of the heavenly world and hence also the only place where a temple for the God of Israel was allowed at all, and therefore the place to which pilgrims came from great distances. The present earthly Jerusalem and the heavenly one above could not be understood as strict opposites, but rather in the relationship of model and copy. At most it was possible to make a critique of the copy in relation to the standard of the model, but not a devaluation such as Paul undertakes here.

Paul also stands in the Jewish tradition when he calls Jerusalem "our mother"; what is new is only that he claims this relationship for believers alone and denies it to those who live under the law. Perhaps this view also makes it clear why Paul was so concerned to carry out the collection he had organized: the Christian church there is the "heavenly Jerusalem," living under the conditions of the earthly city, and to it the peoples bring their gifts. For him Jerusalem is not, as for Matthew, only the city of murderers (cf. Matt. 22:7) that must be destroyed and indeed will be destroyed: it is "mother," the starting point of the gospel for the gathering of all peoples. Thus even here he again takes up a theme from the tradition of the law and claims it for the gospel.

[4:27] Paul substantiates this theme with a quotation from Isa. 54:1, a text that served during the time of exile as a promise to the destroyed Jerusalem when the city and its temple lay in ruins and Israel was in its Babylonian captivity. Perhaps the Sarah story was already brought up to date here in Deutero-Isaiah (cf. Genesis 17); in any case, a connection with it is strongly suggested and was even made in Judaism.

What in Deutero-Isaiah is promised to the earthly Jerusalem is, however, not considered by Paul as having been fulfilled in the return from exile, the repopulation of the city, and the rebuilding of the temple. He holds that the promise of a great progeny will be realized only in a world-encompassing church of Jewish and Gentile Christians.

[4:28-29] In v. 28 Paul echoes 3:29: children of promise are those of faith, as Isaac was born such a child of promise and not "according to the flesh" (cf. v. 23). From this comes, in v. 29, a further parallel with the old Abraham tradition: the persecution of Isaac by Ishmael is repeated in the persecution of the Christian churches by the Jews. Paul himself, of course, had once persecuted the church in the name of the law (cf. 1:13, 23), but now he himself is persecuted for the sake of the gospel (cf. 5:11).

[4:30] The Abraham stories of the Old Testament do not tell of the persecution of Isaac by Ishmael. Paul is apparently referring to Gen. 21:9, because in v. 30 he cites Gen. 21:10. In 21:9, "Sarah saw the son of Hagar the Egyptian . . . playing with her son Isaac," the Jewish tradition also read *play* in the sense of "provoke, do mischief to." Thus Paul is again following an interpretation that developed within Judaism itself. What the "scripture" says according to v. 30 is, in Gen. 21:10, only a request of Sarah's to Abraham. Through the substitution of "with the child of the free woman" for "with my son Isaac," the saying receives in Paul a more definitive character than in its original wording.

The actual story ends in a much more amiable way: Hagar and Ishmael continue to be under God's protection; they are also supposed to become a great people, even if not the people of the promise; they will not become a nation that stands under the curse (cf. Gen. 21:12-21). Islam will subsequently relate this prophecy to the Arabs, and in Ishmael, their own progenitor—not in Isaac as the progenitor of the Jews—they will see the bearer of the promise given to Abraham.

[4:31] Paul here again repeats the conclusion of v. 28 and thereby harks back to 4:7: slaves could become free persons because the promise belongs to the descendants of the free woman, not to the descendants of the slave. Through the offspring for whom the promise is valid (3:16), the believers are free; whoever is under the law remains in slavery. In Paul's opinion, the Galatians want to commit themselves to such slavery when they now convert to that other gospel.

Again, as earlier in 3:6—4:7, the exegesis that Paul gives to the Old Testament Abraham tradition may at many points seem doubtful to us. The allegorical method was, to be sure, less questionable for Paul's contemporaries than for us today, who rely on historical-critical exegesis (and yet who can also correctly say of a biblical text, "Basically, this story is talking about something quite different," and then interpret it allegorically).

The question of truth, however, does not depend on individual interpretations but on the basic question whether the law can really do what it promises and what it is given credit for, or whether and to what extent Paul is right when he asserts that the promise is conveyed by Christ alone through our experience. Here too it is again presupposed that the realization of the promise became possible only through the offspring Christ (cf. 3:16), who on the cross took away the curse (3:13) and thus brought the blessing.

Paul again takes up themes that were developed in Judaism; he does not bring completely foreign conceptual categories into the discussion. This is true for the textual basis itself, but also for the allegorical method of interpretation, for the opposition of the present Jerusalem and the Jerusalem above, and probably even for the geographical explanation in v. 25a.

As in 3:6—4:7, Paul recasts all these elements in terms of Christology. It is obvious that the parallelism he began is not strictly carried out at one point:

two sons (vv. 22-23):

of the slave,	of the free woman,
according to the flesh	through the promise

two covenants (vv. 24-26):

Mount Sinai	—
slavery	freedom
Hagar	our mother
present Jerusalem	Jerusalem above

We are missing a counterpart to the "one" covenant on Mount Sinai (which is not to be tacitly supplied by, say, a covenant of the Mount of Golgotha). Paul had spoken of a covenant, or will, in 3:15 and defined it completely in 3:16 as the promise that is valid for those of faith. The talk of a "new covenant" is missing in Paul, even in 3:6-14. It occurs in his writings only in the cup saying of the Lord's Supper tradition in 1 Cor. 11:25, as well as in very broken form in the discussion of the function of Moses in 2 Cor. 3:7-18. (In Rom. 3:25, a traditional christological text, the key word *covenant* is missing, but the passage is formulated on the basis of the theme of "covenant renewal").

Covenant is not a fundamental category of Paul's definition of the relationship of righteousness, Christology, faith, law, and so forth, which is all the more astonishing, since mention of the covenant in the Jewish tradition is appropriate here, and Paul makes the promises given with the covenant the substantiation of his new orientation of the whole matter. Apparently, for him the covenant (cf. also Rom. 9:4; 11:27), and even the "new covenant" of Jer. 31:31-34, is defined too much by the law, and therefore he speaks only of the promise.

Freedom from the Law

Text

5:1 For freedom Christ has set us free. Stand firm, therefore, and do not submit again to a yoke of slavery.

2 Listen! I, Paul, am telling you that if you let yourselves be circumcised, Christ will be of no benefit to you.

3 Once again I testify to every man who lets himself be circumcised that he is obliged to obey the entire law.

4 You who want to be justified by the law have cut yourselves off from Christ; you have fallen away from grace.

5 For through the Spirit, by faith, we eagerly wait for the hope of righteousness.

6 For in Christ Jesus neither circumcision nor uncircumcision counts for anything; the only thing that counts is faith working through love.

7 You were running well; who prevented you from obeying the truth?

8 Such persuasion does not come from the one who calls you.

9 A little yeast leavens the whole batch of dough.

10 I am confident about you in the Lord that you will not think otherwise. But whoever it is that is confusing you will pay the penalty.

11 But my friends, why am I still being persecuted if I am still preaching circumcision? In that case the offense of the cross has been removed.

12 I wish those who unsettle you would castrate themselves!

Commentary

Once more, Paul goes directly back to the developments in Galatia, which had caused him in 4:21-31 to give a fundamental substantiation of the gospel on the basis of the law itself (cf. 4:21). Again, the style resembles that of 4:8-20: short statements with underlying reasons, not long lines of argumentation. Striking is Paul's emphasis on himself in vv. 2, 10, 11. From this section we can finally demonstrate that one theme of

94

the other gospel was the new teachers' requirement of circumcision, which had nowhere been addressed so directly, but which already had to be considered in various places in commenting on the letter. Of course, the original readers of the letter, in contrast to us later ones, did not have to wait until this point to learn about such a requirement.

The most important key word in the section is carried over from 4:21-31: *freedom,* which together with the opposite concept, *slavery,* forms the last of the great antitheses that Paul arranges under the fundamental alternative of faith and law. In our language there are two different levels of freedom. On the one hand, *freedom* designates national independence from foreign domination (cf. wars of liberation, freedom movements). On the other hand, it means the modern freedoms of the individual as wrestled away from the absolute state, which are formulatted as universal human rights (freedom of religion, of the press, of opinion, etc.).

The two levels are not always kept clearly separated, particularly in political discussions, and are even consciously lumped together. The very concept of civil freedom of the nineteenth century is in a crisis, since in the modern constitutional state, which is no longer the old authoritarian state, these "freedoms" are in danger of becoming the privileges of particular individuals at the expense of others. The privilege of a liberty granted by the state (e.g., freedom from import duties, freedom of markets) is an additional source of our concept of freedom.

It is common to set "Christian freedom" apart from the foregoing freedoms as being not freedom *from* something but freedom *for* something, or to define it as "freedom in dependence," but neither idea approaches what Paul means. Freedom for him is absolutely a "freedom from," namely, from the law and thus also from sin and death. And freedom is the opposite of a dependence on the law and is defined not by dependence but by liberation.

[5:1] What Paul means by freedom, however, is also not to be reduced to ethical assertions, even though starting in v. 13 he develops ethics precisely as a description of freedom. Yet freedom plays a role not only in the question What should I do? but also in the question Who am I? For Paul the answer to this question lies, as we would expect, in Christ (here too echoing the titular sense), who freed us for freedom when he made possible blessing, righteousness, and life. Accordingly, the actual alternative to the concept of civil freedom lies in believers gaining their identity not from their own rights as privileges or asserting and maintaining them at the expense of others but, according to 2:20, from the death of the self with its rights and privileges and from the life of Christ, who by renouncing his own rights (cf. Phil. 2:6-8) made life possible.

Once again Paul asserts an alternative where Judaism does not have one. For the Jews, submitting to the yoke of the law means the realization of freedom, for this yoke is not perceived as heavy, but light. Freedom is defined here dialectically as voluntary subjection to the law. For Paul, however, according to 4:1-7, this service has the negative connotation of enslavement; freedom is one of the signs of the new world defined by Christ, faith, righteousness, life, and blessing.

[5:2] The antithesis of Christ and law, which has already permeated the letter thus far, is now complemented with the antithesis of Christ and the demand of circumcision. Circumcision is one of "the works of the law" established in Genesis 17, that is, precisely in connection with the Abraham tradition and the Abrahamic promise, which Paul lays claim to for his antithesis of law and faith. When his opponents demanded circumcision, he had to question their appeal to Abraham, although on the basis of Scripture, they at first seemed to have more right to claim this theme for themselves. As one of the most important works of the law, circumcision had to be included in Paul's disagreement with the possibility that the law could create life.

The origin of this ritual of circumcision, which then as now was not only Jewish, may lie in the realm of magic (cf. also Exod. 4:24-26), and then as now there are rationalizing interpretations, especially of the medical kind. In any case, for Judaism circumcision was and is a decisive mark of belonging to Israel and thus a sign of expectation of the promises given in the covenants of Abraham and of Sinai. It acquired that meaning above all in the time of the exile, when Israel lived in Babylon among people who were unfamiliar with this custom, and then again in the time of the Maccabees, when attempts were made from within Judaism itself to do away with this and other differentiating marks vis-à-vis the surrounding world. Must the lawless Gentile mission not have seemed like merely a renewal of such tendencies, which had been warded off with much blood?

Under Roman rule circumcision, as the sign of belonging to Judaism, was at the same time a guarantee of participation in certain privileges that the state granted to the synagogue. Thus a Christianity that renounced circumcision also renounced its claim to rights accorded Judaism. Not until later, after the Jewish insurrections, did the Roman emperor Hadrian prohibit circumcision.

[5:3] In a solemnly stated declaration, v. 2 sets up the alternative of Christ or circumcision. In the same form, v. 3 states the obligation of the circumcised to keep the whole law. According to the interpretation of Deut. 27:26 in 3:10, this keeping of the law stands under the curse, and according to the reading of Lev. 18:5 in 3:12, it stands in opposition to righteousness. For Paul there is no purified selection from the law—for example, a reduction to the moral law without the ceremonial law. There is only the rigorous standpoint that was also Paul's as a Pharisee: if the law at all, then the whole law.

In the Greek there is a play on words that links vv. 2 and 3, but it cannot be emulated in English. The word translated "be of benefit to" in v. 2 comes from the same stem as the one rendered "be obliged to" in v. 3; thus the two verses are two sides of the same coin.

[5:4-5] For Paul, having oneself be circumcised is an attempt to achieve righteousness through the law (v. 4). He demonstrated that this is impossible in 2:15-17; righteousness belongs to faith alone (v. 5). It is the content of the hope promised to Abraham, which Christians as heirs of Abraham expect through the Spirit, the same Spirit that lets them as "children" of God pray, "Abba! Father!" (4:6). Through Christ their righteousness can be within reach of this promised righteousness.

[5:6] Paul summarizes this point again in one sentence, which in its negatively formulated first part points back to 3:28. Circumcision is not something that can effect anything, nor is uncircumcision simply an advantage. Rather, both are basically on the same level, before Christ (cf. 2:15-16; Rom. 3:22-23) and in Christ (cf. 3:28; 1 Cor. 7:19). A similar principle will then be formulated again by Paul in his personally written conclusion to the letter (6:15). Decisive is faith alone, working through love. The verb form in Greek could also be translated passively: "faith that is effected through love," and love would then be God's love that goes before faith. This understanding was favored especially by Augustine. Against it, however, is the taking up of v. 6 again in vv. 13-14, where this faith that is effected through love is summed up in the love commandment of Lev. 19:18. Circumcision involves the "works" of the law, which are under the curse; blessing comes with faith, which knows works no more but works itself out in love. At this point Paul is getting ready for the ethical part of the letter, which will provide a description of freedom and love (5:13—6:10).

[5:7-9] In v. 7 Paul returns to the behavior of the Galatians. They were "running well," just as Paul himself had not run in vain with his gospel (cf. 2:2). They have obeyed "the truth" of the gospel as he has (cf. 2:5, 14; 4:16) and harkened to it (cf. 1:10). Amazed, Paul can only wonder who is keeping them from continuing to do so. The persuasion to another gospel (cf. 1:10) does not come from the one who calls them (v. 8)—calls them indeed to freedom (cf. v. 13), as he, Paul himself, called them to the proclaiming of this very gospel (cf. 1:15). With the image of yeast in v. 9, Paul uses a proverbial maxim for which evidence is found both in Greek as well as in Jewish tradition (cf. 1 Cor. 5:6). He understands it here in the negative sense: a little bit of proclaiming of the other gospel can cause great harm!

[5:10] In contrast to the obvious perplexity of 4:20, v. 10 sounds a hopeful note. Paul is convinced that the Galatians will turn away from that other gospel and turn again to the gospel in which there is no other gospel (cf. 1:6-7). This hope, however, is based in nothing other than the gospel itself. In the context of the letter, this means that Paul assumes that the situation has not been decided, that the falling away is not yet complete. In an echo of the curses of 1:8-9, he submits anyone who troubles the Galatians to the divine judgment. "Whoever it is that is confusing you" does not hide an anonymous authority; it means an extension of the announcement of judgment to anyone who claims to proclaim another gospel, even if that one is an angel from heaven (cf. 1:8-9).

[5:11] For Paul, the fact that he is persecuted is proof that he now preaches nothing but Christ. This, and not circumcision, has been the content of his proclamation right from the beginning, as 1:13—2:21 shows, and this was indeed why he persecuted the church earlier when he was still preaching circumcision. The stumbling block of the cross (1 Cor. 1:23) is the content of the proclamation, because the crucified One himself stands under the curse of the law (cf. 3:13), and therefore circumcision and gospel are incompatible.

[5:12] Paul closes with a cynical remark, in which he places Jewish circumcision on a level with the self-castration of the Cybele-Attis cult and at the same time presumably adopts the Gentile's scorn for circumcision (cf. also Phil. 3:2). Moveover, according to the law, castrated males are excluded from the people of God (cf. Deut. 23:1).

This section of 5:1-12 clearly reaches back even in its formulations to 1:6-10. This brings to an end the first large part of the letter, which in the interpretation more and more turns out to be a unit. At the same time, Paul is preparing here for the ethical part of the letter, 5:13—6:10. It will also continue the quarrel with the new teachers, based now not on the history of the gospel and on its content but on the working out of faith in love.

As we have seen in the first part of the letter, Paul arranges under the basic alternative of law and faith a series of further antitheses:

law	faith
death	life
curse	blessing
sin	righteousness
flesh	Spirit
slavery	freedom

Time and again, it is evident that in the Jewish tradition each antithesis belongs to the law as such, which in turn rests on the covenant as God's graceful devotion to his people. Related to this covenant, however, is also the promise that Paul asserts exclusively for faith. Ultimately, faith in the Jewish tradition is not understood as the antithesis of the law, but as behavior in accordance with the law. Thus, with his pairs of opposites, Paul splits apart what in the law belongs together: whoever holds to the law can experience life, blessing, righteousness, Spirit, and freedom; whoever rejects the law lands in death, curse, sin, flesh, and slavery—this would be the Jewish counterposition, which Paul is calling into question.

In the Letter to the Galatians, Paul addresses former Gentiles, even if their new teachers come from the Jewish tradition, as does Paul. He is certainly laying before his readers consequences of which they could not have been conscious when they wanted to win a share in the promises of the law and the promise of Abraham through circumcision as a sign of the covenant. What Paul sees as a step backward could have seemed to them a step forward.

In the Letter to the Romans, Paul shifts the themes a little because there he is dealing with a church of Gentile and Jewish Christians. There one of the main themes is the role of sin (Romans 5–8), which in the Letter to the Galatians he actually never really considers, even though beginnings in that direction can be recognized in 2:17 and 3:22. There we also find in Rom. 7:12, 14 statements on the law that are more positive than we might expect after Gal. 3:19. They stand in Romans precisely in the description of the impotence of the law and of those who live with this good law when faced with sin; the result is the splitting of the law into a "law of sin and of death" and a "law of the Spirit of life" (Rom. 8:2).

With all of this, Paul delivers more than a summary of his individual history and the current situation. In this whole part of the letter from 1:11 to 5:12, the argument is oriented to his biography, which runs like a thread through the whole section. From the beginning, however, the apostle is totally absorbed in the gospel; his own biography becomes a path of the gospel itself. The presentation of this gospel is indeed provoked by the developments in Galatia, but the gospel, as he presents it, is none other than what he preached from the very beginning.

For Paul the question at issue at that time in Galatia was not the question of the legitimacy of his individual religious experiences (his revelation, his consciousness, his calling, or whatever), which were not transmittable as such. At stake, rather, was the question of life itself: How can a person, Jew or Gentile, gain life? How can one find one's identity? This issue was independent of what was happening at that time in Galatia, and Paul's answer also went beyond the current situation in Galatia.

Thus the theme of the proclamation is not the apostle himself but the Christology of the cross as the place where Paul sees the experience of humanity reconciled with the promise of life. Paul presupposes that the law denies experience in favor of the promise. Behind this are the experiences that people had with the law in general—since Moses, Paul would say, but with more historical reflection, we would say, since the time of the exile, when the law, based on Moses, received its definitive meaning for Judaism.

Certainly, "law" was previously something different from "the five books of Moses." But would Paul not reply to such an objection that a consideration going back to the beginning, as proposed in Deuteronomy and then also more or less carried out, remains illusionary as long as it does not really and consistently reach beyond the law to Abraham? In any case, he maintains that such a point of view comes from the law itself if one only reads it correctly.

As we have seen repeatedly, Paul remains within Jewish conceptual categories and argumentative processes; he does not present his critique of the law from a position outside the law. He simply takes the experiences that those within Judaism had had with the law and already formulated as such and fundamentally reinterprets them from the standpoint of Christology.

Theology for Paul is not an articulation of religious experiences that are only to be admired by others but not emulated. It is, rather, an effort to answer this question: How can one succeed in formulating a valid interpretation of experiences that people have with themselves, with God, and with the world, instead of attributing these experiences to the arbitrary nature of the world, which can be confronted only with the confession of faith? The key to such theological work, in Paul's opinion, lies in the Christology of the cross, in which confession and experience coincide.

Life in Freedom

Introduction

In conformity with the pattern of the ancient "friendship letter," Paul opens his letters with a thanksgiving (to God; see above, p. 11) and introduces the second part with "I/we exhort" (Rom. 1:8/12:1; 1 Cor. 1:4/1:10; 2 Cor. 1:3/10:1; Phil. 1:3/4:2; 1 Thess. 1:2/4:1; Phlm. 4/9). A twofold division can also be observed in Galatians. However, as in the introduction to the letter (1:6-10), so here Paul departs from the usual form. Instead of "exhortation" there is a fundamental description of behavior that is no longer oriented to the given norms of the law but that is realized through the freedom that is given by Christ. In Romans, which again has the form of a friendship letter, Paul will broaden this, since there the whole section from 12:1 through 15:13, which stands under the heading "I exhort" (12:1), describes the behavior appropriate to justification. Later, in Colossians and Ephesians, which are probably not from Paul himself, the ethic is still further developed (Col. 3:5—4:6; Eph. 4:1—6:20).

Paul departs from the usual form because he is also still arguing with the "other gospel" in Galatia. We have already seen that in v. 6, in a polemical context, he sets the stage for the love commandment of vv. 13-14 as the foundation of the ethical section. With *freedom* the summons in v. 13 takes up one of the key words of the previous argumentation. The issue of the law also does not disappear here (cf. 5:14, 23; 6:2); finally, the alternative of flesh versus Spirit (3:2) is now really developed for the first time.

This interconnection shows that with ethics Paul is not raising a second theme that is more or less independent from the discussion of the gospel. What the law offered throughout—in addition to all the other things that had to be the center of attention up to this point—was rules for communal life on the basis of God's devotion to his people. But how was meaningful community life for Christians to be described if one followed Paul and based everything no longer on the law, but on faith?

100

We must guard against the hasty conclusion that one could read the negative descriptions in this part as a picture of the actual conditions in Galatia. This is prohibited by insight into the polemical character of the whole letter, for in an argument it is easy to charge an opponent with every imaginable outrage. And what Paul names here is actually nothing that would be thinkable only under the law.

Above all, however, we must see that to a large extent Paul takes up traditional ethical material already formulated in Judaism, which he did not work out for the first time for the special situation in Galatia. This is true of the love commandment of 5:14 adopted from the Old Testament, as well as the lists of negative and positive ways of behaving in 5:19-23 and many other individual instructions. Being bound to tradition, however, is not something characteristic of the Pauline ethic alone; it corresponds to the adoption, throughout the earlier parts of the letter, of conceptual and interpretive categories already developed in Judaism. From now on it will be a question of the ways in which Paul reorders such inherited traditional material under his fundamental alternative of faith and law. Paul faults the law also in the realm of ethics for promising more than it can accomplish: bestowing blessing, righteousness, and life. And he asserts that only freedom from the law makes it possible for human beings to live meaningfully with one another.

Love as the Realization
of Freedom

Text

5:13 For you were called to freedom, brothers and sisters; only do not use your freedom as an opportunity for self-indulgence, but through love become slaves to one another.

14 For the whole law is summed up in a single commandment, "You shall love your neighbor as yourself."

15 If, however, you bite and devour one another, take care that you are not consumed by one another.

Commentary

[5:13] Here, at the beginning of the ethical section, a reminder of the conversion of the Galatians serves as a reminder of the call to freedom, which repeats v. 1. Freedom for Paul is possible only outside the law, since the law, in his opinion, leads to slavery. In the Jewish tradition, in contrast, freedom is realized precisely in submission to the law. For Paul the following clause only appears to limit this proclamation of freedom, which, in the face of the alleged dangers of caprice and libertinism, is all too gladly taken back faintheartedly even by Christians.

Freedom is threatened by the "flesh" (NRSV: "self-indulgence")— what that is will be seen in vv. 16-24. The gospel promised the Spirit (3:14); the new teachers in Galatia questioned this claim and held that the Spirit comes only as a result of works of the law (3:12). Paul, however, again asserts that the "other gospel" let the Galatians end up in the flesh after they had already experienced the Spirit (3:3). In Romans, Paul goes even further and asserts that sin turns the law itself into an instrument of sin and that the law does not have the power to prevent such misuse by sin (cf. Rom. 7:8-12).

Paul wants not to restrict freedom but to designate love as the criterion of freedom: the love that he identified in v. 6 as the working out of faith. In the place of enslavement under the law and the elements of the world comes mutual service within the church, which no longer means slavery, but the realization of freedom. Hence love becomes the criterion even in church order (cf. v. 6 and 3:28).

[5:14] Paul bases the love commandment once again on the law itself, as he had already done earlier in his substantiation of the gospel based on the law. In Lev. 19:18 this commandment of love stands in a series of mostly negatively formulated commandments, each of which is based on "I am the Lord." Presupposed is the covenant that God had made with Israel; the sanctification of Israel (cf. Lev. 19:2) is Israel's answer to this devotion of God.

In the context the "neighbor" is the "brothers and sisters" (cf. especially the parallel in Lev. 19:17: "You shall not hate in your heart anyone of your own kin"), those who likewise belong to the people of Israel. In Lev. 19:34 this commandment is then also extended to the stranger who lives in the land without belonging to the people of Israel but who enjoys, within certain limitations, the rights of an Israelite. The Jewish tradition applies such Old Testament passages that speak of strangers to the proselytes, former Gentiles who have joined the synagogue.

What *love* means in Lev. 19:18, 34 becomes clear in the phrases used there in parallel: "not hate," "not take vengeance," "not bear a grudge against." As the gift of God, the covenant establishes a communion of those who live with one another in accordance with the law, which is also understood as the gift of God. "As yourself" here sets very high standards, for it is obviously based on the simple assumption that everyone addressed will seek the best for himself or herself.

Thus it is quite understandable that in a later period the commandment of love can be interpreted through the so-called Golden Rule, which comes from the Greek tradition. Stated negatively, it says: "What you do not want others to do to you, do not do that to them either"; in the positive version, "What you want others to do to you, do that to them also" (cf. also Matt. 7:12; Luke 6:31).

In the Old Testament the commandment of love is one commandment among many others, and it receives no recognizable systematic meaning. In Judaism, however, it is occasionally linked with the commandment to love God. Thus it appears also in the Jesus tradition in Mark 12:28-34 par. together with Deut. 6:5 ("You shall love the Lord your God with all your heart, and with all your soul, and with all your might") as a double commandment of love and a short summary of the whole law.

Jesus himself probably intensified the Old Testament commandment of love with the demand to love one's enemies, which can probably still be reconstructed in its original wording: "Love your enemies, so that you will be children of God"; the substantiation comes from God's own mercy, which is not only for the righteous (cf. Luke 6:27, 35; Matt. 5:44-45). The promise to the righteous to be "children of God" (cf. above, p. 30) is oriented here toward a new standard. Love is the overcoming of hostility and therefore not simply the confirmation of ongoing fellowship that exists in contrast to the "others," the enemies, but rather the establishment of a new fellowship based on openness toward those others.

In early Christian tradition the commandment of love is a fundamental theme of very different layers of tradition, which otherwise have little in common with each other. This assertion, however, must not obscure the fundamental differences. Without citing the basic Old Testament text of Lev. 19:18, the Johannine tradition expressly states the "new" commandment that Jesus leaves his followers and that he bases on his own love for them (John 13:34-35; 15:12-17).

In the First Letter of John this "new" commandment has already become the old one, which from the very beginning was valid in the church and which is based here in the love of God (1 John 2:28—4:21; cf. 5:2; 2 John 5). As in the commandment to love one's enemies (Luke 6:27, 35; Matt. 5:44-45), here too it is related to the themes of righteousness and of being children of God.

Paul, however, bases the commandment of love not, like John, on the words of Jesus but on the law itself. And thus the later author who wrote in the name of James reaches back precisely to the Old Testament commandment of love in order to pursue ad absurdum the Pauline alternative of law and faith (cf. Jas. 2:8: the commandment of love as the "royal law"). Paul calls it the fulfillment, the summary of the law (cf. Rom. 13:8-10). What he means by this is not the *doing* of the law, which stands under the curse (3:10), but the working out of faith in love (v. 6), whose content was designated in 2:20 as the love of Christ in the giving of himself.

[5:15] With this thought, however, he questions whether love is possible under the law, and as proof he points to the desolate state of the Galatian churches after their turning to the works of the law. Those who want to convert to the law live for that very reason in conflict with one another and show absolutely nothing of the love that is demanded by the law to which they want to commit themselves.

Such a proof must always remain inconclusive, for Paul occasionally complains of similar conditions in other places as well; in the ongoing history of the church, such conditions do not depend only on one's position regarding the law, even if lawfulness and lovelessness can certainly appear as siblings. More important is the fact that here, as throughout the whole letter, Paul is again exclusively promoting faith, which the law promised to give. *Love* is the only great concept of the letter that remains without an antithesis such as *hate* or *enmity* and, unlike the others, is not sharpened through contrast. Love is also, according to 1 Corinthians 13, the only thing that does not remain temporary but can really last.

The following development of the love commandment in the description of freedom, which follows in 5:16—6:10, will show that this commandment of love is transposed quite concretely into the situation of the Christian church and does not remain a general, theoretical principle or a mere impulse. This ethic is structured on the basis of faith and thus of its content, which is given as Christ. That freedom, for which Christ has made us free, is realized in love as the working out of faith. Thus, here again, a connection that was developed earlier in the Jewish tradition is redefined on the basis of Christology.

Since faith offers the opportunity to find one's identity, believers no longer need to seek their identity through deeds, in which they cannot find themselves, as dealing with the law demonstrates (cf. Rom. 7:7-25). The new identity that lies in the cross of Christ (cf. 2:20) enables us to see others and makes us free for mutual ministry. Even in their deeds, believers are not always occupied with themselves alone but can devote themselves to the "neighbor."

Flesh or Spirit

Text

5:16 Live by the Spirit, I say, and do not gratify the desires of the flesh.
17 For what the flesh desires is opposed to the Spirit, and what the Spirit desires is opposed to the flesh; for these are opposed to each other, to prevent you from doing what you want.
18 But if you are led by the Spirit, you are not subject to the law.
19 Now the works of the flesh are obvious: fornication, impurity, licentiousness,
20 idolatry, sorcery, enmities, strife, jealousy, anger, quarrels, dissensions, factions,
21 envy, drunkenness, carousing, and things like these. I am warning you, as I warned you before: those who do such things will not inherit the kingdom of God.
22 By contrast, the fruit of the Spirit is love, joy, peace, patience, kindness, generosity, faithfulness,
23 gentleness, and self-control. There is no law against such things.
24 And those who belong to Christ Jesus have crucified the flesh with its passions and desires.

Analysis

Paul and his opponents disagreed on how to answer the question, Where does the Spirit come from? (3:2). He asserts in 3:3 that with the Galatians' conversion to that "other gospel," they fell back into the flesh again after they had already experienced the Spirit. Hence the alternative of *flesh and Spirit* is part of the series of antithetical pairs that Paul places under the fundamental antithesis of law and faith. In his opinion, the law does not lead one out of the fleshly existence that he characterizes in vv. 19-21; as the working out of faith, however, there can certainly be life in the Spirit in the sense of vv. 22-23.

Flesh and Spirit here do not indicate different inner qualities or even parts of a person, as, for example, the distinction in a long tradition of ethics (also Christian) between negatively characterized sensuality and

106

positively viewed rationality. It is, rather, a question of powers that attempt to determine a person's behavior in this way or that. This behavior, however, is not something that is acquired secondarily: a human being is by nature a creature that behaves and acts.

Thus it depends on how this behavior and action are determined. In other words, faith is not something that basically concerns only a person's thinking and self-understanding, with one's actions arising as secondary matters. A human being never exists without behaving and acting—usually so spontaneously that reflection can only come afterward. Hence, faith always expresses itself directly in behavior, which is by no means arbitrary.

Commentary

[5:16] Only to "live by the Spirit"—not to "gratify the desires of the flesh"—can be appropriate to the commandment of love (v. 14). *Desire* here is not a neutral concept but is clearly negative; for Paul there are no "good" desires in the realm of ethics. Yet this does not mean sexuality as such, as interpreted by moralistic exegesis, but everything "the flesh" is after when it becomes the determining power in human action, the results of which are listed in vv. 19-21.

In the Letter to the Romans, Paul sees the cause of desire in the law itself, whose prohibitions awaken the urge to transgress (Rom. 7:7-8). Thus he expands there what he had already indicated in the Letter to the Galatians with the ordering of sin and flesh under the law, not under faith.

[5:17] Flesh and Spirit are mutually exclusive opposites that battle for control of a person. Life in the flesh divides a person, so that will and actual behavior cannot be brought into agreement with each other, although that is certainly the goal. This is also taken up by Paul in Romans and placed in the familiar context of law, sin, and flesh (Rom. 7:15, 23). The law itself promised the removal of this division, but it cannot deliver on its promise.

[5:18] Here, in the Letter to the Galatians, Paul only suggests this state of affairs: possession of the Spirit (3:14) means freedom from the law, and only thus can a person overcome internal division. One achieves the desired identity with oneself not through the law but, for Paul, only in the cross, which overcomes the contradiction after the murder of the self by the law (2:20). This identity is no longer an aim to be sought through action; rather, it is already basic to the action.

[5:19-23] Here Paul opposes a listing of the *works of the flesh* (vv. 19-21) with a series that designates the *fruit of the Spirit* (vv. 22-23). It should be noted that up to this point he has spoken of works in the context of "works of the law" (2:16; 3:2, 5, 10), which the reader now associates with the negatively valued "works of the flesh." This is all the more evident insofar as Paul opposes them not with the *works* of the Spirit but with the *fruit* of the Spirit—something that issues of itself from the Spirit. It is not the work but the working out of faith in love. Also, it is probably not accidental that we have the singular *fruit,* which suggests that the working out of faith is not the sum of individual modes of behavior listed in vv. 22-23 but a unified picture of what love can mean in reality.

Such listings of positive and negative ways of behaving recall the widespread genre of the catalog of so-called virtues and vices. From the Greek tradition we have the list (sometimes varying in detail) of the four cardinal virtues of wisdom, courage, prudence, and justice, and on the other side the likewise variable four vices of imprudence, licentiousness, injustice, and cowardice. For us the terms *virtue* and *vice* evoke somewhat misleading associations, since in our present understanding one only *has,* and does not *do,* virtues; and vices indicate primarily the lack of virtue or perhaps just bad habits. For Paul, however, even here it was a matter of ways of behaving: Paul's ethic aims not only at certain basic human attitudes or orientations but at concrete behavior, including the resulting consequences, for which one is responsible.

In the Old Testament one finds comparable listings, for example, in Hos. 4:1: faithfulness, loyalty, knowledge of God; in Jer. 7:9: stealing, murder, adultery, swearing falsely, making offerings to Baal, idolatry; and even in the Decalogue, which presents not so much a systematic ethic as a collection of possible misbehaviors toward God.

The lists that Paul uses here and elsewhere are more comparable to texts from Judaism, which in varying degrees show connections with Greek ethical instruction. For Paul, in contrast to the Jewish tradition, it is decisive that in that tradition the positive side naturally goes with keeping the law, while the negative is only a description of falling from the law. Thus Paul again adopts a tradition developed in Judaism and claims it for faith, not for the law.

In early Christianity such lists are a part of church instruction, although there is no obligatory, stereotypically recurring order of items. This is shown by the variability of the listings even with Paul himself. For positive lists in Paul we have only 2 Cor. 6:6 and Phil. 4:8 (cf. Col. 3:12-13; Eph. 4:2, 32; 5:9; 1 Tim. 4:12; 6:11; 2 Tim. 2:22; 3:10; 1 Pet. 3:8; 2 Pet. 1:3-7). More frequent are the lists of negative modes of behavior: Rom. 1:29-31; 13:13; 1 Cor. 5:10-11; 6:9-10; 2 Cor. 12:20-21 (cf. Col. 3:5-8; Eph. 4:31; 5:3-5; 1 Tim. 1:9-10; 2 Tim. 3:2-7; Titus 3:3; 1 Pet. 2:1; 4:3, 15; Mark 7:21-22/Matt. 15:19; Rev. 9:21; 21:8; 22:15).

Such lists are similar to comparable Jewish texts. What is new with Paul is the exclusive connection of the positive modes of behavior—and of the Spirit itself as their cause—with faith alone. The fruit of the Spirit for him is the fruit of the Spirit that has the Christians crying, "Abba! Father!" (4:6).

Paul presupposes that a person naturally wills the good but that behavior tends to go in the opposite direction (v. 17), and the law can do nothing to stop it. This tension in a person between intention and actual behavior corresponds to the tension between one's creed and one's experience, which cannot verify the truth of the creed. As in the question of faith defined thus (see above, p. 47), so also in the realm of human action, the answer for Paul is to be found in Christology as the mediation between the two. In this connection also, faith and action are not to be separated.

The lists have their effect through the simple juxtaposition of nouns, which are not usually qualified by additional attributes. No special order is indicated; the listing as such becomes the comprehensive description. Nevertheless, with each word used we must attempt to understand what is intended. Even for the first readers, the words probably evoked a certain breadth of associations, so that a simple lexical identification of the words—if that is at all possible—would not be appropriate to the text. Indeed, here it is not a question of the conceptual establishment of an elaborate ethical system but of lists that attempt to promote certain human behavior. Difficulties arise, first of all, from the fact that such lists are handed down through an essentially moralizing tradition, which causes us to read them as "typically Christian" in the negative sense, with special emphasis in the realm of sexuality and with an understanding of "vices" or "bad habits" based on a middle-class morality that is oriented toward "decency." This morality then creates the impression that basically we are only concerned with things that a "decent" person would do or not do anyway, with or without Christianity. Such decency can become identified with Christianity, and Christian ethics then becomes merely a legitimation of middle-class morality. Paul, however, asserts that of ourselves we do indeed will what is good, but against our will we repeatedly end up doing the opposite.

[5:19] The first five of "the works of the flesh" belong together in that traditionally they have a certain connection with idolatry. This is true even for "fornication" as the falling away from the God of Israel to other gods. The term designates any illegitimate sexual activity, as measured against Jewish family law.

Something similar can be said for "impurity": in addition to cultic impurity, which excludes one from participation in worship, there are sexual excesses. "Licentiousness" means excesses of every kind, including those in the area of sex. The traditional emphasis on sexual shortcomings, which is also seen here in Paul, goes back to the prohibition against exaggerated sexuality (including cultic life), both in the environment of ancient Israel and in the Hellenistic period.

[5:20] Thus in the naming of these wrong ways of behaving, the warning against "idolatry" is always included. For Jews and Christians, the problem of idolatry did not lie in pagan worship, which could fairly easily be avoided, but rather—as 1 Cor. 8:1-13, for example, shows—especially in the religious permeation of life as a whole. Here one could repeatedly argue the question of where idolatry really begins.

Actually, however, something similar can be said for the whole list. Its purpose is not to give casuistic definitions of what one may still do or no longer do, but to indicate a rough framework. In individual cases, it is a matter of clarifying whether a shortcoming involves the consequence of exclusion from the kingdom of God. Examples of this are presented by the cases treated in 1 Corinthians, where Paul obviously draws the line differently from certain groups in the Corinthian church.

"Sorcery" also belongs to the realm of encounter with the world of idols. The Greek word here has entered our language as the loanword *pharmacy* and can also have the positive meaning of a therapeutic means of healing. Then as now, drugs seem to be dangerously close to magic, so that here too it can be an open question in individual cases where medicine ends and magic begins.

After these shortcomings, which are also rooted in the area of religion, there is a series that basically concerns interpersonal modes of behavior, although this change is not indicated syntactically in any fashion. Moreover, as we have seen, the first five designate not only one's relationship to God but also interpersonal relations.

"Enmities" is the opposite of love. The Greek plural here shows that for Paul it is a question not of a fundamental attitude of hostility but of concrete ways of behaving, in which another person is deprived of the right to be human. Indeed, for me an enemy can only be someone who, in my opinion, is in the wrong and behaves in a wrong way—otherwise I would not perceive him or her as a danger. Likewise, in "strife" a person abandons a sense of commonality and tries to prevail against someone else.

"Jealousy" (literally, "zeal") is a concrete mode of behavior, not a general trait. Although according to 4:17 there is also a good sense of the term, here it is understood negatively as behavior that treats the other person solely as the object of one's exaggerated efforts and not as a person with rights of his or her own. Zeal and jealousy are thus related to "anger," in which aggressiveness tries to annihilate the other person.

In the political realm the Greek word rendered as "quarrels" also designated the recruiting of followers by unfair means and thus is close to *intrigue.* It means attempts to secure one's own advantage through any means and to use the fellowship for that purpose, thus endangering the common life of the fellowship.

"Dissensions" refers to fragmentation within a fellowship, whose unity is threatened by those who pursue their own interests at the expense of others. Here, no doubt, the original readers of Galatians could not have avoided also thinking about their own situation. This is also true of the "factions" that split them into individual groups that then tried to subjugate each other.

[5:21] "Envy" here translates a Greek plural that can only awkwardly be rendered as "envyings" (KJV). The plural shows that here, as earlier, it is a question not just of simple attitudes but of concrete actions.

From "enmities" through "envy" identifies modes of behavior in which one attempts to assert one's own presumed right and fails to grant the rights of others. The last two vices—"drunkenness" and "carousing" —are to be grouped with the first five works of the flesh.

The list could be expanded at will. It is neither complete nor systematically ordered, and therefore it allows no casuistry along the lines of "everything is permitted that is not here expressly forbidden." Indeed, it lacks such offenses as murder and theft, which are found in similar lists. One almost gets the impression that the list names only modes of behavior that are not the first to come to mind.

Paul reminds his readers that they have known all of this since his mission with them and that it is not a question of something new that has just been added to the gospel. The matter is settled: whoever does these things will not inherit the kingdom of God. Paul also speaks of the "kingdom of God," the central theme of Jesus' proclamation, in 1 Cor. 4:20; 6:9-10; 15:50; Rom. 14:17, and in those places, as here, lists wrong ways of behaving, mostly in negatively formulated sentences only. In the Jewish tradition also, exclusionary formulas like these belong to such catalogs. There the "kingdom of God" is the eschatological world in which God's righteousness will clearly be the order of the world, which is now still hidden.

In the whole list Paul is not enumerating attitudes, approaches to life, or ways of thinking, but specific ways of behaving. They are alike in being attempts to find oneself through one's behavior, whether in the orgiastic intensification of life or in the imposition of one's rights at the expense of the rights of others. Both are escapes from one's own self with the aim of finding a new self. But that is not what faith is all about, according to 2:19-20.

As much as the things named here must certainly have rung in the ears of the Galatians, the list is not intended to be a description of the conditions in Galatia. Their new teachers, however, could not accept what Paul asserted: the law is powerless in regard to matters of the flesh. They would have objected all the more if they had read in the Letter to the Romans that all of this is even provoked by the law (cf. Rom. 7:7).

[5:22-23] Against this list Paul sets a somewhat shorter, positive list under the heading "The fruit of the Spirit." The two lists are not symmetrically arranged so that for each wrong way of behaving a corresponding right way is named. And here also it is a matter not merely of attitudes or ways of thinking but of concrete ways of behaving.

At the top is "love," which in the context cannot be simply one item beside others. The Old Testament commandment of love, through its prior placement in vv. 13-14, holds this prominent position as the foundation of all the results of faith, and thus the following concepts are actually only paraphrases of the love that does not insist on its own way (cf. 1 Cor. 13:5). Again, we can only attempt to indicate generally the possible associations of the original readers and cannot arrive at exact lexical equivalents.

"Joy" is not so much a psychic condition of the individual as it is something that is at work within the community, something that is given reciprocally. The opposite is grief. Likewise, "peace" involves more than simply an attitude of peaceableness; it is the end of hostility. Joy and peace appear as complementary concepts in Rom. 14:17 and 15:13.

According to 1 Cor. 13:4, "patience" is also a part of love. In contrast to jealousy or anger, it designates perseverance in listening to another person and allowing that one to speak, without immediately and impatiently jumping in with the right answer. As the opposite of enmity, "kindness" is the attempt not to weaken one's relationship with another person, even under heavy strain. "Generosity" is to be understood in a similar way.

For "faithfulness" the Greek text has the same word that is usually translated "faith" (so rendered in this verse by the kjv). The corresponding Hebrew word also has these two possible meanings (cf. the expression *in good faith*). Faithfulness is a mark of friendship; it is reliability in all conceivable situations. "Gentleness" also belongs within the scope of friendship. It means the opposite of anger, the enduring of another in spite of that one's obvious mistakes.

"Self-control" refers especially to the shortcomings of immorality, drunkenness, and carousing named in vv. 19 and 21. Here, however, it is not a question of an absolute asceticism, but of a renunciation of pleasure seeking for its own sake.

None of this fruit of the Spirit is in any way against the law, as Paul says with perhaps an undertone of irony. Conversion to the works of the law, however, produces nothing in this regard; it brings nothing different and nothing new. On the contrary, this is a paraphrasing of the commandment of love, which was taken from the law itself, as the initial position of love in v. 22 shows. If the Galatians believe that they did not attain all of this fruit until their conversion to the other gospel, then they are deceiving themselves, for the Spirit whose fruit is enumerated here comes not from the law but from the preaching of faith (cf. 3:14).

For Paul it is not a question here of requirements, of commandments; the exclusionary formula of v. 21b is not followed by a positive promise. Rather, Paul sees in all of this simply the "fruit" of the Spirit, something that human beings on their own may certainly intend, but that for them—with or without the law—repeatedly changes into the opposite (v. 17).

[5:24] Only in faith—and its content is recalled here again by Paul with *Christ*—does all of this become possible. In faith the "flesh," as the power driving people into conflict between the will and actual behavior, is crucified, and with it the passions and desires that draw people into what they in themselves do not want at all.

This verse refers back to 2:20 and the crucifixion of the self through the law. It is therefore only logical that in the context of Romans 7 (where Paul characterizes the law more positively than he does in Galatians), Paul connects the law with flesh, desires, and sin. In 6:14 he will summarize this connection once more in his personal postscript as the crucifixion of the world.

The new identity that is gained in the crucifixion of the self according to 2:19-20 relieves one of the attempt to gain one's identity through one's actions by trying to find oneself at the cost of others or to indulge oneself sexually. Thus the Pauline thesis of justification by faith as the finding of one's identity through the cross logically includes a quite definite ethic, not an arbitrary one, which is oriented toward this very cross.

Comparable assertions in the Greek and Jewish traditions show that human beings certainly know what is good and have the will to do good. Paul asserts, however, that on our own we do not escape the conflict between our will and our actual behavior. In his view, "good will," or the assurance that we "meant well" and could not have known what would come out of it, is not enough. The withdrawal into one's own moral integrity belongs, rather, to the realm of the "flesh," since such integrity comes at the expense of others, who are sacrificed to the self and cannot receive their rights because the self seeks only its own right.

An action based on faith, however, also includes reflection on the consequences of the action: what will be the actual result of a behavior? The person of faith is not relieved of the responsibility for the consequences of his or her action. For this very reason, talk of "virtues" and "vices," which we rejected right from the start, is so misleading. For us, "virtues" are certain human qualities, characteristics, or fundamental attitudes, whereas "vices" are modes of behavior that result from a lack of such "virtues."

There is, however, a process by which virtues become independent; even a tyrant can have everything that we call virtues, including a kind of perverted sense of justice. Secondary virtues such as duty, loyalty, and decency were also demanded of concentration camp guards; offenses against them were severely punished. One should speak of virtues only when one also speaks of the norms to which they are related.

For Paul, however, ethics can be based neither on the good will of human beings nor on their virtues, but only on justification by faith. Thus love becomes the realization of the freedom that is based on the cross of Christ (v. 1).

Life in the Spirit

Text

5:25 If we live by the Spirit, let us also be guided by the Spirit.

26 Let us not become conceited, competing against one another, envying one another.

6:1 My friends, if anyone is detected in a transgression, you who have received the Spirit should restore such a one in a spirit of gentleness. Take care that you yourselves are not tempted.

2 Bear one another's burdens, and in this way you will fulfill the law of Christ.

3 For if those who are nothing think that they are something, they deceive themselves.

4 All must test their own work; then that work, rather than their neighbor's work, will become a cause for pride.

5 For all must carry their own loads.

6 Those who are taught the word must share in all good things with their teacher.

7 Do not be deceived; God is not mocked, for you reap whatever you sow.

8 If you sow to your own flesh, you will reap corruption from the flesh; but if you sow to the Spirit, you will reap eternal life from the Spirit.

9 So let us not grow weary in doing what is right, for we will reap at harvest time, if we do not give up.

10 So then, whenever we have an opportunity, let us work for the good of all, and especially for those of the family of faith.

Analysis

After the general admonitions in vv. 16-24 there now follows a series of short, individual instructions, some of which are formulated positively, some negatively. A systematic order is not perceivable, and syntactically also they are only loosely connected. Paul could certainly have also concluded them with "and things like these" (cf. 5:21). The basic tendency of the previous section continues: the rejection of the attempt to

114

find one's own identity in deeds. The text concludes by pointing to the judgment at the end of days (6:7-9). Not even those who live in the Spirit are relieved of the responsibility for their actions. Summarizing the entire ethical section, 6:10 then closes with the admonition to utilize the time remaining before the end.

Commentary

[5:25] In this verse Paul addresses the Galatians again on their possession of the Spirit. Life in the Spirit, according to 2:20, is nothing other than life in the faith whose content is the love of the Son of God in his giving of himself. Used here in the conclusion drawn by Paul is the word translated "be guided" (cf. v. 16), which appears again in 6:16 (and which is also used in Phil. 3:16 and Rom. 4:12). For the original readers of the text, this word may have had associations with the theme of the elements of the world (4:3, 9), since the Greek verb for "be guided" in 5:25 and 6:16 has the same root as the Greek noun meaning "elements." If the opponents in Galatia asserted a connection between the elements of the world and the law, then ethics for them meant the orientation of action toward the world order; cosmology and ethics, natural law and moral law, belong together, as in another area the basic ethical assertion of the Stoics is "to live in harmony with nature," a maxim whose force survives today in the call to make the "natural life" the norm of ethics.

For Paul, however, the foundation of ethics cannot be harmony with the world, since this world is destroyed in the cross (cf. 6:14); rather, it must be agreement with the Spirit that is the Spirit of the Son (4:6), the Son who gave himself out of love (2:20). Thus even this criterion of action, which takes up the love commandment of 5:13-14, is involved in the disagreement with the other gospel, which promised the possession of the Spirit through the works of the law, including observation of the world elements (4:9-10).

[5:26] In an initial specific prohibition Paul rejects relations with "one another" that only seek confirmation of oneself in comparison with others. Conceit characterizes those who constantly expect from others approval for their own achievements, whose description must therefore always be exaggerated. "Competing against" refers to the challenging of another to comparison, with the aim of coming out better oneself. And "envy" arises almost necessarily from such behavior, because none of us, no matter how much we overestimate ourselves, can be so superior to another person that we cannot see that the other person is still a little better in some area.

Such attitudes and behavior belong not to the Spirit but to the realm of the flesh. Here too the Galatians must have felt themselves addressed, without, however, any specific reference to the disagreements.

[6:1] With the new form of address "my friends," Paul warns them against such arrogance, even in a situation where they have caught a person in a trespass. They should not use such a situation to magnify their own worth or to conclude that they are different from that one; rather, because they have the Spirit, they are supposed to put the sinner straight. Their own standing in the Spirit is not defined by the fact that others are sinners (cf. 2:15), but by the faith that has made possession of the Spirit possible. Gloating, even the spiritual kind, can all too easily turn into one's own fall.

[6:2] In a positive way Paul initially summarizes all of this in the admonition to bear one another's burdens. This is another formulation of the love commandment of 5:14, and "one another's" no doubt includes the idea that we ourselves must also be ready to have our own burdens taken from us and no longer be among those who believe that they should always heroically—and unilaterally—bear the burdens of others.

Paul calls this the fulfillment of the "law of Christ," just as, with the commandment of love, he spoke of the fulfillment of the law. This may be the way the new teachers in Galatia characterized the law from Sinai as also still valid in the Christian community. For Paul, however, the law of Christ can only be the opposite of the law of Sinai (cf. 3:19), and *Christ* here again is not merely the personal name of the founder of this law but, rather, in the titular sense, anchors this law in the content of faith and of the gospel.

In 5:17, after asserting that the law does not deliver humanity from the conflict between will and actual deed, Paul proceeds logically to the division between the law of Sinai and the law of Christ, which in the Letter to the Romans is then completed with the opposition of the "law of the Spirit of life" and the "law of sin and of death" (Rom. 8:2). The "law of Christ" is possible only through freedom from the law that was given on Sinai.

[6:3-4] Such renunciation of using another solely as a standard for establishing one's own superiority excludes the overestimation of oneself (v. 3). Self-testing should be restricted to consideration of one's own work (v. 4). It certainly does not always have to lead to a negative result, contrary to what a long tradition of religious practice in self-examination asserts. But the worth of one's own deeds lies precisely not in the idea that at least they are always a little bit better than those of someone else but rather in a sober taking stock of what one has done, what the results were, and what remains to be done.

[6:5] In this process, furthermore, we will probably also discover that not everything is simply marvelous; there is always a residue, however, that does not need to be repressed, but rather can be lifted up in the common life of the church. The ambiguity of one's own action cannot be made unambiguous through denying the negative side, or through concentrating on the negative side alone. This ambiguity is bearable if the present life in the flesh is understood as life by faith in the Son (2:20), life in the Spirit that is the Spirit of the Son (4:6).

Inherent in justification is the possibility of finding one's identity, and thus openness for others is also possible precisely in the assumption of responsibility for one's own actions with all their ambiguity and for the no less ambiguous consequences of those actions because identity does not have to be achieved through deeds. Only where this connection between justification and ethics is no longer realized does one have to appeal to institutions such as confession and penance.

[6:6] Now follows, without close connection to the context, an admonition for the material support of the teacher by the students. Paul thus adopts a principle that he also cites in 1 Cor. 9:7-14 but that he rejects for himself in regard to the Corinthians (1 Cor. 9:12, 15; 2 Cor. 11:7), although he certainly accepted gifts from the Macedonian churches (cf. 2 Cor. 11:8-9; Phil. 4:10-20). Perhaps at this point the Galatians are also reminded of the offering for Jerusalem (cf. 1 Cor. 16:1), which in Rom. 15:27 Paul derives from the principle cited here.

[6:7-8] The gravity of the admonitions is underlined by the solemn-sounding "Do not be deceived" with which Paul introduces an allusion to the eschatological revelation of works (cf. in a similar connection 1 Cor. 6:9; 15:33). When it comes to the relationship between flesh and Spirit, God does not play games. A kind of "farmer's rule," such as is also found in similar form in Greek and Jewish texts, shows the unavoidable connection between sowing and reaping, start and finish. So it is also with life in the flesh and life in the Spirit (v. 8): the outcome in the one case is corruption; in the other, eternal life. The decision will come in the eschatological judgment, for which the harvest was already a symbol in the Old Testament. At stake in the alternative between flesh and Spirit, law and faith, is nothing less than life, including eternal life. This may seem offensive to an ethic that is based purely on attitude, because now the suspicion is that a good deed no longer occurs for its own sake. But Paul's concern is to maintain the ambiguity of action and not dissolve it in good will, an ambiguity that only in the eschatological judgment will become unambiguously apparent as good and evil. Not even those who live in the Spirit are relieved of the responsibility for their actions, including the consequences of those actions.

[6:9-10] What Paul previously described as "life in Christ" he now summarizes again in the rather sober words "doing what is right." Faith also requires a bit of endurance when vigilance threatens to vanish and the most personal question of faith comes up again—the question of translating creed, promise, and hope into action. Paul underlines this need to act again in v. 10: to use the time that remains—and Paul is certainly not counting on a long span—to work for the good of everyone, especially fellow Christians. This is not to limit the commandment of love but to identify a concrete beginning. Throughout church history there will again and again be occasion to remind Christians of these their closest neighbors, for there will always be those who believe that the commandment of love applies primarily to those at a distance, while other standards may be valid in dealing with neighbors in the church.

The word *family* designates those in the house who live and work together under one roof: the larger family, including the slaves of the house. Sociologically, this group designation shows that the Christian churches, when they no longer had a place in the synagogue, were organized as churches in the houses of the more affluent believers.

Unlike in our present understanding, however, the *house* was not the private realm in contrast to the public as the area of actual social relations; rather, as the social structure of the larger family, including servants living in the house, it was the model for the polis as well as for the more extensive organizational forms of the state. That was true throughout the Middle Ages and well into the modern period before, as a result of the separation of private and public ethics, individual and social ethics also went their own ways. With this separation, however, the social dimension of such an ethic was also lost, and it now reads as though intended only for the private realm.

Moreover, politics and economics have now also split off from ethics as independent disciplines and are oriented primarily toward objectives and not toward ethical decision. For us, this situation makes the application of such an ethic to the concrete situation very difficult in the private realm as well as in the public realm, especially since its moralistic interpretation and the retreat to attitude alone go hand in hand with this development, and thus the ethic no longer seems practical, even in the private realm.

A possible new beginning is offered by the connection between justification and ethics as described here by Paul. Justification through faith alone offers the possibility of life to human beings, whose humanity already includes behaving and acting. Thus what ethics involves is not the idea that humans are first concerned with themselves and their faith and then, in a second step, act in relation to their surroundings. Nor, however, is it a question of directly implementing justification in action. We should always keep in mind that in the ethical section of the Letter to the Galatians, we no longer find the concept of righteousness, which in our tradition we are accustomed to interpreting ethically. Even more surprising, the concept of sin, which much more readily invites such an understanding, is also missing. For Paul the question What should I do? always includes the question Who am I? because there is no humanity without the action of human beings.

The Pauline ethic is not the application of justification to social relations but its execution in the lives of people who never live for themselves but who always find themselves in a web of social relationships. These, however, do not then become the means of self-realization and self-satisfaction but are the locus of love as the working out of faith. This is also true of the church as a whole, which does not need to misuse the practice of adducing a proof of the truth of the gospel but which, rather, is grounded in the unambiguous nature of the gospel and through it can be free to do what is needed. If faith for Paul is the reconciliation of confession and experience in the cross of Christ, then the same is also true of love, which does not give up, in spite of the ambiguity of experience, because in view of the cross it sees no reason to give up.

Postscript in Paul's Own Hand

Text

6:11 See what large letters I make when I am writing in my own hand!

12 It is those who want to make a good showing in the flesh that try to compel you to be circumcised—only that they may not be persecuted for the cross of Christ.

13 Even the circumcised do not themselves obey the law, but they want you to be circumcised so that they may boast about your flesh.

14 May I never boast of anything except the cross of our Lord Jesus Christ, by which the world has been crucified to me, and I to the world.

15 For neither circumcision nor uncircumcision is anything; but a new creation is everything!

16 As for those who will follow this rule—peace be upon them, and mercy, and upon the Israel of God.

17 From now on, let no one make trouble for me; for I carry the marks of Jesus branded on my body.

18 May the grace of our Lord Jesus Christ be with your spirit, brothers and sisters. Amen.

Commentary

[6:11] Paul closes the letter with a few lines from his own hand. Perhaps he is filling up the rest of a page already begun or is adding a final sheet. Earlier he dictated (cf. Rom. 16:22, where we also learn the name of one writer), as he probably did for all of his letters, with the exception of the Letter to Philemon, which he wrote himself (cf. Phlm. 19).

With his own hand Paul also places a greeting at the close of the First Letter to the Corinthians (16:21). Yet nowhere in the other letters do we find a postscript as detailed as here. As with other deviations from the normal form of a letter (see above, pp. 11, 100), the explanation here is also to be found in the peculiar situation of the Letter to the Galatians: the dispute causes Paul once again, urgently, to call to the attention of the Galatians the choice that is at stake.

119

The past form in the Greek (literally, "I wrote") is used in reference to the point in time when the Galatians will be reading this letter. The mention of "large letters"—in contrast to which we can imagine an elegant calligraphy—contains perhaps an understatement or a compliment to the scribe, but perhaps also an indication of the urgency of what Paul is writing. Naturally, we can no longer verify this difference in the written image, since we possess the original neither of the Letter to the Galatians nor of any other Pauline letter or any other New Testament writing.

What we have are copies of copies. The oldest available manuscript of the Letter to the Galatians (which is not quite complete) is relatively old: it dates from around 200, that is, about 150 years after Paul dictated the letter. The hundreds and even thousands of other manuscripts—which all pass on this notice of writing "in my own hand"—all come from a later time.

In the region of the Pauline churches around the Aegean Sea, the letters Paul wrote from there were gathered, reworked, and placed together in a collection. That happened after Paul traveled from there via Jerusalem to Rome, where he suffered martyrdom. The Pauline letters are preserved for us through copies of this collection, not directly through copies of the original letters.

From the beginning this collection also included two letters that likewise contain the notice of writing in Paul's own hand (Col. 4:18; 2 Thess. 3:17), although one can, for good reasons, dispute their composition by Paul himself. Thus the notice serves here to legitimize the authorship. This was, of course, verifiable only in the original and not even in the first copy.

[6:12-13] Once again, Paul gives a polemical sketch of the position of his opponents. He charges them with only wanting to gain prestige for themselves—and that in the realm of the flesh. Against this attitude stands the proverbial statement of God's impartiality already cited in 2:6. As the actual reason for their requirement of circumcision, Paul states, again clearly polemically, that they only want to avoid persecution for the sake of the cross of Christ. A Christianity that could not, if need be, identify itself through circumcision as a part of Judaism did indeed renounce the legal protection that the Jewish religion enjoyed in the Roman Empire. Beyond this, however, for Paul there is a direct connection between the gospel and persecution for the sake of the gospel (cf. 1:13, 23; 5:11); persecution is tantamount to proof of the authenticity of the gospel, for in this way Christians are only suffering the same fate as their Christ.

In v. 13 Paul charges further that his opponents are not concerned with keeping the law, but only with using the circumcision of the Galatians to gain glory for themselves as successful missionaries. Apparently, boasting "about your flesh" has an intentional double meaning here. First, it is a boasting about the flesh and not the boasting about the Lord with which Paul immediately counters in v. 14. Second, it is a boasting whose basis, through circumcision, becomes visible in the flesh of the Galatians. Through this double meaning Paul manages once again to place the other gospel on the side of the flesh and not of the Spirit (cf. 3:3).

According to 6:4, boasting about another person does not belong to the life of the Spirit.

[6:14] The opponents probably reacted indignantly to such charges, but for the Galatians the alternative was clear: circumcision or the cross, law or faith. There can be true boasting only when one boasts in the Lord, as Paul says in 1 Cor. 1:31 and 2 Cor. 10:17, following Jer. 9:24. This Old Testament text probably also stands behind the present formulation. Here, however, we have the connection of the christological title *Lord* with the cross, which is unusual for Paul (otherwise occurring only in 1 Cor. 2:8); elsewhere—and even in the Letter to the Galatians (cf. 3:1)—he always speaks of the cross of *Christ.*

In general it is striking how much the title *Lord,* which appears so very often in the other letters, yields to *Son of God* (see pp. 30–31) and *Christ* (see p. 13) in the Letter to the Galatians. It occurs only incidentally in the fixed formulations of 1:3, 19; 5:10; 6:18. Thus all the more surprising is its pointed use here at the close of the letter. Jesus is *Lord* as the resurrected One and the one enthroned as Sovereign in his glory (cf. Phil. 2:11). Thus to speak of the "cross of our Lord" means to bind tightly together extreme opposites and probably also the point that Christ's glory does not exist without his cross.

If this crucified One is Lord of the world, however, then it is not a lordship that allows the world to continue to have its order in itself; rather, the world is crucified. Here Paul picks up statements about the crucifixion of the self (2:19-20) and the flesh (5:24). *World* is then the comprehensive designation for everything that is connected with the law. This stands against the other gospel, which promised through the law knowledge of "the elemental spirits of the world" (4:3, 9) and integration into the law of the world in the observation of cosmic processes (4:10) as well as in ethics (see p. 115).

For Paul, however, confession of the crucified One as Lord of the world means freedom from the world as well as from the law. In the cross the world order is exposed as broken and rendered impotent (cf. 1:4). Attempts to create such order in thought and action through the law are excluded by this radical interpretation of Christology, as it is asserted by Paul.

[6:15] As substantiation he states again the principle that he cited in 5:6 and that in 3:28 proclaimed in more detail the abolition of all apparently natural differences in humanity. Circumcision no longer has any advantage, nor does uncircumcision; it is a question, rather, of a "new creation" in place of the old, crucified world, whose categories have been abolished. The old, including the law, has passed away; the new has come—righteousness, life, blessing, freedom, Spirit, love—in Christ as the crucified One (cf. 2 Cor. 5:17).

[6:16] Paul calls this the new rule that Christians follow and that he hopes the Galatians will again follow, whereas the new teachers are not following it when they try to introduce the difference between circumcision and uncircumcision and promise knowledge of this world. Thus for them the benediction that comes from Jewish tradition is not valid: that the peace and mercy of God be upon them (cf. Pss. 125:5; 128:6). In contrast to this prayer is the curse that applies to anyone who preaches another gospel that is not oriented toward this rule (cf. 1:8-9). Paul extends his benediction to the whole "Israel of God," the church of Jews and Gentiles in contrast to the "Israel after the flesh" (1 Cor. 10:18, KJV). Or should this Israel also be included, the Israel to whom the original promises were made (cf. Rom. 9:4)—which will be the theme of Romans 9–11?

[6:17] Paul inserts a rather gruff remark with which he forbids any further annoyance. As a basis for this he refers to the *stigmata* of Jesus on his body. In seeking to understand this comment, we must exclude the idea of stigmatization with the wound marks of Jesus in accordance with the medieval piety tradition. What Paul refers to is clear: scars on his body that he has acquired on his missionary journeys for the sake of the gospel. Where they came from can be gleaned from 2 Cor. 11:23-27; Paul is marked by service to this Lord.

But why does Paul use the coined term *stigmata?* His readers probably associated it especially with the marking of slaves through branding, which made possible their identification as property of a certain master, as was also the case with soldiers and—even today—with animals. There was also, however, a religious stigmatization in various cults of the Hellenistic period, which made their members property of their god and at the same time placed them under that god's protection. Thus whoever still made trouble for Paul in the future was, in this view, not actually dealing with Paul himself, but with the Lord, whom Paul served as slave (1:10). It is possible, however, that the sentence contains an additional point if, perhaps, the opponents designated as stigma the mark of circumcision, the property and protection sign of belonging to the law. In any case, such an interpretation of circumcision can be demonstrated in Jewish texts (cf. also Gen. 17:11: "sign of the covenant"; Rom. 4:11: "seal" of circumcision).

[6:18] Paul closes the letter with the benediction usually found in this position (cf. Phil. 4:23; Phlm. 25; also Rom. 15:33; 16:20; 1 Cor. 16:23; 2 Cor. 13:13; 1 Thess. 5:28). Noteworthy, however, is the emphatic final position of the vocative "brethren" (KJV). Even with all of the pointedness of the disagreement, the Galatians remain Paul's brothers (cf. 1:11; 3:15; 4:12, 28, 31; 5:11, 13; 6:1); his opponents are their new teachers, not the Galatians themselves, and he is obviously counting on the fact that their falling away from the gospel is not yet final. Now it is up to them to react to his letter. We, however, do not know how they decided.

Missing at the end of the letter are the usual personal greetings from people who are with Paul and greetings to persons mentioned by name in the receiving churches. This omission may have been due to special circumstances of the composition, but it allows the letter to end all the more clearly with the repetition of the possibilities for decision that the readers have; they are not diverted by the remembrance of special personal relations from their decision between the alternatives, which Paul again has briefly summarized.

Appendix

The Galatians' Alternative: Gospel versus Gospel

The Opponents' Gospel

One cannot expect Paul to paint a picture of his opponents that does justice to their real intentions. He is biased because for him there can only be bias toward the gospel, and he wants to call his readers back from what in his eyes is a fateful path; in the theology of the new teachers he actually sees nothing that could even be worthy of a serious discussion. Thus the letter is not apologetic but rather is defined by polemic, as well as by suppositions and, certainly, exaggerations; at the same time and above all, however, it is an argumentative presentation of what in his opinion is the one and only gospel, with which he seeks to court his readers.

Since we have no other sources at our disposal, we are dependent on the information in this letter alone for a reconstruction of what may have constituted the temptation that came from this other gospel and caused the Galatians to fall away so precipitously to a gospel that their new teachers designated as such, and that only in the eyes of Paul was actually no gospel at all. Had it not been a question of a theology really to be taken seriously, Paul would not have needed to react so pointedly to its proclamation and to set against it such a thoroughgoing, detailed presentation of his own theology.

What the new teachers offered can be derived least of all from the places in which Paul claims to know what their basic intentions are (1:7; 4:17; 6:12, 13). Here it is a question of polemical reproaches, which they could, with some justification, reject as gross suppositions.

The safest point of departure in describing their preaching is their demand that those who want to convert to their gospel, and thus to Christianity in general, must undergo circumcision. This is expressly stated in 5:2 and 6:12-13, and also in other places in the letter special attention is given to circumcision. Paul stresses that as an uncircumcised

Gentile Christian in Jerusalem, Titus was not forced to have himself circumcised (2:3); from this fact Paul derives the recognition by Jerusalem of the "gospel for the uncircumcised" (2:7) and the concomitant abolition of the nature-given (cf. 2:15) difference between circumcision and uncircumcision in Christ (3:28; 5:6; 6:15); this finally leads him to the cynical remark of 5:12 that brings circumcision close to castration.

Since in 3:27 Paul uses baptism in his argument, this rite seems not to have been a point of contention, however much the opponents may have tied it to circumcision. Thus it is a question here of Christian missionaries who linked Christ with the law of Sinai and not of Jewish ones, who would simply have opposed the gospel of Christ with a theology of the law without Christ, perhaps in the fashion of the zeal for the law that Paul reports for himself during the time before his conversion (1:13-14).

A second clue to the theology of the opposition is offered by Paul's reproach that the Galatians were now observing days, months, seasons, and years (4:10). The immediate context of 4:8-9 is, to be sure, quite polemical, for at this point Paul is denigrating their devotion to that other gospel as a return to their heathen past. The series in 4:10, however, is not a usual theme in the contention with idolatry and therefore probably refers to a particular content of the opposing proclamation.

The wording does not require one to think of cultic celebrations, nor does it list certain holidays. That is different from the nearest parallel to this text in the New Testament, Col. 2:16, in which holidays are indeed intended: festival, new moon, Sabbath. In Gal. 4:10, in contrast, it is a question of the repeating rhythms of the world, which are determined by the movement of heavenly bodies and are to be noticed. In the interpretation of the passage (cf. pp. 83–84 above) this can be understood as a continuation of what was already set out in the creation report of the "law" in Gen. 1:14. Indeed, the law offered a comprehensive orientation to the way of the world.

A third clue is the expression "elemental spirits" (4:3, 9), which Paul uses only in the Letter to the Galatians. In its place one would expect in 4:3 to find "the law" (cf. 3:23) and in 4:9 "beings that by nature are not gods" (cf. 4:8). Again, the nearest parallel is offered by the Letter to the Colossians, where in similar fashion the elemental spirits are polemically disqualified (2:8, 20). The expression refers to the foundations of the order of the universe, which hold it together and keep it from falling back into chaos. This was not a special tenet of the earlier pagan religion of the Galatians but, as the interpretation has showed (cf. p. 84), is again a theme set out in the law itself, which in its first chapters offers knowledge concerning the ordering of what human beings experience as the world.

Thus both the series in 4:10 and the term "elemental spirits"—and even more the requirement of circumcision—are quite appropriate to a Christian mission with the law. They cannot be used as an argument that Paul wrongly estimates the situation in Galatia when he ties the position of his opponents to the law (3:1-5).

In 4:21 Paul addresses his readers as people who, on the basis of the opponents' preaching, want to be under the law, and in 5:4 as people who want to be justified by the law. In the two middle chapters he substantiates the gospel with the law itself and can well assume that this procedure, including the methods of interpretation, will be recognized as a basis for argumentation in Galatia. The reproach, though, that in reality his opponents do not keep the law at all (6:13) can be attributed to polemics (cf. Rom. 2:21-25).

Furthermore, it can be shown that the Old Testament texts referred to by Paul, including the complex of the Abraham tradition, in no way prove his theses unambiguously. Rather, they at least allow other interpretations along the line of the opponents' relating of Christ and law, whether or not this connection was advocated in Galatia.

Finally, in the first two chapters and then again in 4:21-31, Jerusalem plays a major role, and here too we may presume that this was a theme of the opponents' preaching. Yet Paul demonstrates that the other gospel cannot base itself on Jerusalem. His opponents had authorities there only among such people as those whom he (turning directly to his readers) discounted in 2:4 as "false believers secretly brought in," but not among the "pillars" (2:9) of the Jerusalem church.

Out of all these intimations comes one possible image of the representatives of that other gospel. What they could offer was an interpretation, on the basis of the law, of human experiences in the world and an assurance that these experiences are meaningful. The law was the possibility of life, including the ethical realm of everyday interactions between people.

This question of life is also concealed under the key word *Spirit;* the opponents asserted that they brought to Galatia what the Galatians, in Paul's view, had already received through the preaching of faith. According to the proclamation of the new teachers, however, the promises inherent in the law, including possession of the Spirit, were answers to the question of the coherence of life in general; circumcision was the seal of these promises and perhaps even, as "stigma" (cf. 6:17), the sign of God's property and protection and the claim to participation in these promises.

The fact that angels took part in the giving of the law (cf. 3:19) could only underline its distinctiveness—even more if the angels were somehow brought into relationship with the elemental spirits. Whether or not the term *law of Christ* (6:2) was their slogan, they—unlike Paul— did not see the law called into question in Christ, but we do not learn any details about their Christology. It was probably not very different from the christological traditions adopted by Paul (cf. pp. 129–31 below), except that they drew from it conclusions that were different from those of Paul with his Christology of the cross and his alternative of law and faith.

In the background stood Jerusalem, the "city set on a hill," with all its promises. In keeping with all of this focus, the new teachers may have made Abraham the illustration of their proclamation as the first proselyte and as the wise man from ancient times, to whom circumcision and law ultimately go back. Such an emphasis may have caused Paul to feel compelled to present his own interpretation of the Abraham heritage, which stood against every tradition.

Such a theology united impressive, ancient traditions from the East with the figure of Christ, proven wisdom, and present issues. The result was a tradition that promised to unlock and interpret meaningfully the experiences of humankind. Such theology could exercise great charm, as indeed Judaism itself was at this time achieving astonishing missionary successes with the law in the Hellenistic world.

Just as Paul himself in his mission began with the Jewish congregations spread out over the whole Roman Empire—offering, of course, an alternative to the law—so also other Christian missionaries apparently did the same thing, which resulted in a broad spectrum of different kinds of relation to and distinction from Judaism. This Judaism of the Diaspora, however, also offered in itself a distinctive picture of various theological currents, as even the relatively small literary heritage of this Judaism permits us to surmise. Thus the various types of early Christian theology reflect not least of all such preexisting differences.

If we now seek a label for the representatives of the other gospel in Galatia, we will be able to get no further than a very general characterization: Jewish Christian missionaries of a kind positively oriented toward the law; their classification with one of the currents known to us within Judaism is not possible. Even less can be said as to where they were theologically at home within early Christianity. Antioch and the Christian church in Jerusalem, however, are no doubt out of the question as their missionary base, since it would be inconceivable—at least according to Paul's presentation—that from either of these two places missionary work could be carried on among the Gentiles with the obligation of circumcision. Yet there may have been some sort of division there: indeed, an example of division in general is the independent missionary work of Paul around the Aegean after his separation from the Antiochene church.

This very region, however, was also penetrated by Jewish Christian missionaries other than those we know from the Letter to the Galatians. Paul had to deal with them in the Letter to the Philippians and in the Second Letter to the Corinthians. And in this region we also encounter a man like Apollos (cf. 1 Cor. 3:6; 4:6; 16:12; Acts 18:24; 19:1), with whom Paul seems to have worked together well over long years but who cannot be considered simply a follower of Paul.

In Asia Minor during the following period there were various theological traditions that could not have gone back to the activity of Paul alone; among them was a later development of the "other gospel" of Galatia, which the author of the Letter to the Colossians addressed in Paul's name. Thus at its beginning Christianity did not present itself at all as a uniform entity, as it has never been in later church history.

The Christian theology of the law, which was represented by the new teachers in Galatia, was not designed from the beginning as a frontline position against Paul, and their representatives were not hard on his heels, as it were, in order that churches founded by him might be converted to what in their opinion was the right gospel. In their own missionary work in the middle of Asia Minor, however, they came upon an island of Gentile Christian churches that had been founded by this Paul and that they now attempted to incorporate into their missionary effort.

They may have already been familiar with such a type of Christianity, for it was not essentially different from the churches that Paul and others from Antioch had founded in the provinces of Syria and Cilicia; at this time even Paul was no longer unknown in Christian circles (cf. 1:23).

Perhaps they were only surprised to come upon his tracks here also, since they must have presumed that he was farther to the west.

Not until Galatia did they find it really necessary to deal with this Paul. Had they crossed paths with him earlier in Jerusalem or Antioch or elsewhere, Paul for his part would have been able in such an early encounter to make clear what he is now trying to show his readers with the example of the "false believers secretly brought in" (2:4).

The fact that in the first two chapters of the letter Paul so fully details his path from Damascus to Galatia—actually also the path of the gospel to the Galatians—was no doubt occasioned by the falsified representations of his opponents, especially concerning his relationship with Jerusalem, whose legitimate representatives they claimed to be. On the one side, they apparently asserted that his gospel, as he preached it in Galatia, lacked true legitimation by Jerusalem, because Jerusalem stood not behind his gospel but behind their gospel of circumcision. On the other side, however, Paul himself had earlier represented the gospel of circumcision (cf. 5:11), and information on his Christian activity (cf. 1:13-14, 23) may have been mixed up with reports of his many trips to Jerusalem. With all of this, his claim to be an apostle of Jesus Christ (1:1) was called into question.

Also at stake, no doubt, were other interpretations of the incident in Antioch (2:11-21), which, as a matter of fact, had not ended well for Paul. If one can determine from Paul's writing that he worked with polemic and suppositions, then they for their part were not inferior to him in this regard. At any rate, we later readers have this circumstance to thank for such a detailed and coherent biographical presentation of Paul himself.

For Paul, nevertheless, more was at stake here in Galatia than his personal honor. In his opinion it was a question of the gospel itself, and therefore he felt it necessary to reflect so thoroughly on the fundamental alternative of faith or law, which for him resulted from his own conversion. It was the basic presupposition of his missionary work and not its later result. Its consequences were the churches of Jewish and Gentile Christians that he founded in the Aegean region as he had earlier around Antioch. But since apparently nowhere else was this basic presupposition so radically called into question as in Galatia, in none of his other letters did he need to give such detailed reasoning for evangelizing not with the law but with the crucified Christ.

Only in the letter to the Roman Christians, who at best may have known his gospel from hearsay, does he again lay out this fundamental alternative in detail—but then forgoing all biographical information. There even more than in the Letter to the Galatians, the apostle is totally absorbed in the gospel.

A secret addressee of this later Letter to the Romans, however, is the church in Jerusalem, for at the time of its composition Paul was preparing to convey an offering to that church (cf. Rom. 15:25-26) and was not at all sure (cf. Rom. 15:31) that those in Jerusalem still stood by what was agreed upon almost a decade earlier. In the meantime Paul had also separated himself from his actual negotiating partner Antioch, and the incident there had moreover been triggered by a group of Jerusalem Christians (2:12).

We do not know whether the Galatians reversed their falling away. It must have been clear to Paul that here it was a question of more than just some who were trying to sow confusion (1:7; 5:10) and some unsettling elements (5:12), of people who had only their own advantage in mind. It would in no way be incomprehensible if the Galatians preferred the enticements of the "other gospel" to the radical gospel of Christ. In any case, the Letter to the Colossians demonstrates that such a theology survived in Asia Minor, developed further, and a generation later could still mean a threat for the churches that came out of the Pauline tradition.

Paul's Gospel of Christ

Against this "other gospel" Paul placed his interpretation of Christology, which is the content of the gospel as well as the faith that comes from the gospel. The following table shows how all the further alternatives of the letter that are developed from the basic alternative of law and faith are also grounded in Christology. The list is the same as that on page 98, but now each pair of concepts is connected with a christological assertion from Paul's letter. We can see here that such christological statements, with the exception of hymns (here: Phil. 2:7), always include an indication of the benefit of the salvation event for the believer.

law	faith	Gal. 4:4-5	"so that"
death	life	Gal. 2:19-20	"for me"
curse	blessing	Gal. 3:13-14	"for us . . . in order that"
sin	righteousness	2 Cor. 5:21	"so that"
flesh	Spirit	Rom. 8:3-4	"in order that"
slavery	freedom	Phil. 2:7	—

To this list we would have to add *love,* which remains without an opposite and would also refer to 2:20. Thus the alternatives that convey the argumentation of the letter are not merely the result of the Christology but are anchored in the Christology itself.

In this way the whole letter is filled with christological assertions, some in the form of terse summaries of the salvation event, others in christological titles that, almost cipherlike, evoke broader associations. The two also occur in combination.

Among the summaries are 1:1, 4; 2:20; 3:13. These statements were assuredly not worked out by Paul but rather take up basic assertions that had already been developed before him and that can be considered the common possession of wider circles of early Christianity, even if one need not regard each set formulation as a composed "confession of faith."

Common to them and to the long list of comparable passages in other Pauline letters is a concentration on Jesus' death and resurrection alone as the actual salvation event. There is no trace here of the tradition of the teachings and actions of Jesus that we know from the Gospels. When Paul speaks of salvation, he—unlike the tradition that underlies the Gospels—is not referring to what Jesus said and did, but only to what happened to him in death and resurrection.

As we have seen (see p. 13 above), all of this meaning is also represented in Paul by the title *Christ,* which occurs almost forty times in the Letter to the Galatians. It would certainly be exaggerated to conclude that his readers actually understood the titular sense in every case. Nonetheless, for them it still must have remained an unusual word—in a modern translation of the New Testament we must consistently replace *Christ* with *the anointed One* in order to convey how the Greek word *Christos* might have sounded to original readers like those in Galatia.

This Greek word is understandable, not in connection with the Greek language, but only as the translation for *Messiah.* In contrast to the two names *Cephas* and *Peter* (see pp. 32–33 above), here Paul uses the Greek translation and not the Hebrew equivalent (as in John 1:41; 4:25); this makes the titular sense immediately clear.

Naturally, Paul is not the first one to apply this title to Jesus: that was done in quite different layers of early Christian tradition. Nor is the connection of this title alone with the death and resurrection of Jesus the original work of Paul; it was already a part of the tradition in which he stood, as was also, no doubt, the consistent use of this title to indicate the content of gospel and faith. New with Paul is the special emphasis on the manner of death, by crucifixion (cf. 3:1), which seems to have played no role in previous tradition (cf. p. 52 above).

Paul is also not the first to give Jesus the title *Son of God* (1:16; 2:20; 4:4, 6) but rather adopts it likewise from the tradition in which he stands (cf. p. 30 above). Here we must distinguish between the mission statement (4:4), which is also found in John's Gospel, and the approximation of the complex of Jesus' death and resurrection, connected with the title *Christ,* in the formulations of the self-sacrifice of the Son (2:20)—which, however, was no doubt also already present in the tradition that Paul adopted. This is one more indication of how much everything here is focused on the salvation event.

It is difficult to say anything about the possible associations with the title on the part of readers who, like the Galatians, came from a Greek language area. Naturally, they were familiar with the gods and demigods who as children belonged to the Greek pantheon that was portrayed as a family unit. There, however, it was a question of being the children of certain specific gods, for example, Heracles, the son of Zeus. In contrast to this, the combination *Son of God* must have seemed rather abstract, especially since it was used with the definite article: not *a* Son of God, but *the* Son of God.

In any case, what Paul connects with this title goes back to Jewish tradition, and it is doubtless not coincidental that he uses the title *Son of God* almost exclusively in the context of the alternative of faith or law in Romans and Galatians, where there is never any mention of Jesus as the "Son of God" in the sense of a physical descent from God in the manner of Greek gods and demigods. Jesus is rather the "Son of God" as the exemplary righteous one, who has been made righteous by God himself.

The title *Lord,* which is so frequent in Paul's other letters (in all, occurring about two hundred times) is avoided in the Letter to the Galatians, perhaps even intentionally. Except in certain set phrases it appears only in 6:14, and then very pointedly (see p. 121 above). Jesus is "Lord" as the exalted One (cf. Phil. 2:11), who is active in his church as the Lord of the cosmos and is confessed by the church as *her* Lord (cf. 1 Cor. 8:5-6). This is not the issue in Galatia, however, but rather whether one can speak of Jesus' lordship apart from his cross (cf. 6:14).

This overview makes clear again how strongly Christology shapes the whole letter and how much Paul concentrates his Christology on statements about the death and resurrection of Jesus; in this emphasis he follows his tradition but goes beyond it in stressing the manner of death. In looking back, he thus can summarize the whole of his earlier missionary preaching in Galatia and characterize it as the proclamation of Jesus Christ, the crucified (3:1), limit himself to *Christ* as the statement of content of his preaching, and label this "the message about the cross" (1 Cor. 1:18), although his actual sermons naturally could not have consisted of the one word *Christ* or of only the one sentence "The crucified One is the anointed One."

We have at our disposal, however, no such missionary preaching, since the speeches of Paul reported in Acts give only a vague hint of how he might have proclaimed this "message about the cross." What we have in his letters are opinions expressed about problems in churches that originated from his mission. The Letter to the Galatians shows how his Christology becomes the key to the interpretation of the Old Testament and how Paul develops this Christology in the pairs of opposites that follow from the basic alternative of law and faith and that, in his view, are contained in it. He asserts that he is able from the standpoint of Christology to interpret the Old Testament more properly than it can interpret itself.

With this Christology provided for him in terse formulations and titles, Paul also took up the question of righteousness. We have seen (see pp. 30–31 above) how the title *Son of God* is not to be understood only as an ethical concept but, rather, refers in a more comprehensive way to the ordering of the world in general, including the orderly behavior of Israel. As shown by, for example, so important a text as Gen. 15:6 (see pp. 55–56 above), it is a matter here of the question, discussed by Paul in Galatians, of how one can find life, blessing, and so forth.

The question continues in Judaism and becomes more urgent in the face of experiences that less and less allow righteousness in this sense to be verified. If ultimately the righteous person is called the "Son of God," then it is precisely not as the one who experiences the realization of God's promise in this life but as one who nonetheless relies on the certainty of finally receiving righteousness vis-à-vis the unrighteous, who in this world only seem to have it better than the righteous (cf. Wis. 2:1-20; 5:1-23).

The norm for this righteousness in Judaism is the law, first as the document of God's promises, which are valid for anyone who holds to the law, and second as the book that gives a comprehensive orientation to the nature of the world, right down to everyday life. Whoever read the law could glean from its narrated histories of the patriarchs and the fate of Israel in Egypt and in the wilderness that it paid to hold to the law and its promises. Readers could also learn what happened to those who believed they could not endure a life with only promise.

The title *Christ* is also subject to the question of righteousness from the standpoint of the messiah/king tradition. We have seen (cf. p. 13

above) how the Jerusalem king, no different from the kings in the ancient Orient in general, was considered the guarantor of such righteousness in the broad sense, including peace, welfare, and fertility (cf. Psalm 72). After the collapse of Israel and the concomitant end of the Davidic dynasty in Jerusalem, some groups held during the time of the exile that the kingdom had now been given the death sentence and that one must ask anew how God's righteousness can succeed. Others, however, expected a renewal of the kingdom, based on the ongoing validity of the promise given to David in 2 Sam. 7:16: "Your house and your kingdom shall be made sure forever before me; your throne shall be established forever."

Thus, when early Christianity designated Jesus as *the* Son of God, not *a* Son of God, it was confessing that he is absolutely the righteous One, who maintains his righteousness before God and is made righteous by God. And when one confesses him as the *Christ,* one sees fulfilled in him the petition expressed in Psalm 72 that through him righteousness might be established. The tradition Paul adopts relates this righteousness in both cases to the death and resurrection of Jesus, not to Jesus' teachings and actions before the Passion.

The theme of righteousness is also contained in the assertion of the resurrection of Jesus by God (1:1) as the fulfillment of the promise of life to the righteous. It is found also in the expressions that speak of his sacrifice "for our sins" (1:4), "for me" (2:20), and "for us" (3:13), and in the manner of suffering, so that in Jesus' death, as in cultic sacrifice, the righteousness is reestablished that was lost through the shortcomings of the people (cf. Rom. 3:25). The Christology that Paul adopts is thus clearly formulated on the plane of Jewish expectations, and it is the answer to the question of faith, likewise developed in this tradition (cf. p. 47 above); it is the question, namely, of how confession is to be reconciled with experience, or whether God's promises for the righteous can become reality. A new way of making such a reconciliation was offered when in this Christology the extreme experience of suffering even with death on the cross was incorporated into the confession itself.

Summaries of the Christian proclamation to Gentiles, who came from a polytheistic environment, had a different appearance, as shown, for example, by 1 Cor. 8:5-6. Nonetheless, in what was formulated in the Jewish tradition as a question of faith, a fundamental experience was addressed that is not limited to that tradition: the tension between design and execution, between the will and actual behavior, between hope and failure—in the extreme, the contradiction between life and death.

Therefore both Jews and Gentiles could be addressed with such preaching and offered meaningful interpretation of their experiences, especially when the Christian mission built on the previous work of the Jewish synagogue. In both cases, however, the content of the proclamation was not the formulation of the fundamental question as such, but certain answers to it: in Judaism on the basis of the law, in early Christianity on the basis of Christology with various connections to the law. One of the basic elements of these answers was the idea that the world is God's creation and thus does not come from the devil and also, therefore, cannot go to the devil.

Curiously unsettled in this christological tradition, however, was the relationship of Christology to the law. It is related to hopes and issues that developed in the Jewish tradition of the law, and in 1 Cor. 15:3b-5, one of these summaries of the Christian proclamation, we read that Christ died and was raised "in accordance with the scriptures," without, however, defining more closely what the relationship between Christology and the "scriptures" might be like.

Acts 6:1-7 suggests that in the early days of the Jerusalem church there were disagreements over the question of the meaning of the law (cf. p. 23 above). Also, Jesus' own behavior relative to the law was open to various interpretations in the early churches. It is likely that in the various circles of early Christianity there was simply a silent rejection of parts of the law that were held to be superfluous, as was also quite possibly the case in parts of contemporary Judaism. The abolition of circumcision and the relaxing of the purity regulations—for example, in regard to the table fellowship of Jewish and Gentile Christians—was understood neither here nor there as a fundamental problem.

This is indicated also by what we learn in 2:12 about the conditions in Antioch. And even the Jerusalem church did not place the law above or even beside the gospel, as shown by their ready acceptance of the agreement referred to in 2:9-10. The gospel was one and the same, whether it was proclaimed by Gentiles or Jews (2:7; cf. 1 Cor. 15:11).

Paul, however, sees a more fundamental problem here. From the very beginning he—as no one had done before him—understands Christology as calling the law into question. He asserts that in Christology the law gives itself up on behalf of faith; this is what his argumentation with the Old Testament seeks to demonstrate. It is quite possible that the new teachers in Galatia adopted the same Christology as Paul but did not draw from it the same consequences.

As we have seen, Paul does not begin his critique of the law with some kind of degenerate phenomena of the so-called late Jewish legal piety, but with the central structures of the Old Testament itself. And we have also seen that such traditional structures in themselves in no way prove his theses as clearly as it might seem to us, who through Paul are accustomed to reading the Old Testament from the standpoint of the New. This applies particularly to his interpretation of the Abraham tradition in 3:6—4:7.

For Paul the alternative to faith is also not merely "works righteousness," for we saw that the Jewish tradition is in no way primarily interested in achieving righteousness through human accomplishments but, on the contrary, must deal with the experience that the blessing has not been ratified, although Israel and individual righteous people hold to the law. With categories such as "works righteousness" we are prisoners of our tradition and probably less of the Reformation tradition than of a certain neo-Protestantism to which, after idealism, everything seemed suspect that did not happen for its own sake; such ethical theology was then legitimized historically in interpretations of the Reformation and of Pauline theology.

Paul held fast to the promises of righteousness, blessing, and life. So did the Jewish tradition in that in the law they saw these promises reconciled with experience, which as such was not able to verify the promises. Thus arose apocalypticism, in which verification lies in a future world, and thus also arose dualistic wisdom theology, which tries to go beyond worldly experience to another, otherworldly level of experience.

Against such attempts, however, Paul places the assertion that the law cannot do what it promises at all, and the assertion that such reconciliation is offered by Christology and by it alone. In this we have seen how Paul repeatedly brings these assertions to the law not from the outside but out of Jewish tradition itself, fundamentally reordering the conceptual and linguistic possibilities developed within it.

In Christology, for Paul, not only suffering and death but also sin and a death on the cross, which is placed under the curse by the law, are integrated into the confession—that is, the whole living reality of human life, including its extreme experiences. Here at the cross, promise and experience are really together; here also the opposition between God and humanity is lifted. In contrast, the law, in his opinion, can only ascertain or outmaneuver this tension; instead of establishing the promised state of blessing, it only drives under the curse the very ones who hold to the law. The question of righteousness in the biblical sense can be comprehended as the question of the interpretation and assurance of the experiences that one has with oneself, with God, and with the world, in regard not only to one's thinking but also to one's behavior. The Jewish tradition sees the answer to this question in the law; Paul takes issue with that conclusion and finds the answer in Christology alone.

The solution for Paul also relates to his anthropology (cf. 2:19-20), as well as to ethics (cf. p. 113 above) and ecclesiology (cf. 3:28). Those who base themselves in the cross as the content of the proclamation as well as of faith, would not need first to find themselves through their actions, and the consequence of the gospel was the formation of groups whose programmatic principle is named in 3:28. Here they were "one in Christ"; as with the ethics, however, finding one's identity was the presupposition, not the result, of fellowship formation.

It may seem almost self-evident to us that proclamation produces churches as social entities, because we are only familiar with present-day missions carried on by missionary societies in this way. Throughout church history, however, there has also been a quite different type of Christianity as isolation, asceticism, and hermitism in consequence of the gospel—a type that does not aim primarily at the formation of community. That may have already been a possibility in early Christianity as well. For Paul, however, the "formation" of Christ (cf. 4:19) means the church as the place where apparently natural oppositions are lifted.

Thus 3:28 names the consequences of Christology for the structure of the church. For Paul, Christology is the only criterion for the situation that, according to 2:12-13, arose in Antioch, as well as for the situation in Galatia. On this foundation stand the churches founded by him in his own missionary area. Here new and different problems then ensued, some from the churches themselves as in Thessalonica and in Corinth at the time of the First Letter to the Corinthians, some caused by the penetration of other Christian missionaries to Philippi and to Corinth at the time of the Second Letter to the Corinthians.

Only in Galatia, however, was the foundation of everything so radically called into question that Paul was moved again to give to himself and his readers an account of the basic alternative of faith and law, which was the presupposition of his gospel proclamation. In doing so, his argumentation may also go beyond the current situation in Galatia; what he develops from the standpoint of Christology under the theme of justification is not a product of this special discussion but, as he himself presents it, the foundation of his missionary activity in general, which was given earlier in his conversion.

In the process Paul works through his own biography in the first, large section, 1:11—5:12, yet not in order to legitimize himself and his gospel with a special religious experience (conversion, revelation, or whatever); rather, he lets his biography be absorbed into the way of the gospel from Damascus to Galatia, as he then, in the Letter to the Romans, can also present the gospel without any biographical details. It is legitimized not by Paul but by its content. Only then does it become a theology that is transmittable to others and achievable by others.

If today the traditional Protestant "doctrine of justification" is felt in all quarters as an embarrassment and supposedly can no longer be the answer to the questions of the "modern" person, in the Reformation understanding the fate of the church hangs in the balance at this very point. Perhaps, however, as once in the context of late medieval issues at the time of the Reformation, a return to Pauline Christology can make accessible, from the standpoint of the cross, a meaningful interpretation and assurance of even our present-day experiences. Perhaps also our situation is not basically different from that of the Hellenistic cities in which Paul missionized—with their polarizing tendencies, their unrest caused by new experiences no longer secured in tradition, their endangerment by puzzling developments, and their threatening by powers that could not be handled even with the help of a technology already widely developed for that time. Pauline theology is not analysis of this situation for its own sake and also not simply profession against the situation but an opening up of profession as experience in Christology. In this theology the seemingly irreconcilable is rethought and relived as a unified whole, based on the premise that in the cross itself the world is broken (6:14). A harmonious world view does not have to be postulated with the help of the law or a Christology in order to make life a little more bearable while pointing to another, "real" world or another, otherworldly level of experience. Under the cross, the very radicality of the Pauline basic alternative makes life possible in this world, which is not whole, whose character as creation of God is not to be read from the world itself, but in which, nonetheless, the promises of blessing, life, and righteousness can be realized for the individual and for the church.

Paul's Career

Year	Paul's Letters	The Acts of the Apostles
		21:39; 22:3: from Tarsus
		18:3: tentmaker trade
		16:37; 22:28: Roman citizen
	Phil. 3:5: Pharisee	22:3: Pharisee in Jerusalem
30 Jesus' crucifixion		
	Gal. 1:13, 23; Phil. 3:16; 1 Cor. 15:9: persecutor of the church	7:58; 8:3; 22:4; 26:9-11
	Gal. 1:15-16: Conversion in Damascus	9:1-19a; 22:3-21; 26:9-20
35	Gal. 1:17: Arabia	
	Return to Damascus	
	Gal. 1:18: Damascus-Jerusalem	9:26-29
	(cf. 2 Cor. 11:32-33)	
		9:30: Caesarea-Tarsus
40		
	Gal. 1:21: Syria and Cilicia	11:25-26: Tarsus-Antioch
		(11:30: Antioch-Jerusalem)
45		12:25: Jerusalem-Antioch
	(cf. 2 Tim. 3:11)	13–14: Cyprus/Asia Minor
	Gal. 2:1: Antioch-Jerusalem	15:1–35
	Gal. 2:11-21: Conflict in Antioch;	15:36-39
	Gal. 3:1-5; 4:13: Galatia; Phil. 4:15-16:	
50	Philippi; 1 Thess. 2:2: Thessalonica;	15:40—18:17
	1 Thess. 3:1: Athens; 1–2 Cor.: Corinth	in Corinth 18 months
51/52 Gallio proconsul	1 Cor. 16:8: Ephesus; from there several trips to Macedonia and Corinth	18:19-21; 19:1-40: in Ephesus 2 years and 3 months (18:21-23: Ephesus-Jerusalem-Antioch-Ephesus)
55	Letter to the Romans from Corinth (Rom. 15:25, 27)	20:1-2: Ephesus-Corinth 20–21: Corinth-Jerusalem
	to Jerusalem: Rom. 15;25, 31	
	Plan: from Jerusalem by Rome to Spain (Rom. 15:25, 28-29)	27–28: Jerusalem-Rome
		The death of Paul in Rome (58/60) is not reported in Acts
60	Paul gives connected biographical information only in Galatians; the individual notes in the other letters can be ordered only with the help of Acts.	yet is presupposed in 20:18-35.

Bracket annotations: 3 years (35 to ~38); 14 years and 11 years (spanning ~35 to 50); Letters come from this period.

135

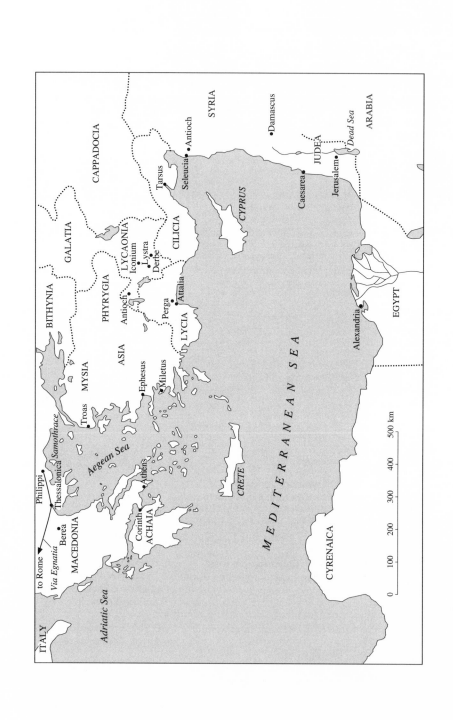

A Select Bibliography

Achtemeier, Paul J. "An Elusive Unity: Paul, Acts, and the Early Church [Acts 15; Gal 2:11–14]." *CBQ* 48 (1986) 1-26.

Arichea, Daniel C., Jr., and Eugene A. Nida. *A Translators Handbook on Paul's Letter to the Galatians*. Helps for Translators 18. Stuttgart: United Bible Societies, 1976.

Arndt, William F. "Galatians: A Declaration of Christian Liberty." *CTM* 27 (1956) 673-92.

Baasland, Ernst. "Persecution: A Neglected Feature in the Letter to the Galatians." *ST* 38 (1984) 135–50.

Baird, William. "What is the Kerygma? A Study of 1 Cor 15:3-8 and Gal 1:11-17." *JBL* 76 (1957) 181–91.

____. "Visions, Revelation, and Ministry: Reflections on 2 Cor 12:1-5 and Gal 1:11-17." *JBL* 104 (1985) 651-62.

Bammel, E. "Gottes *diathēkē* (Gal 3:15-17) und das jüdische Rechtsdenken." *NTS* 6 (1959-60) 313-19.

____. "*nomos Christou*." In *Studia Evangelica*, vol. 3, edited by F. L. Cross, 120-28. TU 88. Berlin: Akademie, 1964.

Bandstra, A. J. *The Law and the Elements of the World: An Exegetical Study in Aspects of Paul's Teaching*. Kampen: J. H. Kok, 1964.

Barclay, John M. G. "Mirror-reading a Polemical Letter: Galatians as a Test Case." *JSNT* 31 (1987) 73-93.

____. *Obeying the Truth: A Study of Paul's Ethics in Galatians*. Studies of the New Testament and Its World. Edinburgh: T. & T. Clark, 1988; Minneapolis: Fortress Press, 1991.

Barclay, William. *Flesh and Spirit: An Examination of Galatians 5.19-23*. Naperville: SCM 1962.

Barrett, C. K. "Paul and the 'Pillar' Apostles." In *Studia Paulina in honorem Johannis de Zwaan septuagenarii*, edited by J. N. Sevenster and W. C. van Unnik, 1-19. Haarlem: Bohn, 1953.

Compiled by David J. Lull. This bibliography is limited to works published in the present century. For lists of works before 1900, see Betz, *Galatians*, 336-40, and Mussner, *Der Galaterbrief*, xi-xvii. For abbreviations, see: *Journal of Biblical Literature*, "Instructions for Contributors, 1991."

Bibliography

——. "The Allegory of Abraham, Sarah, and Hagar in the Argument of Galatians." In *Rechtfertigung: Festschrift für Ernst Käsemann zum 70. Geburtstag*, edited by J. Friedrich, W. Pohlmann, and P. Stuhlmacher, 1-16. Tübingen: Mohr (Siebeck); Göttingen: Vandenhoeck & Ruprecht, 1976.

——. "Galatians as an 'Apologetic Letter': *Galatians: A Commentary on Paul's Letter to the Churches in Galatia*, by Hans Dieter Betz." *Int* 34 (1980) 414-17.

——. *Freedom and Obligation: A Study of the Epistle to the Galatians*. Philadelphia: Westminster, 1985.

Barth, Markus. "The Kerygma of Galatians." *Int* 21 (1967) 131-46.

——. "Text to Sermon on Galatians 2:11-21." *Int* 22 (1968) 147-57.

——. "Jews and Gentiles: The Social Character of Justification in Paul." *JES* 5 (1968) 241-67.

Becker, Jürgen, Hans Conzelmann, and Gerhard Friedrich. *Die Briefe an die Galater, Epheser, Philipper, Kolosser, Thessalonicher und Philemon*. 15th ed. NTD 8. Göttingen: Vandenhoeck & Ruprecht, 1981.

Belleville, Linda L. "'Under Law': Structural Analysis and the Pauline Concept of Law in Galatians 3:21-4:11." *JSNT* 26 (1986) 53-78.

Berchman, Robert M. "Galatians (1:1-5): Paul and Greco-Roman Rhetoric." In *Judaic and Christian Interpretation of Texts: Contents and Contexts*, vol. 3 of *New Perspectives on Ancient Judaism*, edited by Jacob Neusner and Ernest S. Frerichs, 1-15. Lanham: University Press of America, 1987.

Berger, Klaus. "Abraham in den paulinischen Hauptbriefen." *MTZ* 17 (1966) 47-89.

Betz, Hans Dieter. "Spirit, Freedom, and Law: Paul's Message to the Galatian Churches." *SEÅ* 39 (1974) 145-60.

——. "The Literary Composition and Function of Paul's Letter to the Galatians." *NTS* 21 (1975) 353-79.

——. "In Defense of the Spirit: Paul's Letter to the Galatians as a Document of Early Christian Apologetics." In *Aspects of Religious Propaganda in Judaism and Early Christianity*, edited by Elisabeth Schüssler Fiorenza, 99-114. Studies in Judaism and Christianity in Antiquity 2. Notre Dame: University of Notre Dame Press, 1976.

——. "Paul's Concept of Freedom in the Context of Hellenistic Discussions About Possibilities of Human Freedom." In *Protocol Series of the Colloquies of the Center for Hermeneutical Studies in Hellenistic and Modern Culture* 26, edited by W. Wuellner, 1-13. Berkeley: Graduate Theological Union and University of California Press, 1977.

——. *Galatians: A Commentary on Paul's Letter to the Churches in Galatia*. Hermeneia. Philadelphia: Fortress, 1979.

——. "The Problem of Rhetoric and Theology according to the Apostle Paul." In *L'Apôtre Paul: Personnalité, style et conception du ministère*, edited by Albert Vanhoye, 16-48. BETL 73. Leuven: Leuven University Press, 1986.

Blank, Josef. "Warum sagt Paulus: 'Aus Werken des Gesetzes wird niemand gerecht'?" In *Evangelisch-Katholischer Kommentar zum Neuen Testament*, Vorarbeiten Heft 1, Josef Blank et al., 79-95. Zürich: Benziger Verlag; Neukirchen-Vluyn: Neukirchener Verlag, 1969.

——. "Zu welchen Freiheit hat uns Christus befreit? Die theologische Dimension der Freiheit." *Stimmen der Zeit* 207 (1989) 460-72.

Bligh, John. *Galatians in Greek: A Structural Analysis of St. Paul's Epistle to the Galatians, With Notes on the Greek*. Detroit: University of Detroit Press, 1966.

——. *Galatians: A Discussion of St. Paul's Epistle*. Householder Commentaries 1. London: St. Paul Publications, 1969.

Blinzer, Josef. "Lexikalisches zu dem Terminus *ta stoicheia tou kosmou* bei Paulus." In *Studiorum Paulinorum Congressus Internationalis Catholicus (1961)*, vol. 2, 429-444. AnBib 17-18. Rome: Pontifical Biblical Institute, 1963.

Boers, Hendrikus. "The Significance of Abraham for the Christian Faith." In

    Theology out of the Ghetto: A New Testament Exegetical Study concerning Religious Exclusiveness, 74-106. Leiden: Brill, 1971.

Bonnard, Pierre. *L'épître de Saint Paul aux Galates*. 2nd ed. CNT 9. Neuchâtel: Delachaux & Niestlé, 1972.

Borgen, Peder. "Observations on the Theme 'Paul and Philo': Paul's Preaching of Circumcision in Galatia (Gal. 5:11) and Debates on Circumcision in Philo." In *Die paulinische Literatur und Theologie*, edited by S. Pedersen, 85-102. Teologiske Studier 7. Århus: Aros; Göttingen: Vandenhoeck & Ruprecht, 1980.

———. "Paul Preaches Circumcision and Pleases Men." In *Paul and Paulinism: Essays in Honour of C. K. Barrett*, edited by M. D. Hooker and S. G. Wilson, 37-46. London: SPCK, 1982.

———. "Catalogues of Vices, the Apostolic Decree, and the Jerusalem Meeting." In *The Social World of Formative Christianity and Judaism: Essays in Tribute to Howard Clark Kee*, edited by Jacob Neusner et al., 126-41. Philadelphia: Fortress, 1988.

Bornkamm, Günther. "Die christliche Freiheit (Gal 5)." In *Das Ende des Gesetzes: Paulusstudien*, vol. 1 of *Gesammelte Aufsätze*, 133-38. 5th ed. Munich: Kaiser, 1966.

———. "The Revelation of Christ to Paul on the Damascus Road and Paul's Doctrine of Justification and Reconciliation." In *Reconciliation and Hope: New Testament Essays on Atonement and Eschatology Presented to Leon L. Morris on his 60th Birthday*, edited by Robert J. Banks, 90-103. Grand Rapids: Eerdmans, 1974.

Borse, Udo. *Der Standort des Galaterbriefes*. BBB 41. Bonn: Hanstein, 1972.

———. *Der Brief an die Galater*. RNT. Regensburg: Pustet, 1984.

Böttger, Paul C. "Paulus und Petrus in Antiochien: Zum Verständnis von Galater 2:11-21." *NTS* 37 (1991) 77-100.

Bousset, Wilhelm. "Der Brief an die Galater." In *Die Schriften des Neuen Testaments*, vol. 2, edited by J. Weiss, 28-72. 2nd ed. Göttingen: Vandenhoeck & Ruprecht, 1908.

Bouttier, Michel. "*Complexio Oppositorum*: Sur les Formules de I Cor. xii.13; Gal. iii.26-28; Col. iii.10, 11." *NTS* 23 (1976) 1-19.

Bouwman, Gijs. "Die Hagar- und Sara-Perikope (Gal 4:21-31): Exemplarische Interpretation zum Schriftbeweis bei Paulus." *ANRW* 2.25.4 (1987) 3135-55.

Bovon, François. "Une formule prepaulinienne dans l'épître aux Galates (Gal 1:4-5)." In *Paganisme, Judaïsme, Christianisme: Influences et affrontements dans le monde antique. Mélanges offerts à Marcel Simon*, F. F. Bruce et al., 91-107. Paris: E. de Boccard, 1978.

Bring, Ragnar. *Commentary on Galatians*. Translated by Eric Wahlstrom. Philadelphia: Muhlenberg, 1961.

———. "Die Mittler und das Gesetz: Eine Studie zu Gal 3,20." *KD* 12 (1966) 292-309.

Brinsmead, Bernard Hungerford. *Galatians–Dialogical Response to Opponents*. SBLDS 65. Chico: Scholars Press, 1982.

Brooten, Bernadette J. "The Gospel in Conflict. Paul's Opponents in Galatians." *Bible Today* 18 (1980) 89-95.

Bruce, F. F. "Galatian Problems, 1. Autobiographical Data." *BJRL* 51 (1969) 292-309.

———. "Galatian Problems, 2. North or South Galatians?" *BJRL* 52 (1970) 243-66.

———. "Galatian Problems, 3. The 'Other' Gospel." *BJRL* 53 (1970-71) 253-71.

———. "Galatian Problems, 4. The Date of the Epistle." *BJRL* 54 (1972) 250-67.

———. "Galatian Problems, 5. Galatians and Christian Origins." *BJRL* 55 (1973) 264-84.

———. "Further Thoughts on Paul's Autobiography (Galatians 1:11-2:14)." In *Jesus und Paulus: Festschrift für Werner Georg Kümmel zum 70. Geburtstag*, edited by E. Earle Ellis and Erich Grässer, 21-29. Tübingen: Mohr (Siebeck); Göttingen: Vandenhoeck & Ruprecht, 1975.

———. *Commentary on Galatians*. NIGTC. Grand Rapids: Eerdmans, 1982.

Bibliography

_____. "The Curse of the Law." In *Paul and Paulinism: Essays in Honour of C. K. Barrett*, edited by M. D. Hooker and S. G. Wilson, 27-36. London: SPCK, 1982.

_____. "'Called to Freedom': A Study in Galatians." In *The New Testament Age: Essays in Honor of Bo Reicke*, vol. 1, edited by William C. Weinrich, 61-72. Macon: Mercer University Press, 1984.

_____. "The Spirit in the Letter to the Galatians." In *Essays on Apostolic Themes: Studies in Honor of Howard M. Ervin Presented to him by Colleagues and Friends on his Sixty-Fifth Birthday*, edited by Paul Elbert, 36-48. Peabody: Hendrickson, 1985.

Buck, Charles H. "The Date of Galatians." *JBL* 70 (1951) 113-22.

Bultmann, Rudolf. "Zur Auslegung von Galater 2.15-18." In *Exegetica: Aufsätze zur Erforschung des Neuen Testaments*, edited by Erich Dinkler, 394-99. Tübingen: Mohr (Siebeck), 1967.

Burton, Ernest de Witt. *A Critical and Exegetical Commentary on the Epistle to the Galatians*. ICC. Edinburgh: T. & T. Clark, 1921.

Caird, George B. "Paul and Women's Liberty." *BJRL* 54 (1972) 268-81.

Callan, Terrance. "Pauline Midrash: The Exegetical Background of Gal 3:19b." *JBL* 99 (1980) 549-67.

Callaway, Mary C. "Mistress and the Maid: Midrashic Traditions Behind Galatians 4:21-31." *Radical Religion* 2 (1975) 94-101.

Carson, Donald A. "Pauline Inconsistency: Reflections on 1 Corinthians 9:19-23 and Galatians 2:11-14." *Churchman* 100 (1986) 6-45.

Cavallin, H. C. C. "Demythologizing the Liberal Illusion [Gal 3:28]." *Churchman* 83 (London, 1969) 263-74.

_____. "'The Righteous Shall Live by Faith': A Decisive Argument for the Traditional Interpretation." *ST* 32 (1978) 33-43.

Chamblin, Knox. "Revelation and Tradition in the Pauline *Euangelion*." *WTJ* 48 (1986) 1-16.

Corsani, Bruno. "*Ek pisteōs* in the Letters of Paul." In *The New Testament Age: Essays in Honor of Bo Reicke*, vol. 2, edited by William C. Weinrich, 87-93. Macon: Mercer University Press, 1984.

Cosgrove, Charles H. "The Mosaic Law Preaches Faith: A Study in Galatians 3." *WTJ* 41 (1978) 146-64.

_____. "The Law Has Given Sarah No Children (Gal. 4:21-30)." *NovT* 29 (1987) 219-35.

_____. "Arguing Like a Mere Human Being: Galatians 3:15-18 in Rhetorical Perspective." *NTS* 34 (1988) 536-49.

_____. *The Cross and the Spirit: A Study in the Argument and Theology of Galatians*. Macon: Mercer University Press, 1989.

Cousar, Charles B. *Galatians*. IBC. Atlanta: John Knox, 1982.

_____. "Redefining the People of God" and "Boasting in the Cross." In *A Theology of the Cross: The Death of Jesus in the Pauline Letters*, 111-21 and 137-48. OBT 24. Minneapolis: Fortress, 1990.

Craffert, P. F. "Paul's Damascus Experience as Reflected in Galatians 1: Call or Conversion?" *Scriptura* 29 (1989) 36-47.

Cranfield, C. E. B. "St. Paul and the Law." *SJT* 17 (1964) 43-68.

Crownfield, Frederic R. "The Singular Problem of the Dual Galatians." *JBL* 64 (1945) 491-500.

Dahl, Nils A. "Der Name Israel: Zur Auslegung von Gal. 6,16." *Judaica* 6 (1950) 161-70.

_____. "Contradictions in Scripture." In *Studies in Paul*, 159-77. Minneapolis: Augsburg, 1977.

_____. "The Atonement–An Adequate Reward for the Akedah?" In *Jesus the Christ: The Historical Origins of Christological Doctrine*, edited by Donald H. Juel, 149-66. Minneapolis: Fortress, 1991.

Danker, Frederick W. "Faith Without Works." *CTM* 27 (1956) 513-35.

_____. "Faith With Works: Galatians 5 and 6." *CTM* 27 (1956) 593-612.

Dautzenberg, Gerhard. "'Da ist nicht männlich und weiblich': Zur Interpretation von Gal 3:28." *Kairos* 24 (1982) 181-206.

Davies, W. D., Paul W. Meyer, and David E. Aune. Reviews of *Galatians: A Commentary on Paul's Letter to the Churches of Galatia*, by Hans Dieter Betz. *RelSRev* 7 (1981) 310-28.

Davis, J. J. "Some Reflections on Galatians 3:28, Sexual Roles, and Biblical Hermeneutics." *JETS* 19 (1976) 201-208.

de Lacy, D. R. "Jesus as Mediator [Gal 3:19]." *JSNT* 29 (1987) 101-21.

de Merode, M. "Une théologie primitive de la femme [Gal 3:28]?" *RTL* 9 (1978) 176-89.

Dietzfelbinger, Christian. *Die Berufung des Paulus als Ursprung seiner Theologie.* WMANT 58. Neukirchen-Vluyn: Neukirchener Verlag, 1985.

Dinkler, Erich. "Der Brief an die Galater." *VF* 1-3 (1953/55) 175-83.

Donaldson, T. L. "The 'Curse of the Law' and the Inclusion of the Gentiles: Galatians 3.13-14." *NTS* 32 (1986) 94-112.

Dülman, Andrea van. "Das Gesetz im Galaterbrief." In *Die Theologie des Gesetzes bei Paulus*, 12-71. SBM 5. Stuttgart: Katholisches Bibelwerk, 1968.

Duncan, George S. *The Epistle of Paul to the Galatians*. MNTC. London: Hodder & Stoughton, 1934.

Dunn, James D. G. "The Early Paulines." In *Baptism in the Holy Spirit: A Reexamination of the New Testament Teaching on the Gift of the Spirit in Relation to Pentecostalism Today*, 103-15. SBT 2/15. London: SCM, 1970.

_____. "Ethical Emphases in Galatians." *Southwestern Journal of Theology* 15 (1972) 53-66.

_____. "The Relationship between Paul and Jerusalem according to Galatians 1 and 2." *NTS* 28 (1982) 461-78.

_____. "The Incident at Antioch (Gal 2.11-18)." *JSNT* 18 (1983) 3-57.

_____. "The New Perspective on Paul [Gal 2:16]." *BJRL* 65 (1983) 95-122.

_____. "Works of the Law and the Curse of the Law (Galatians 3:10-14)." *NTS* 31 (1985) 523-42.

_____. "Once More–Gal 1:18: *historēsai Kēphan*; In Reply to Otfried Hofius." *ZNW* 76 (1985) 138-39.

_____. "'A Light to the Gentiles': The Significance of the Damascus Road Christophany for Paul." In *The Glory of Christ in the New Testament: Studies in Christology in Memory of G. B. Caird*, edited by L. D. Hurst and N. T. Wright, 251-66. Oxford: Clarendon, 1987.

_____. *Jesus, Paul and the Law: Studies in Mark and Galatians.* Louisville: Westminster/John Knox, 1990.

_____. "The Theology of Galatians: The Issue of Covenantal Nomism." In *Thessalonians, Philippians, Galatians, Philemon*, vol. 1 of *Pauline Theology*, edited by Jouette M. Bassler, 125-46. Minneapolis: Fortress, 1991.

_____. "Once More, *PISTIS CHRISTOU*." In *Society of Biblical Literature 1991 Seminar Papers*, edited by Eugene H. Lovering, Jr., 730-44. Atlanta: Scholars Press, 1991.

Duprez, Antoine. "Note sur le rôle de l'Esprit-Saint dans la filiation du chrétiien, à propos de Gal. 4:6." *RSR* 52 (1964) 421-31.

Ebeling, Gerhard. *The Truth of the Gospel: An Exposition of Galatians.* Translated by David Green. Philadelphia: Fortress, 1984.

Eckert, Jost. *Die urchristliche Verkündigung im Streit zwischen Paulus und seinen Gegnern nach dem Galaterbrief.* Biblische Untersuchungen 6. Regensburg: Pustet, 1971.

_____. "Paulus und die Jerusalemer Autoritäten nach dem Galaterbrief und der Apostelgeschichte: Divergierende Geschichtsdarstellung im NT." *Schriftauslegung: Beiträge zur Hermeneutik des Neuen Testamentes und im Neuen Testament*, edited by Josef Ernst, 281-311. Munich: F. Schöningh, 1972.

_____. "Die Verteidigung der apostolischen Autorität im Galaterbrief und im zweiten Korintherbrief. Ein Beitrag zur Kontroverstheologie." *TGl* 65 (1975) 1-19.

Elliott, John H. "Paul, Galatians, and the Evil Eye." *CurTM* 17 (1990) 262-73.

Epp, Eldon J. "Paul's Diverse Images of the Human Situation and His Unifying Theme of Freedom." In *Unity and Diversity in New Testament Theology:*

Essays in Honor of George E. Ladd, edited by R. Guelich, 100-16. Grand Rapids: Eerdmans, 1978.

Farmer, William R. "Galatians and the Second Century Development of the *Regula Fidei*." *SecCent* 4 (1984) 143-70.

Fatum, Lone. "Women, Symbolic Universe and Structures of Silence: Challenges and Possibilities in Androcentric Texts." *ST* 43 (1989) 61-80.

Feld, Helmut. "'Christus Diener der Sunde': Zum Ausgang des Streites zwischen Petrus und Paulus." *TQ* 153 (1973) 119-31.

Feuillet, A. "Structure de la section doctrinale de l'Epître aux Galates (III, 1-VI,10)." *RevThom* 82 (1982) 5-39.

Fiorenza, Elisabeth Schüssler. "Neither Male nor Female: Galatians 3:28–Alternative Vision and Pauline Modification." In *In Memory of Her: A Feminist Theological Reconstruction of Christian Origins*, 205-41. New York: Crossroad, 1983.

———. "Justified by All Her Children: Struggle, Memory, and Vision." In *On the Threshold of the Third Millennium*, edited by Philip Hillyer, 19-38. Concilium 1990/1. Philadelphia: Trinity Press International, 1990.

Fitzmyer, Joseph A. "Saint Paul and the Law." *The Jurist* 27 (1967) 18-36.

Flusser, D. "'Durch das Gesetz dem Gesetz gestorben' (Gal 2,19)." *Judaica* 43 (1987) 30-46.

Foerster, Werner. "Abfassungszeit und Ziel des Galaterbriefes." In *Apophoreta: Festschrift für Ernst Haenchen zu seinem 70. Geburtstag*, edited by W. Eltester and F. H. Kettler, 135-41. BZNW 30. Berlin: Töpelmann, 1964.

Fredriksen, Paula. "Paul and Augustine: Conversion Narratives, Orthodox Traditions, and the Retrospective Self." *JTS* 37 (1986) 3-34.

Fridrichsen, Anton. "Die Apologie des Paulus Gal. 1." In *Paulus und die Urgemeinde*, Lyder Brun and Anton Fridrichsen, 53-76. Giessen: Töpelmann, 1921.

Fuller, D. P. "Paul and 'the Works of the Law'." *WTJ* 38 (1975-76) 28-42.

Fung, Ronald Y.K. *The Epistle to the Galatians*. NICNT. Grand Rapids: Eerdmans, 1988.

Gaston, Lloyd. *Paul and the Torah*. Vancouver: University of British Columbia Press, 1987.

Gaventa, Beverly R. "Conversion in the Letters of Paul." In *From Darkness to Light: Aspects of Conversion in the New Testament*, 17-51. OBT 20. Philadelphia: Fortress, 1986.

———. "Galatians 1 and 2: Autobiography as Paradigm." *NovT* 28 (1986) 302-26.

———. "The Maternity of Paul: An Exegetical Study of Galatians 4:19." In *The Conversation Continues: Studies in Paul & John in Honor of J. Louis Martyn*, edited by Robert T. Fortna and Beverly R. Gaventa, 189-201. Nashville: Abingdon, 1990.

———. "The Singularity of the Gospel: A Reading of Galatians." In *Thessalonians, Philippians, Galatians, Philemon*, vol. 1 of *Pauline Theology*, edited by Jouette M. Bassler, 147-59. Minneapolis: Fortress, 1991.

Gese, H. "*To de Hagar Sina oros estin en tē Arabia* (Gal 4,25)." In *Vom Sinai zum Sion: Alttestamentliche Beiträge zur biblischen Theologie*, 49-62. BEvT 64. Munich: Kaiser, 1974.

Getty, Mary Ann. *A Commentary on Galatians and Romans*, vol. 1 of *Invitation to the New Testament Epistles*. Doubleday New Testament Commentary. Garden City: Image Books, 1982.

Gordon, T. David. "The Problem in Galatia." *Int* 41 (1987) 32-43.

———. "A Note on *paidagōgos* in Galatians 3:24-25." *NTS* 35 (1989) 150-54.

Grant, Robert M. "Hellenistic Elements in Galatians." *ATR* 34 (1952) 223-26.

Grässer, Erich. "Das eine Evangelium: Hermeneutische Erwägungen zu Gal 1,6-10. Rudolf Bultmann zum 85. Geburtstag." *ZTK* 66 (1969) 306-53.

Grundmann, Walter. "Die Häretiker in Galatien." *ZNW* 47 (1956) 25-66.

Haacker, K. "Paulus und das Judentum im Galaterbrief." In *Gottes Augapfel: Beiträge zur Erneuerung des Verhältnisses von Christen und Juden*, edited by Edna Brocke and Jürgen Seim, 95-111. Neukirchen-Vluyn: Neukirchener Verlag, 1986.

Hahn, Ferdinand. "Genesis 15:6 im Neuen Testament." In *Probleme biblischer*

Theologie: Gerhard von Rad zum 70. Geburtstag, edited by Hans Walter Wolff, 90-107. Munich: Kaiser, 1971.

_____. "Das Gesetzesverständnis im Römer- und Galaterbrief. Günther Bornkamm zum 70. Geburtstag." *ZNW* 67 (1976-77) 29-63.

_____. "Die Bedeutung des Apostelkonvents für die Einheit der Christenheit einst und jetzt (Acts 15; Gal 2)." In *Auf Wegen der Versöhnung: Beiträge zum ökumenischen Gespräch*, edited by Peter Neuner and Franz Wolfinger, 15-44. Frankfurt: J. Knecht, 1982.

Hall, Robert G. "The Rhetorical Outline for Galatians: A Reconsideration." *JBL* 106 (1987) 277-87.

Halter, H. "Gal 2,15-21: Mit Christus gestorben dem Gesetz, frei zum Leben in Glaube und Liebe," "Gal 3,26-29: 'In Christus' Söhne Gottes und Erben der Verheißung durch Glaube und Taufe," and "Gal 5,13-25: Freiheit im Kampf zwischen Fleisch und Geist." *Freiburger Theologische Studien* 106 (1977) 98-108, 108-17, and 117-33.

Hamerton-Kelly, Robert G. "Sacred Violence and 'Works of Law': 'Is Christ Then an Agent of Sin?' (Galatians 2:17)." *CBQ* 52 (1990) 55-75.

_____. "Sacred Violence and the Curse of the Law (Galatians 3:13): The Death of Christ as a Sacrificial Travesty." *NTS* 36 (1990) 98-118.

Hansen, G. Walter. *Abraham in Galatians: Epistolary and Rhetorical Contexts.* JSNTSup 29. Sheffield: JSOT, 1989.

_____. "Paul's Three-Dimensional Application of Genesis 15:6 in Galatians." *Trinity Theological Journal* 1 (1989) 59-77.

Hanson, Anthony T. "The Origin of Paul's Use of *paidagōgos* for the Law." *JSNT* 34 (1988) 71-76.

Harnisch, Wolfgang. "Einübung des neuen Seins: Paulinische Paränese am Beispiel des Galaterbriefs." *ZTK* 84 (1987) 279-96.

Hasler, V. "Glaube und Existenz: Hermeneutische Erwägungen zu Gal. 2,15-21." *TZ* 25 (1969) 241-51.

Hays, Richard B. *The Faith of Jesus Christ: An Investigation of the Narrative Substructure of Galatians 3:1-4:11.* SBLDS 56. Chico: Scholars Press, 1983.

_____. "Jesus's Faith and Ours: A Rereading of Galatians 3." In *Conflict and Context: Hermeneutics in the Americas*, edited by Mark Lau Branson and C. René Padilla, 257-68. Grand Rapids: Eerdmans, 1986.

_____. "Christology and Ethics in Galatians: The Law of Christ." *CBQ* 49 (1987) 268-90.

_____. "Scripture Prefigures the Blessing of Gentiles." In *Echoes of Scripture in the Letters of Paul*, 105-21. New Haven: Yale University Press, 1989.

_____. "Crucified With Christ: A Synthesis of the Theology of 1 and 2 Thessalonians, Philemon, Philippians, and Galatians." In *Thessalonians, Philippians, Galatians, Philemon*, vol. 1 of *Pauline Theology*, edited by Jouette M. Bassler, 227-46. Minneapolis: Fortress, 1991.

_____. "*PISTIS* and Pauline Christology: What Is at Stake?" In *Society of Biblical Literature 1991 Seminar Papers*, edited by Eugene H. Lovering, Jr., 714-29. Atlanta: Scholars Press, 1991.

Heiligenthal, Roman. "Soziologische Implikationen der paulinischen Rechtfertigungslehre in Galaterbrief am Beispiel der 'Werke des Gesetzes.' Beobachtungen zur Identitätsfindung einer frühchristlichen Gemeinde." *Kairos* 26 (1984) 38-53.

Helminiak, Daniel A. "Human Solidarity and Collective Union in Christ [Gal 3:28]." *ATR* 70 (1988) 34-59.

Hemer, Colin J. "Acts and Galatians Reconsidered." *Themelios* n.s. 2 (1977) 81-88.

Hester, James D. "The 'Heir' and *Heilsgeschichte*: A Study of Galatians 4:1ff." In *Oikonomia: Heilsgeschichte als Thema der Theologie; Oscar Cullmann zum 65. Geburtstag gewidmet*, edited by Felix Christ, 118-25. Hamburg: Reich, 1967.

_____. "The Rhetorical Structure of Galatians 1:11-2:14." *JBL* 103 (1984) 223-33.

_____. "The Use and Influence of Rhetoric in Galatians 2:1-14." *TZ* 42 (1986) 386-408.

Bibliography

Hirsch, Emanuel. "Zwei Fragen zu Galater 6." *ZNW* 29 (1930) 192-97.
Hofius, Otfried. "Das Gesetz des Mose und das Gesetz Christi." *ZTK* 80 (1983) 262-86.
_____. "Gal 1:18: *historēsai Kēphan*." *ZNW* 75 (1984) 73-85.
Holtz, Traugott. "Die Bedeutung des Apostelkonzils für Paulus." *NovT* 16 (1974) 110-48.
_____. "Der antiochenische Zwischenfall (Gal 2:11-14)." *NTS* 32 (1986) 344-61.
Holtzmann, O. "Zu Emanuel Hirsch, 'Zwei Fragen zu Galater 6'." *ZNW* 30 (1931) 76-83.
Hong, In-Gyu. "The Perspective of Paul in Galatians." *Scriptura* 36 (1991) 1-16.
Hooker, M. D. "Interchange in Christ [Gal 3:13; 2 Cor 5:21]." *JTS* 22 (1971) 349-61.
_____. *Paul, Apostle to the Gentiles*. St. Paul's Lecture, 1989. London: London Diocesan Council for Christian-Jewish Understanding, 1989.
_____. "*PISTIS CHRISTOU*." *NTS* 35 (1989) 321-42.
Howard, George. "On the 'Faith of Christ'." *HTR* 60 (1967) 459-65.
_____. "The Faith of Christ." *ExpTim* 85 (1974) 212-15.
_____. *Paul: Crisis in Galatia*. 2nd ed. SNTSMS 35. Cambridge: Cambridge University Press, 1990.
Hübner, Hans. "Gal 3,10 und die Herkunft des Paulus." *KD* 19 (1973) 21-31.
_____. "Das ganze und das eine Gesetz: Zum Problemkreis Paulus und die Stoa [Gal 5:14]." *KD* 21 (1975) 239-56.
_____. "Identitätsverlust und paulinische Theologie: Anmerkungen zum Galaterbrief." *KD* 24 (1978) 181-93.
_____. "Der Galaterbrief und das Verhältnis von antiker Rhetorik und Epistolographie (H. D. Betz, *Galatians*)." *TLZ* 109 (1984) 241-50.
_____. "Nomos in Galatians" and "Boasting in Galatians." In *Law in Paul's Thought*, edited by J. Riches, 15-50 and 101-11. Translated by James C. G. Greig. Studies of the NT and its World. Edinburgh: T. & T. Clark, 1984.
_____. "Galaterbrief." *TRE* 12 (1984) 5-15.
_____. "Was heisst bei Paulus 'Werke des Gesetzes'?" In *Glaube und Eschatologie: Festschrift für Werner Georg Kümmel zum 80. Geburtstag*, edited by Erich Grässer and Otto Merk, 123-33. Tübingen: Mohr (Siebeck), 1985.
Hultgren, Arland J. "Paul's Pre-Christian Persecutions of the Church: Their Purpose, Locale, and Nature." *JBL* 95 (1976) 97-111.
_____. "The *pistis Christou* Formulation in Paul." *NovT* 22 (1980) 248-63.
Hurtado, Larry W. "The Jerusalem Collection and the Book of Galatians." *JSNT* 5 (1979) 46-62.
Jegher-Bucher, Verena. *Der Galaterbrief auf dem Hintergrund antiker Epistolographie und Rhetorik: Ein anderes Paulusbild*. ATANT 78. Zürich: Theologischer Verlag, 1991.
Jewett, Robert. "Agitators and the Galatian Congregation." *NTS* 17 (1971) 198-212.
Jones, F. Stanley. "*eleutheria* im Galaterbrief." In *"Freiheit" in den Briefen des Apostels Paulus: Eine historische, exegetische und religionsgeschichtliche Studie*, 70-109. GTA 34. Göttingen: Vandenhoeck & Ruprecht, 1987.
Kamlah, Erhard. "Gal. 5,19-23." In *Die Form der katalogischen Paränese im Neuen Testament*, 14-18. WUNT 7. Tübingen: Mohr (Siebeck), 1964.
Kern, W. "Die antizipierte Entideologisierung oder die 'Weltelemente' des Galater- und Kolosserbriefes heute." *ZKT* 96 (1974) 185-216.
Kertelge, Karl. "Zur Deutung des Rechtfertigungsbegriffs im Galaterbrief." *BZ* 12 (1968) 211-22.
_____. "Apokalypsis Jesou Christou (Gal 1, 12)." In *Neues Testament und Kirche: Für Rudolf Schnackenburg*, edited by Joachim Gnilka, 266-81. Freiburg: Herder & Herder, 1974.
_____. "Gesetz und Freiheit im Galaterbrief." *NTS* 30 (1984) 382-94.
_____. "Autorität des Gesetzes und Autorität Jesu bei Paulus." In *Vom Urchristentum zu Jesus: Für Joachim Gnilka*, edited by Hubert Frankemoelle and Karl Kertelge, 358-76. Freiburg: Herder & Herder, 1989.
_____. "Freiheitsbotschaft und Liebesgebot im Galaterbrief." In *Neues Testament*

144

und Ethik: Für Rudolf Schnackenburg, edited by Helmut Merklein, 326-37. Freiburg: Herder & Herder, 1989.

Kieffer, René. *Foi et justification à Antioch: Interprétation d'un conflit (Gal 2,14-21)*. LD 111. Paris: Cerf, 1982.

Kilpatrick, G. D. "Gal 2.14 *orthopodousin*." In *Neutestamentliche Studien für Rudolf Bultmann zu seinem 70. Geburtstag*, edited by Walther Eltester, 269-74. BZNW 21. Berlin: Töpelmann, 1954.

_____. "Galatians 1:18, *HISTORĒSAI KĒPHAN*." In *New Testament Essays: Studies in Memory of Thomas Walter Manson (1893-1958)*, edited by Angus John Brockhurst Higgins, 144-49. Manchester: Manchester University Press, 1959.

_____. "Peter, Jerusalem and Galatians 1:13-2:14." *NovT* 25 (1983) 318-26.

Kim, Seyoon. *The Origin of Paul's Gospel*. WUNT 2/4. 2nd ed., rev. and enl. Tübingen: Mohr (Siebeck), 1984.

Kittel, Gerhard. "*pistis Iēsou Christou* bei Paulus." *TSK* 79 (1906) 419-36.

Klein, Günter. "Galater 2,6-9 und die Geschichte der Jerusalemer Urgemeinde." *ZTK* 57 (1960) 275-95.

_____. "Individualgeschichte und Weltgeschichte bei Paulus: Eine Interpretation ihres Verhältnisses im Galaterbrief." *EvT* 24 (1964) 126-65.

_____. "Werkruhm und Christusruhm im Galaterbrief und die Frage nach einer Entwicklung des Paulus: Ein hermeneutischer und exegetischer Zwischenruf." In *Studien zum Text und zur Ethik des Neuen Testaments: Festschrift zum 80. Geburtstag von Heinrich Greeven*, edited by Wolfgang Schrage, 196-211. BZNW 47. New York: de Gruyter, 1986.

Klostermann, Erich. "Zur Apologie des Paulus Galater 1,10-2,21." In *Gottes ist der Orient: Festschrift für Otto Eissfeldt zu seinem 70. Geburtstag*, Konrad v. Rabenau et al., 84-87. Berlin: Evangelische Verlagsanstalt, 1959.

Klumbies, P.-G. "Zwischen Pneuma und Nomos. Neuorientierung in den galatischen Gemeinden." *WD* 19 (1987) 109-35.

Knox, John. "On the Meaning of Galatians 1:15." *JBL* 106 (1987) 301-4.

Kraftchick, Steven J. "Why Do the Rhetoricians Rage?" In *Text and Logos: The Humanistic Interpretation of the New Testament* [in honor of Hendrikus Boers], edited by Theodore W. Jennings, 55-79. Scholars Press Homage Series. Atlanta: Scholars Press, 1990.

Krentz, Edgar, John Koenig, and Donald H. Juel. *Galatians, Philippians, Philemon, 1 Thessalonians*. Augsburg Commentary on the New Testament. Minneapolis: Augsburg Pub. House, 1985.

Kümmel, Werner G. "'Individualgeschichte' und 'Weltgeschichte' in Gal. 2:15-21." In *Christ and Spirit in the New Testament: In Honour of Charles Francis Digby Moule*, edited by Barnabas Lindars and Stephen S. Smalley, 157-73. Cambridge: Cambridge University Press, 1973.

Ladd, George E. "The Holy Spirit in Galatians." In *Current Issues in Biblical and Patristic Interpretation* [in honor of M. C. Tenney], edited by Gerald F. Hawthorne, 211-16. Grand Rapids: Eerdmans, 1975.

Lagrange, Marie-Joseph. *Saint Paul Epître aux Galates*. 2nd ed. Ebib. Paris: Gabalda, 1950.

Lake, Kirsopp. *The Earlier Epistles of St. Paul: Their Motive and Origin*. 2nd ed. London: Rivingtons, 1914.

Lamarche, P. "'Ni mâle, ni femelle' (Gal 3,28)." *Christus* 24 (1977) 349-55.

Lambrecht, Jan. "The Line of Thought in Gal. 2.14-21." *NTS* 24 (1978) 484-95.

_____. "Gesetzesverständnis bei Paulus." In *Das Gesetz im Neuen Testament*, edited by Karl Kertelge and Johannes Beutler, 88-127. QD 108. Freiburg: Herder & Herder, 1986.

_____. "Once Again Gal 2:17-18 and 3:21." *ETL* 63 (1987) 148-53.

Lategan, Bernard C. "Is Paul Defending his Apostleship in Galatians? The Function of Galatians 1:11-12 and 2:19-20 in the Development of Paul's Argument." *NTS* 34 (1988) 411-30.

_____. "Is Paul Developing a Specifically Christian Ethics in Galatians?" In *Greeks, Romans, and Christians: Essays in Honor of Abraham J. Malherbe*, edited by David L. Balch, Everett Ferguson, and Wayne A. Meeks, 318-28. Minneapolis: Fortress, 1990.

Bibliography

Legrand, L. "'Il n'y a ni esclave ni homme libre, ni homme ni femme'; St. Paul et l'émancipation sociale." *Indian Theological Studies* 18 (1981) 135-63.

Léon-Dufour, Xavier. "Une lecture chretienne de L'Ancien Testament: Galates 3:6 à 4:20." In *L'Evangile, hier et aujourd'hui: Mélanges offerts au professeur Franz-J. Leenhardt*, edited by P. E. Bonnard, 109-15. Genève: Labor et fides, 1968.

Lietzmann, Hans. *An die Galater*. 4th ed., with a postscript by Philipp Vielhauer. HNT 10. Tübingen: Mohr (Siebeck), 1971.

Liftin, A. D. "Evangelical Feminism: Why Traditionalists Reject It [Gal 3:28]." *BSac* 136 (1979) 258-71.

Lindemann, Andreas. "Die biblischen Toragebote und die paulinische Ethik." In *Studien zum Text und zur Ethik des Neuen Testaments: Festschrift zum 80. Geburtstag von Heinrich Greeven*, edited by Wolfgang Schrage, 242-65. BZNW 47. New York: de Gruyter, 1986.

Linton, Olof. "The Third Aspect–A Neglected Point of View: A Study in Gal. I-II and Acts IX and XV." *ST* 3 (1950) 79-95.

Loisy, Alfred. *L'Epître aux Galates*. Paris: Nourry, 1916.

Longenecker, Richard N. "The 'Faith of Abraham' Theme in Paul, James and Hebrews: A Study in the Circumstantial Nature of New Testament Teaching." *JETS* 20 (1977) 203-12.

———. "The Pedagogical Nature of the Law in Galatians 3:19-4:7." *JETS* 25 (1982) 53-61.

———. *Galatians*. WBC 41. Dallas: Word Books, 1990.

Lönning, Inge. "Paulus und Petrus: Gal 2,11ff. als kontroverstheologisches Fundamentalproblem." *ST* 24 (1970) 1-69.

Lührmann, Dieter. "Offenbarung und Gesetz im Galaterbrief." In *Das Offenbarungsverständnis bei Paulus und in Paulinischen Gemeinden*, 67-81. WMANT 16. Neukirchen-Vluyn: Neukirchener Verlag, 1965.

———. *Glaube im frühen Christentum*. Gütersloh: G. Mohn, 1976.

——— and D. Stollberg. "Identität und der Tod des Ich (Gal 2,19-20)." In *Doppeldeutlich. Tiefendimensionen biblicscher Texte*, edited by Yorick Spiegel, 227-33. Munich: Kaiser, 1978.

———. "Abendmahlsgemeinschaft: Gal 2,11ff." In *Kirche: Festschrift für Günther Bornkamm zum 75. Geburtstag*, edited by Dieter Lührmann and Georg Strecker, 271-86. Tübingen: Mohr (Siebeck), 1980.

———. "Tage, Monate, Jahreszeiten, Jahre (Gal 4,10)." In *Werden und Wirken des Alten Testaments: Festschrift für Claus Westermann zum 70. Geburtstag*, edited by R. Albertz, 428-45. Göttingen: Vandenhoeck & Ruprecht, 1980.

———. "Gal 2:9 und die katholischen Briefe: Bemerkungen zum Kanon und zur *regula fidei*." *ZNW* 72 (1981) 65-87.

———. "Die 430 Jahre zwischen den Verheißungen und dem Gesetz (Gal 3,17)." *ZAW* 100 (1988) 420-23.

Lull, David J. "The Spirit and the Creative Transformation of Human Existence." *JAAR* 47 (1979) 39-55.

———. *The Spirit in Galatia: Paul's Interpretation of PNEUMA as Divine Power*. SBLDS 49. Chico: Scholars Press, 1980.

———. "'The Law Was Our Pedagogue': A Study in Gal 3:19-25." *JBL* 105 (1986) 481-98.

———. "Salvation History: Theology in 1 Thessalonians, Philemon, Philippians, and Galatians: A Response to N. T. Wright, R. B. Hays, and R. Scroggs." In *Thessalonians, Philippians, Galatians, Philemon*, vol. 1 of *Pauline Theology*, edited by Jouette M. Bassler, 247-65. Minneapolis: Fortress, 1991.

Lütgert, Wilhelm. *Gesetz und Geist: Eine Untersuchung zur Vorgeschichte des Galaterbriefes*. BFCT 22/6. Gütersloh: Bertelsmann, 1919.

Lux, W. *Zur Freiheit befreit: Zur Wirkungsgeschichte des Galaterbriefs*. Studienhefte Religion 3. Stuttgart: Calwer, 1982.

Luz, Ulrich. "Gesetz, Verheißung und Geschichte (Rom. 4; Gal. 3)." In *Das Geschichtsverständnis des Paulus*, 168-86. BEvT, Theologische Abhandlungen 49. Munich: Kaiser, 1968.

Lyonnet, Stanislas. *Les épîtres de saint Paul aux Galates, aux Romains*. 3rd ed. Paris: Cerf, 1966.

Lyons, George. *Pauline Autobiography: Toward a New Understanding.* SBLDS 73. Atlanta: Scholars Press, 1985.

MacDonald, Dennis R. *There Is No Male and Female: The Fate of a Dominical Saying in Paul and Gnosticism.* HDR 20. Philadelphia: Fortress, 1986.

MacGorman, J. W. "The Law as *paidagōgos*: A Study in Pauline Analogy." *New Testament Studies: Essays in Honor of Ray Summers in His Sixty-fifth Year*, edited by Huber L. Drumwright and Curtis Vaughan, 99-111. Waco: Markham Press Fund, 1975.

Manson, T. W. "St. Paul in Ephesus: (2) The Problem of the Epistle to the Galatians." *BJRL* 24 (1940) 59-80.

Martin, Ralph P. *1 Corinthians, 2 Corinthians, Galatians.* Understanding the New Testament. Philadelphia: Holman, 1978.

Martyn, J. Louis. "A Law-Observant Mission to Gentiles: The Background of Galatians." *Michigan Quarterly Review* 22 (1983) 221-36.

_____. "Apocalyptic Antinomies in Paul's Letter to the Galatians." *NTS* 31 (1985) 410-24.

_____. "Paul and his Jewish-Christian Interpreters." *USQR* 42 (1988) 1-15.

_____. "The Covenants of Hagar and Sarah." In *Faith and History: Essays in Honor of Paul W. Meyer*, edited by John T. Carroll, Charles H. Cosgrove, and E. Elizabeth Johnson, 160-92. Scholars Press Homage Series. Atlanta: Scholars Press, 1990.

_____. "Events in Galatia: Modified Covenantal Nomism versus God's Invasion of the Cosmos in the Singular Gospel: A Response to J. D. G. Dunn and B. R. Gaventa." In *Thessalonians, Philippians, Galatians, Philemon*, vol. 1 of *Pauline Theology*, edited by Jouette M. Bassler, 160-79. Minneapolis: Fortress, 1991.

Marxsen, Willi. "Sündige tapfer. Wer hat sich beim Streit in Antiochen richtig verhalten?" *EvK* 20 (1987) 81-84.

Matera, Frank J. "The Culmination of Paul's Argument to the Galatians: Gal 5:1-6:17." *JSNT* 32 (1988) 79-91.

Mauser, Ulrich. "Galater iii.20: Die Universalität des Heils." *NTS* 13 (1966-67) 258-70.

Meeks, Wayne A. "The Image of the Androgyne: Some Uses of a Symbol in Earliest Christianity." *HR* 13 (1973) 165-208.

_____. "A Review of *Galatians: A Commentary on Paul's Letter to the Churches in Galatia*, by Hans Dieter Betz." *JBL* 100 (1981) 304-7.

Merk, Otto. "Der Beginn der Paränese im Galaterbrief." *ZNW* 60 (1969) 83-104.

Minear, Paul S. "The Crucified World: The Enigma of Galatians 6,14." In *Theologia Crucis-Signum Crucis: Festschrift für Erich Dinkler zum 70. Geburtstag*, edited by Carl Andresen and Günter Klein, 395-407. Tübingen: Mohr (Siebeck), 1979.

Modalsli, O. "Gal. 2,19-21; 5,16-18 und Röm. 7,7-25." *TZ* 21 (1965) 22-57.

Motyer, Stephen. "The Relationship Between Paul's Gospel of 'All One in Christ Jesus' (Galatians 3:28) and the 'Household Codes'." *Vox Evangelica* 19 (1989) 33-48.

Moule, C. F. D. "Death 'to sin,' 'to law' and 'to the world': A Note on Certain Datives." In *Mélanges bibliques en hommage au R. P. Béda Rigaux*, edited by Albert Descamps and André de Halleux, 367-75. Gembloux: Duculot, 1970.

Munck, Johannes. "The Judaizing Gentile Christians: Studies in Galatians." In *Paul and the Salvation of Mankind*, 87-134. Translated by F. Clarke. Richmond: John Knox, 1959.

Murphy-O'Connor, Jerome. "Pauline Missions Before the Jerusalem Conference." *RB* 89 (1982) 71-91.

Mussner, Franz. "Hagar, Sinai, Jerusalem: Zum Text von Gal 4,25a." *TQ* 135 (1955) 56-60.

_____. "Theologische 'Wiedergutmachung'. Am Beispiel der Auslegung des Galaterbriefes." *Freiburger Rundbrief* 26 (1974) 7-11.

_____. *Theologie der Freiheit nach Paulus.* QD 75. Freiburg: Herder & Herder, 1976.

_____. *Der Galaterbrief.* 5th ed., enl. HTKNT 9. Freiburg: Herder & Herder, 1988.

_____. "'Das Wesen des Christentums ist *synesthiein*': Ein authentischer

Kommentar." *Mysterium der Gnade: Festschrift für Johann Auer*, edited by Herbert Rossmann and Joseph Ratzinger, 92-102. Regensburg: Pustet, 1975.

____. "Gesetz-Abraham-Israel." *Kairos* 25 (1983) 200-22.

Neil, William. *The Letter of Paul to the Galatians*. CBC, *New English Bible*. Cambridge: Cambridge University Press, 1967.

Neitzel, H. "Zur Interpretation von Galater 2,11-21." *TQ* 163 (1983) 15-39 and 131-49.

Neyrey, Jerome H. "Bewitched in Galatia: Paul's Accusations of Witchcraft." In *Paul in Other Words: A Cultural Reading of his Letters*, 181-206. Louisville: Westminster/John Knox, 1990.

Nickelsburg, George W. E. "An *ektrōma*, Though Appointed from the Womb: Paul's Apostolic Self-description in 1 Corinthians 15 and Galatians 1." *HTR* 79 (1986) 198-205.

Oepke, Albrecht. *Der Brief des Paulus an die Galater*. 3rd ed., rev. and enl. by J. Rohde. THKNT 9. Berlin: Evangelische Verlagsanstalt, 1973.

O'Neill, J. C. *The Recovery of Paul's Letter to the Galatians*. London: SPCK, 1972.

Osiek, Carolyn. "Galatians: Paul's Gospel of Freedom." *Bible Today* 18 (1980) 82-88.

____. *Galatians*. New Testament Message 12. Wilmington: M. Glazier, 1980.

Osten-Sacken, Peter von der. "Das paulinische Verständnis des Gesetzes im Spannungsfeld von Eschatologie und Geschichte." *EvT* 37 (1977) 549-87.

Pagels, Elaine H. "Paul and Women: A Response to Recent Discussion [Gal 3: 28; 1 Cor 7; 11]." *JAAR* 42 (1974) 538-49.

Parker, Pierson. "Once More: Acts and Galatians." *JBL* 86 (1967) 175-82.

Patte, Daniel. "Galatians: For Freedom Christ Has Set Us Free." In *Paul's Faith and the Power of the Gospel: A Structural Introduction to the Pauline Letters*, 31-86. Philadelphia: Fortress, 1983.

Paulsen, Henning. "Einheit und Freiheit der Söhne Gottes–Gal 3:26-29." *ZNW* 71 (1980) 74-95.

Pesch, Rudolf. "Peter, in the Mirror of Paul's Letters." In *Paul de Tarse, apôtre de notre temps*, Albert-Louis Descamps et al., with an Introduction by Guiseppe Turbessi and Lorenzo De Lorenzi and a Preface by Giovanni Benelli, 291-309. Série monographique de "Benedictina," Section paulinienne 1. Rome: Abbaye de S. Paul, 1979.

____. "Das jerusalemer Abkommen und die Lösung des antiochenischen Konflikts: Ein Versuch über Gal 2, Apg 10:1-11, Apg 11:27-30; 12-25." In *Kontinuität und Einheit: Festschrift für Franz Mussner*, edited by Paul-Gerhard Müller and Werner Stenger, 105-22. Freiburg: Herder & Herder, 1981.

Pilch, John J. *Galatians and Romans*. Collegeville Bible Commentary 6. Collegeville: Liturgical Press, 1983.

Pinnock, Clark H. *Truth on Fire: The Message of Galatians*. Grand Rapids: Baker Book House, 1972.

Pratscher, Wilhelm. "Der Herrenbruder Jakobus und sein Kreis [Gal 2]." *EvT* 47 (1987) 228-44.

Prümm, Karl. "Gal und 2 Kor: Ein lehrgehaltlicher Vergleich." *Bib* 31 (1950) 27-72.

Quesnell, Quentin. *The Gospel of Christian Freedom*. New York: Herder & Herder, 1969.

Radl, Walter. *Galaterbrief*. Stuttgarter kleiner Kommentar; Neues Testament 9. Stuttgart: Katholisches Bibelwerk, 1985.

Räisänen, Heikki. "Paul's Theological Difficulties with the Law." In *Papers on Paul and Other New Testament Authors*, vol. 3 of *Studia Biblica 1978*, edited by E. A. Livingstone, 301-20. JSNTSup 3. Sheffield: JSOT, 1980.

____. "Legalism and Salvation by the Law: Paul's Portrayal of the Jewish Religion as a Historical and Theological Problem." In *Die paulinische Literatur und Theologie*, edited by Sigfred Pedersen, 63-83. Teologiske Studier 7. Århus: Aros; Göttingen: Vandenhoeck & Ruprecht, 1980.

____. "Galatians 2.16 and Paul's Break with Judaism." *NTS* 31 (1985) 543-53.

____. "Paul's Conversion and the Development of His View of the Law." *NTS* 33 (1987) 404-19.

Ramsay, William M. *A Historical Commentary on St. Paul's Epistle to the Galatians.* New York: G. P. Putnam's Sons, 1900.

Reicke, Bo. "The Law and This World According to Paul. Some Thoughts Concerning Gal. 4:1-11." Translated by W. Schaeffer. *JBL* 70 (1951) 259-76.

____. "Paulus über das Gesetz." *TZ* 41 (1985) 237-57.

Refoulé, François. "Approches de l'épître aux Galates." *Lumière et Vie* 38/192 (1989) 15-28.

Richardson, Peter. "Pauline Inconsistency: 1 Corinthians 9:19-23 and Galatians 2:11-14." *NTS* 26 (1980) 347-62.

Ridderbos, Herman N. *The Epistle of Paul to the Churches of Galatia.* Translated by Henry Zylstra. NICNT. Grand Rapids: Eerdmans, 1953.

Riesenfeld, Harald. "The Misinterpreted Mediator in Gal 3:19-20." In *The New Testament Age: Essays in Honor of Bo Reicke*, vol. 2, edited by William C. Weinrich, 405-12. Macon: Mercer University Press, 1984.

Robinson, Arthur William. *The Epistle of Paul the Apostle to the Galatians.* London: Methuen, 1900.

Robinson, D. W. B. "The Distinction between Jewish and Gentile Believers in Galatians." *AusBR* 13 (1965) 29-48.

____. "'Faith of Jesus Christ'–A New Testament Debate." *Reformed Theological Review* 29 (1970) 71-81.

Ropes, James Hardy. *The Singular Problem of the Epistle to the Galatians.* HTS 14. Cambridge: Harvard University Press, 1929.

Rordorf, Bernard. "L'Evangile de la liberté." *Bulletin du Centre Protestant d'Etudes* 35 (1983) 36-59.

Roux, Hébert. *L'évangile de la liberté: Commentaire de l'épître de Paul aux Galates.* Genève: Labor et fides, 1973.

Ruegg, Uli. "Paul et la Rhétorique Ancienne." *Bulletin du Centre Protestant d'Etudes* 35 (1983) 5-35.

____, Bernard Rordorf, François Bovon, and Joël Allaz, eds. *Chrétiens en conflit: L'Epître de Paul aux Galates: Dossier pour l'animation biblique.* Essais bibliques 13. Genève: Labor et fides, 1987.

Russell, Walt. "Who Were Paul's Opponents in Galatia?" *BSac* 147 (1990) 329-50.

Sampley, J. Paul. "Before God, I Do Not Lie (Gal 1:20): Paul's Self-defence in the Light of Roman Legal Praxis." *NTS* 23 (1977) 477-82.

____. "Romans and Galatians: Comparison and Contrast." In *Understanding the Word: Essays in Honor of Bernhard W. Anderson*, edited by James T. Butler, Edgar W. Conrad, and Ben C. Ollenburger, 315-39. JSOTSup 37. Sheffield: JSOT, 1985.

Sanders, E. P. "On the Question of Fulfilling the Law in Paul and Rabbinic Judaism." In *Donum Gentilicium: New Testament Studies in Honour of David Daube*, edited by E. Bammel, C. K. Barrett, and W. D. Davies, 103-26. Oxford: Clarendon, 1978.

____. *Paul, the Law and the Jewish People.* Philadelphia: Fortress, 1983.

____. "Jewish Association with Gentiles and Galatians 2:11-14." In *The Conversation Continues: Studies in Paul & John in Honor of J. Louis Martyn*, edited by Robert T. Fortna and Beverly R. Gaventa, 170-88. Nashville: Abingdon, 1990.

Sanders, Jack T. "Paul's 'Autobiographical' Statements in Galatians 1-2." *JBL* 85 (1966) 335-43.

Sanders, James A. "Habakkuk in Qumran, Paul, and the Old Testament." *JR* 39 (1959) 232-44.

Schläger, G. "Bemerkungen zu *pistis Iēsou Christou*." *ZNW* 7 (1906) 356-58.

Schlier, Heinrich. *Der Brief an die Galater.* 5th ed. MeyerK 7. Göttingen: Vandenhoeck & Ruprecht, 1971.

Schmidt, Karl Ludwig. *Ein Gang durch den Galaterbrief.* Zollikon-Zürich: Evangelischer Verlag, 1942.

Schmithals, Walter. "The Heretics in Galatia." In *Paul and the Gnostics*, 13-64. Translated by John E. Steely. Nashville: Abingdon, 1972.

149

Bibliography

_____. "Judaisten in Galatien?" *ZNW* 74 (1983) 27-58.

Schoon-Janssen, Johannes. *Umstrittene 'Apologien' in den Paulusbriefen: Studien zur rhetorischen Situation des 1. Thessalonicherbriefes, des Galaterbriefes und des Philipperbriefes.* GTA 45. Göttingen: Vandenhoeck & Ruprecht, 1991.

Schreiner, Thomas R. "Is Perfect Obedience to the Law Possible: A Re-examination of Galatians 3:10." *JETS* 27 (1984) 151-60.

Schrenk, G. "Was bedeutet 'Israel Gottes'?" *Judaica* 5 (1949) 81-94.

Schulz, O. "*Ti oun ho nomos*; Verhältnis von Gesetz, Sünde und Evangelium nach Gal. 3." *TSK* 75 (1902) 5-56.

Schulz, Siegfried. "Katholisierende Tendenzen in Schliers Galater-Kommentar." *KD* 5 (1959) 23-41.

_____. "Zur Gesetztheologie des Paulus im Blick auf Gerhad Ebelings Galaterbriefauslegung." In *Wirkungen hermeneutischer Theologie: Eine Züricher Festgabe zum 70. Geburtstag Gottes Gerhard Ebelings*, edited by Hans F. Geisser and Walter Mostert, 81-98. Zürich: Theologischer Verlag, 1983.

Schürmann, Heinz. "'Das Gesetz des Christus' [Gal 6,2]. Jesu Verhalten und Wort als letztgültige sittliche Norm nach Paulus." In *Neues Testament und Kirche: Festschrift für Rudolf Schnackenburg*, edited by Joachim Gnilka, 282-300. Freiburg: Herder & Herder, 1974.

Schütz, John H. "Tradition, Gospel and the Apostolic Ego: Gal. 1 and 2." In *Paul and the Anatomy of Apostolic Authority*, 114-58. SNTSMS 26. Cambridge: Cambridge University Press, 1975.

Schwartz, D. R. "Two Pauline Allusions to the Redemptive Mechanism of the Crucifixion [Gal 3:13; 4:4-5; Rom 8:32]." *JBL* 102 (1983) 259-68.

Schweizer, Eduard. "Zum religionsgeschichtlichen Hintergrund der 'Sendungsformel' Gal. 4.4f; Röm. 8.3f; Joh. 3.16f; 1 Joh. 4.9." *ZNW* 57 (1966) 199-210.

_____. "Die 'Elemente der Welt' Gal 4,3 9; Kol 2,8 20." In *Beiträge zur Theologie des Neuen Testaments: Neutestamentliche Aufsätze (1955-1970)*, 147-63. Zürich: Zwingli, 1970.

_____. "Slaves of the Elements and Worshipers of Angels: Gal 4:3, 9 and Col 2:8, 18, 20." *JBL* 107 (1988) 455-68.

_____. "Altes und Neues zu den 'Elementen der Welt' in Kol 2,20; Gal 4,3-9." In *Wissenschaft und Kirche: Festschrift für Eduard Lohse*, edited by Kurt Aland and Siegfried Meurer, 111-18. Texte und Arbeiten zur Bibel 4. Bielefeld: Luther-Verlag, 1989.

_____. "What Do We Really Mean When We Say, 'God Sent His Son'?" In *Faith and History: Essays in Honor of Paul W. Meyer*, edited by John T. Carroll, Charles H. Cosgrove, and E. Elizabeth Johnson, 298-312. Scholars Press Homage Series. Atlanta: Scholars Press, 1990.

Scroggs, Robin. "Salvation History: The Theological Structure of Paul's Thought (1 Thessalonians, Philippians, and Galatians)." In *Thessalonians, Philippians, Galatians, Philemon*, vol. 1 of *Pauline Theology*, edited by Jouette M. Bassler, 212-26. Minneapolis: Fortress, 1991.

Silva, Moises. "Betz and Bruce on Galatians." *WTJ* 45 (1983) 371-85.

Smit, Joop. "The Letter of Paul to the Galatians: A Deliberative Speech." *NTS* 35 (1989) 1-26.

Snodgrass, Klyne R. "Galatians 3:28: Conundrum or Solution." In *Women, Authority and the Bible*, edited by Alvera Mickelsen, 161-81. Downers Grove: Inter-Varsity, 1986.

Soards, Marion L. "Seeking (*zētein*) and Sinning (*hamartōlos* and *hamartia*) according to Galatians 2:17." In *Apocalyptic and the New Testament: Essays in Honor of J. Louis Martyn*, edited by Joel Marcus and Marion L. Soards, 237-54. JSNTSup 24. Sheffield: JSOT, 1989.

Stagg, Frank. "Freedom and Moral Responsibility Without License or Legalism [Gal 5-6]." *RevExp* 69 (1972) 483-94.

_____. *Galatians/Romans*. Knox Preaching Guides. Atlanta: John Knox, 1980.

Stalder, Kurt. "Das Gesetz nach dem Galaterbrief" and "Das Gericht nach den Werken [Galatians 5]." In *Das Werk des Geistes in der Heiligung bei Paulus*, 307-49 and 455-63. Zürich: EVZ, 1962.

Standaert, Benoit. "La rhetorique antique et l'épître aux Galates." *Foi et Vie* 84/5 (1985) 33-40.

Stanley, Christopher D. "'Under a Curse': A Fresh Reading of Galatians 3:10-14." *NTS* 36 (1990) 481-511.

Stein, Robert H. "The Relationship of Galatians 2:1-10 and Acts 15:1-35: Two Neglected Arguments." *JETS* 17 (1974) 239-42.

Steinhauser, Michael G. "Gal 4:25a: Evidence of Targumic Tradition in Gal 4:21-31?" *Bib* 70 (1989) 234-40.

Steinmann, Alphons. *Der Leserkreis des Galaterbriefes: Ein Beitrag zur urchristlichen Missionsgeschichte.* NTAbh 1.3-4. Münster: Aschendorff, 1908.

Stenger, Werner. "Biographisches und Idealbiographisches in Gal 1:11-12, 14." In *Kontinuität und Einheit: Festschrift für Franz Mussner*, edited by Paul-Gerhard Müller and Werner Stenger, 123-40. Freiburg: Herder & Herder, 1981.

Stoll, Karlheinz. "Galater 3,26-29: Eine biblische Meditation." In *Frau und Mann, befreundet in Christus*, edited by Friedrich Hauschildt, 9-21. Zur Sache 28. Hannover: Lutherisches Verlagshaus, 1988.

Stolle, Volker. "Die Eins in Gal 3,15-29." In *Festgabe für Karl Heinrich Rengstorf zum 70. Geburtstag*, edited by Wolfgang Dietrich and Heinz Schreckenberg, 204-13. Theokratia 2. Leiden: Brill, 1973.

Strelan, John G. "Burden-Bearing and the Law of Christ: A Re-examination of Galatians 6:2." *JBL* 94 (1975) 266-76.

Strobel, August. "Das Aposteldekret in Galatien: Zur Situation von Gal. I und II." *NTS* 20 (1973/74) 177-90.

Suhl, Alfred. "Der Galaterbrief–Situation und Argumentation." *ANRW* 2.25.4 (1987) 3067-134.

_____. "Die Galater und der Geist: Kritische Erwägungen zur Situation in Galatien." In *Jesu Rede von Gott und ihre Nachgeschichte im frühen Christentum: Beiträge zur Verkündigung Jesu und zum Kerygma der Kirche; Festschrift für Willi Marxsen zum 70. Geburtstag*, edited by Dietrich-Alex Koch, Gerhard Sellin, and Andreas Lindemann, 267-96. Gütersloh: G. Mohn, 1989.

Tannehill, Robert C. "Dying with Christ as the Basis of the New Life." Part I.4-6 of *Dying and Rising With Christ: A Study in Pauline Theology*, 55-65. BZNW 32. Berlin: Töpelmann, 1967.

Taylor, G. M. "The Function of *pistis Christou* in Galatians." *JBL* 85 (1966) 58-76.

Thielman, Frank S. *From Plight to Solution: A Jewish Framework to Understanding Paul's View of the Law in Galatians and Romans.* NovTSup 61. Leiden: Brill, 1989.

Thornton, T. C. G. "Jewish New Moon Festivals, Galatians 4:3-11 and Colossians 2:16." *JTS* 40 (1989) 97-100.

Thyen, Hartwig. "'. . . nicht mehr männlich und weiblich . . .': Eine Studie zu Galater 3,28." In *Als Mann und Frau geschaffen: Exegetische Studien zur Rolle der Frau*, Frank Crüsemann and Hartwig Thyen, 107-97. Kennzeichen 2. Gelnhausen: Burckhardthaus, 1978.

Trummer, Peter. "Wieso 'aus Werken des Gesetzes kein Mensch gerechtfertigt wird' (Gal 2,16) und welche Konsequenzen dies für uns hat." In *Aufsätze zum Neuen Testament*, 81-94. Grazer Theologische Studien 12. Graz: Institut für ökumenische Theologie und Patrologie, 1987.

Tuckett, C. M. "Deuteronomy 21,23 and Paul's Conversion." In *L'Apôtre Paul: Personnalité, style et conception du ministère*, edited by Albert Vanhoye, 344-50. BETL 73. Leuven: Leuven University Press, 1986.

Tyson, Joseph B. "Paul's Opponents in Galatia." *NovT* 10 (1968) 241-54.

_____. "'Works of Law' in Galatians." *JBL* 92 (1973) 423-31.

Vanhoye, Albert. "Un médiateur des anges en Ga 3,19-20." *Bib* 59 (1978) 403-11.

_____. "Mary in Galatians 4,4." *TD* 28 (1980) 257-59.

Venetz, H.-J. "'Christus anziehen.' Eine Exegese zu Gal 3,26-27 als Beitrag zum paulinischen Taufverständnis." *Freiburger Zeitschrift für Philosophie und Theologie* 20 (1973) 3-36.

Bibliography

Viard, André. *Saint Paul, Epître aux Galates*. Sources bibliques. Paris: Gabalda, 1964.

Vielhauer, Philipp. "Gesetzesdienst und Stoicheiadienst im Galaterbrief." In *Rechtfertigung: Festschrift für Ernst Käsemann zum 70. Geburtstag*, edited by J. Friedrich, W. Pöhlmann, and P. Stuhlmacher, 543-55. Tübingen: Mohr (Siebeck); Göttingen: Vandenhoeck & Ruprecht, 1976.

Vos, Johannes Sijko. "Der Geist und das Erbe Abrahams (Gal 2,15-5,12)." In *Traditionsgeschichtliche Untersuchungen zur paulinischen Pneumatologie*, 85-106. Van Gorcum's Theologische Bibliotheek 47. Assen: Van Gorcum, 1973.

Vouga, François. "La construction de l'histoire en Galates 3-4." *ZNW* 75 (1984) 259-69.

____. "Zur rhetorischen Gattung des Galaterbriefes." *ZNW* 79 (1988) 291-92.

Wallace, Daniel B. "Galatians 3:19-20: A *crux interpretum* for Paul's View of the Law." *WTJ* 52 (1990) 225-45.

Walter, Nikolaus. "Paulus und die Gegner des Christusevangeliums in Galatien." In *L'Apôtre Paul: Personnalité, style et conception du ministère*, edited by Albert Vanhoye, 351-56. BETL 73. Leuven: Leuven University Press, 1986.

Wanamaker, C. A. "A Case Against Justification by Faith." *Journal of Theology for Southern Africa* 42 (1983) 37-49.

Watson, F. *Paul, Judaism and the Gentiles. A Sociological Approach*. SNTSMS 56. Cambridge: Cambridge University Press, 1986.

Weiss, B. "Die Sorge, vergebens zu laufen [Gal 2:2]." *Geist und Leben* 44 (1971) 85-92.

Wenham, David. "Paul's Use of the Jesus Tradition: Three Samples." In *The Jesus Tradition Outside the Gospels*, edited by David Wenham, 7-37. Sheffield: JSOT, 1985.

Westerholm, Stephen. "'Letter' and 'Spirit': The Foundation of Pauline Ethics." *NTS* 30 (1984) 229-48.

____. "On Fulfilling the Whole Law (Gal 5.14)." *SEÅ* 51-52 (1986-87) 229-37.

Whiteley, D. E. H. "Galatians: Then and Now." In *Studia Evangelica*, vol. 6, edited by E. Livingstone, 619-27. TU 112. Berlin: Akademie, 1973.

Wilckens, Ulrich. "Die Bekehrung des Paulus als religionsgeschichtliches Problem." *ZTK* 56 (1959) 273-93.

____. "Was heisst bei Paulus: 'Aus Werken des Gesetzes wird kein Mensch gerecht'?" In *Rechtfertigung als Freiheit: Paulusstudien*, 77-109. Neukirchen-Vluyn: Neukirchener Verlag, 1974.

____. "Zur Entwicklung des paulinischen Gesetzesverständnis." *NTS* 28 (1982) 154-90.

Wilcox, Max. "'Upon the Tree'–Deut 21:22-23 in the New Testament [Gal 3:13]." *JBL* 96 (1977) 85-99.

____. "The Promise of the 'Seed' in the New Testament and the Targumim." *JSNT* 5 (1979) 2-20.

Williams, Sam K. "Justification and the Spirit in Galatians." *JSNT* 29 (1987) 91-100.

____. "*Promise* in Galatians: A Reading of Paul's Reading of Scripture." *JBL* 107 (1988) 709-20.

____. "The Hearing of Faith: *akoē pisteōs* in Galatians 3." *NTS* 35 (1989) 82-93.

Wilson, Robert McL. "Gnostics–in Galatia?" In *Studia Evangelica*, vol. 4, edited by Frank L. Cross, 358-67. TU 102. Berlin: Akademie, 1968.

Winger, Joseph Michael. *By What Law? The Meaning of Nómos in the Letters of Paul*. SBLDS 128. Atlanta: Scholars Press, 1992.

Wink, Walter. "The 'Elements of the Universe' in Biblical and Scientific Perspective." *Zygon* 13 (1978) 225-53.

Wire, Antoinette C. "*Not* Male and Female." *Pacific Theological Review* 19 (1986) 37-43.

Witherington, Ben. "Rite and Rights for Women: Galatians 3:28." *NTS* 27 (1981) 593-604.

Wuellner, Wilhelm H. "Toposforschung und Torahinterpretation bei Paulus und Jesus." *NTS* 24 (1978) 463-83.

Yates, Roy. "Saint Paul and the Law in Galatians." *ITQ* 51 (1985) 105-24.

Young, E. M. "'Fulfill the Law of Christ'. An Examination of Galatians 6:2." *Studia Biblica et Theologica* 7 (1977) 31-42.

Young, Norman Y. "*Paidagōgos*: The Social Setting of a Pauline Metaphor." *NovT* 29 (1987) 150-76.

Zahn, Theodor. *Der Brief des Paulus an die Galater*, with a Preface by Martin Hengel. Wuppertal: Brockhaus, 1990 (original, Kommentar zum neuen Testament 9, 3rd ed. [Leipzig: A. Deichert, 1922]).

Zerwick, Maximilian. *Der Brief an die Galater*. Die Welt der Bibel: Kleinkommentare zur Heiligen Schrift 2. Düsseldorf: Patmos, 1964.

Ziesler, J. A. "Galatians." In *The Meaning of Righteousness in Paul: A Linguistic and Theological Enquiry*, 172-85. Cambridge: Cambridge University Press, 1972.

Index of Biblical References

*(The numbers are those of the New Revised Standard Version.
Primary references are in boldface.)*

Genesis
1–2	84
1:14	85, 124
12:3	59–60
12:7	69
13:15	69
14:18–20	91
15	69
15:6	**55, 57,** 58–61, 66, 68–69, 81, 89, 130
15:13	70
15:18	68
16:1	89–90
16:2	90
16:4	89
16:15–16	89
17	69, 89, 92, 96
17:1–14	69
17:10–11	65
17:11	122
17:15–22	89
17:23	90
17:23–27	69, 89
18:18	59–60
21:1–21	89
21:4	69, 89
21:9	92
21:10	92
21:12–13	90
21:12–21	90
22	69
22:1–19	57
23:17–18	69
25:1–2	89
25:6, 9, 18	90
26:5	56
27	70

Exodus
4:24–26	96
12:40	70
19:1	70
25:9	91

Leviticus
17–26	62
18:5	59, 61–62, 96
19:2	103
19:17	103
19:18	97, 103–4
19:34	103
26	**62–63**

Deuteronomy
6:5	103
10:17	37, 39
12–28	63
21:23	59, 61
23:1	98
27:15–26	60
27:26	59, 60–61, 96
28–30	**62–64**
28:36, 49–65	63
28:62	70
29:1	63
29:2–29	64
30:5	70
33:2	71

2 Samuel
7:16	131

1 Chronicles
5:10, 19–20	90

Psalms
2:7	30
24	56
72	30, 63, 131
83:6	90
125:5	122
128:6	122
137	41
143:2	46, 47

Isaiah
52:7	29
54:1	87, 92

Jeremiah
1:5	29
7:9	108
9:24	121
31:31–34	93

Ezekiel
18; 18:9	56
40–48	91

Hosea
4:1	108

Habakkuk
2:4	56, 59, 61

Index of Biblical References

Wisdom
2:1–20	130
2:16	80
5:1–23	130

Sirach
32:16	39
44:19–21	**57, 66**

1 Maccabees
2:50–52	**58**

Matthew
1:1	69
3:9	56
5:44–45	103, 104
6:9	81
7:12	103
15:19	108
16:17–19	33
22:7	91

Mark
1:19–20	40
3:17	40
7:21–22	108
12:28–34	103
14:36	80

Luke
3:8	56
6:27, 35	103, 104
6:31	103
11:2	81

John
1:41–42	33, 129
3:16–17	80
4:25	129
13:34–35	104
15:12–17	104
21:15–17	33
21:18–19	45
21:23	40

Acts
1:8	20
1:21–22	9
4:36–37	23
5:34	21
6:1–7	23, 132
6:8–15	23
6:14	23
7:53	71
7:54–8:3	23
7:58	21
8:3	21
9:1–19a	18
9:2	22
9:15	18
9:20, 22	18
9:25–26	22

9:27	23
9:29	18, 23
9:30	23
11:20	23
11:25–26	23
11:26	18, 23
11:27–30	25
11:28–29, 30	24
12:2	40
12:17	33
12:25	24
13–14	23
13:13	25
13:14, 42	40
13:46	18, 23–24
14:1	40
14:4, 14	9
15:1	24
15:1–35	24, 38
15:4	24
15:5	39
15:12	24
15:13	33
15:22	25
15:23	7, 24
15:23–29	25
15:36–39	25
15:40	39
15:41	24
16:3	25, 39
16:6	25
16:19–40	26
16:37	21
18:2	26
18:3	21
18:12	26
18:18–23	2, 26, 86
18:22	45
18:23	25
18:24	126
19:1	126
19:1–7	10
20:4	41
21:18	33
21:24, 26	25
21:39	21
22:3–16	18
22:3, 4	21
22:5	22
22:17–21	18
22:28	21
23:26	7
23:34	21
26:9, 10	21
26:10–12	22
26:9–20	18
26:16–18	18

Romans
1:1–7	7
1:3–4	30
1:8	100

1:9	30
1:13	26
1:14	76
1:17	30
1:29–31	108
2:21–25	125
3:20–22	46
3:21	53
3:22–23	83, 97
3:25	93, 131
3:28	46
4	58
4:11	66, 90, 122
4:12	115
4:23–25	60, 69
4:24	8
5–8	4, 72, 98
5:20	71
6:1–11	75
6:10	48
7	4, 112
7:1–2, 6	48
7:7	111
7:7–8	107
7:7–11	72
7:7–25	105
7:8–12	102
7:12, 14	98
7:15, 23	107
8:2	99, 116
8:3, 15	80
8:3–4	128
9–11	4, 122
9:4	93, 122
9:15	72
10:4	80
10:5, 19	72
11:27	93
12:1–15:13	100
13:8–10	104
13:13	108
13:14	75
14:17	111
15:13	111
15:22	26
15:25–26	127
15:26	3, 24, 41
15:27	117
15:31	42, 127
15:33	122
16:20	122
16:22	119

1 Corinthians
1:4, 10	100
1:14–17	75
1:18	130
1:23	52, 98
1:24	52
1:30	30
1:31	121
2:4	53

2:8	121	10:1	100	2:7	128
3:6	126	10:17	121	2:11	121, 129
3:11, 16	40	11:7	117	3:2	98
4:6	126	11:8–9	117	3:4–11	18
4:15	87	11:13	9	3:5	21, 39
4:20	111	11:22	21, 69	3:6	21, 47
5:6	97	11:23–27	122	3:16	115
5:10–11	108	11:32–33	22	4:2	100
6:9	117	12:1	17, 38	4:8	108
6:9–10	108, 111	12:7	38, 86	4:10–20	41, 117
7	76–77	12:20–21	108	4:23	122
7:1	76	13:4	48, 86		
7:17–24	**76**	13:13	122	**Colossians**	
7:19	97			2:16	124
7:29	77	**Galatians**		2:17–23	85
8:1–13	109	1:11–12	19	3:5–8	108
8:2–3	83	1:11–16	4, 46	3:5–4:6	100
8:5–6	84, 130–31	1:14	46	3:11	76
9:1	18	1:16	18, 80	3:12–15	108
9:5	45	1:17	4	4:10	24
9:5–6	38	1:20	3, 20–21	4:18	120
9:7–14	117	1:21	4, 23		
9:9	72	2:4	125, 127	**1 Thessalonians**	
9:12, 15	117	2:5, 14	20	1:1	7
9:19–21	76	2:9	33	1:2	100
9:21	86	2:9–10	132	1:9b	83
10:18	122	2:15–21	17, 19, 20	4:1	100
11:3	76	2:19–20	128	4:5	83
11:17–34	44	2:20	30, 65, 74, 75, 77,	5:28	122
11:25	93		78, 80, 95, 104, 105,		
12–14	52		107, 112, 115, 116,	**2 Thessalonians**	
12:13	76		128, 129, 131	3:17	120
13	104	3:1	3, 14, 26		
13:4, 5	111	3:13–14	128	**Philemon**	
13:12	83	3:19	12, 99	4, 9	100
14:6, 26	38	3:22	83	10	87
14:33–36	76	3:23	18, 30	19	119
15:1	16	3:23–24	46	25	122
15:1ff.	17, 19	3:27	3, 52		
15:3b-5	132	3:28	76	**Hebrews**	
15:5, 7	33	4:3, 9	3, 115, 121, 124	6:12–20	58
15:8	18	4:4, 5, 6	30, 128	7:1–10	91
15:9	21	4:10	3, 121, 124	11:8–19	58
15:11	38–39, 132	4:13	3, 52		
15:33	117	4:13–14	12, 52	**James**	
15:50	111	4:13–15	26, 73	1:1	7
16:1	2, 3, 24, 41, 117	4:16	6	2:8	104
16:2	85	4:21–3133, 39, 41, 53, 125		2:14–26	49
16:12	126	5:1	2, 39	2:21–23	57–58
16:21	119	5:13	39	2:21–24	56
16:22	12, 81	6:11–18	1, 2, 14		
16:23	122	6:12–13	3	**1 John**	
				2:28–4:21	104
				5:2	104
2 Corinthians		**Ephesians**			
1:3	100	4:1–6:20	100	**2 John**	
3:7–18	72, 93	4:2, 31, 32	108	5	104
4:5	46	4:24	75		
5:17	121	5:3–5, 9	108	**Revelation**	
5:21	30, 128			1:10	85
6:6	108	**Philippians**			
7:12	86	1:3	100		
8–9	3, 24	2:6–8	95		

Index of Names and Subjects

(Primary references are in boldface.)

Abraham, 2, **53, 55–61, 63–70, 72,** 78, 81, 85, 87–92, 96, 98–99, 125, 132
Achaia, 2, 26
Aegean, 2–3, 40–41, 120, 126–27
Ananias, 18
Andrew, 40
Angel, 12, 71–72, 85–86, 97, 125
Antioch, 2, 14, 15, 23–27, 38, 40–45, 48–49, 51, 81, 86, 126–27 132–33
Apocalypticism, 17–18, 64, 132
Apollos, 3, 126
Apostle, **8–9,** 12, 16, 18, 21–23, 31–34, 39, 46, 99, 127
Arabia, 4, 22, 26, 32, 38, 90
Asia Minor, 1, 2, 10, 20–21, 25, 45, 126, 128
Athens, 26
Baptism, 3, 39, 52, 75–76, 124
Barnabas, 23–27, 38, 44–45, 49
Biography, 4, 14–15, 18–19, 21, 26, 50, 59, 99, 127, 134
Blessing, 53, **56–57, 59–65,** 69–70, 72, 74, 81, 85, 93, 95, 97–9 121, 128, 130, 132–34
Cephas (Simon Peter), 9, 21–27, **31–33, 38–40, 44–45,** 48–49, 12
Christianity, 4–5, 13, 21, 39, 84, 96, 109, 120, 123, 126, 133
Christology, 13, 30, 46–49, 53, 65, 73, 77, 93, 99, 104, 108, 121, 125, 128–134
Christ (Messiah), 2, 4, 6, 8–10, 12–13, 15, 17–19, 24, 26, 29, 36, 40, 45–49, 51–52, 59–62, 65, 69–75, 77–78, 80–81, 85, 93, 95–97, 100, 104–5, 113, 116, 118, **120–21, 124–25, 127–33**

Church, 9, 21–22, 26, 33, 39–42, 44–45, 49, 52, 75, 78, 85, 87, 92, 97, 103–4, 118, 129–30, 133–34
Cilicia, 4, 21, 23, 25–26, 35, 38, 40, 51, 126
Circumcision, 2–3, 13, 24–25, 39–40, 45–46, 54, 57–58, 65–66, 76, 77, 89–90, **94–98,** 120–26, 132
Confession (creed), 31, 47, 56, 64–65, 77, 85, 99, 108, 117–18, 121, 128, 133
Conversion, 9, 13, **18–23,** 26, 28–29, 38, 46, 48–50, 53, 63, 65, 77, 82–83, 90, 102, 106, 112, 124, 134
Corinth, 2, 3, 26, 38, 75–77, 86, 133
Covenant, 57–58, 62–66, 68–70, 79, 89–91, 93, 96, 98, 103, 122
Creation, 85, 121, 124, 131, 134
Curse, 12–13, 41, 48, 52–53, **59–65,** 69–72, 74, 78, 80–81, 92–96–98, 104, 122, 128, 133
Cyprus, 23–25
Damascus, 4, 9, 13, 18–22, 26, 29–30, 32, 34, 46–47, 49–51, 54, 65, 74, 127, 134
David, 30, 131
Death, 47–48, 53, 62, 65, 72, 81, 95, 98–99, 116, 128, 131, 133
Early Christianity, 23, 30, 55, 76–77, 108, 126, 128–29, 131–33
Elements/elemental spirits, 80, 83–85, 102, 115, 121, 124–25
Ephesus, 2–3, 10
Ethics, 14, 84, 95, 100–101, 104, 106–9, **112–13, 115–18,** 121, 125, 132–33
Experience, 46–48, 50, 52–53, 56–57, 64–

65, 73, 77, 84–85, 93, 98–99, 118, 124–26, 130–34

Faith, 1–2, 4, 6, 13, 15–17, 19–20, 29–30, 35–36, 39, 43–48, 52–53, 55–62, 64–67, 69–70, 72, 74–75, 78–81, 86, 88–89, 91–93, 95–99, 102, 104–8, 111–13, 115–16, 118, 121, 125, 12

Flesh, 30, 48, 53, 57, 59, 72, 81, 92–93, 98, 100–102, 106–7, 111–12, 115–17, 120–21, 128

Freedom, 2, 6, 14, 22, 31, 39, 42, 61, 76–77, 88, 93, **94–95, 97–98,** 100–104, 107, 113, 116, 121, 128

Fruit of the Spirit, **107–8, 111–12**

Galatia/Galatians, 1–4, 6, 8–15, 20, 23–28, 31, 33–35, 38–39, 41–42, 44, 49, 51–54, 56, 62, 65–66, 68–69, 72, 75, 77, 79–87, 89–92, 94–97, 99–102, 106, 111–12, 115–17, 119–30, 132–34

Gentiles, 18, 22–23, 29–32, 38–41, 45–46, 48–49, 56, 58–61, 65, 75–76, 83, 98–99, 103, 122, 126, 131–32

Gentile Christians/Christianity, 3, 21, 23–25, 27, 39–42, 44–45, 49, 60, 75, 83, 92, 98, 124, 126–27, 132

Gentile mission, 18, 22–26, 34–35, 38, 40–41, 49, 96

Gospel, 1–5, **8–20,** 26, 28–31, 33–34, 36, 38–46, 49–54, 59–61, 65, 69, 75–78, 83–87, 89–92, 94, 97–100, 102–3, 110, 116, 118, 120, 122–24, 127–29, 132–34

Grace, 8, 12, 48, 62

Greece, 2, 20, 26, 45

Hagar, 88–93

Ignatius of Antioch, 45

Isaac, 57–58, 69, 89–92

Ishmael, 69, 89–92

Israel, 4, 30, 56, 60, 63–64, 69–70, 72, 89, 91–92, 96, 103, 109, 122, 130, 132

James (brother of Jesus), 22–26, **32–33, 38, 40, 44,** 49

James (son of Zebedee), 40

Jerusalem, 2–4, 14, 17–18, 20–27, 31–35, 38–42, 44–45, 49, 51, 53, 63, 86, 88, 90–93, 116, 120, 124–27, 131–32

Jesus, 9, 13, 17–18, 22, 30, 32, 40, 46–48, 52, 60, 69, 73–75, 85–86, 104, 111, 122, 128–31

Jewish Christians/Christianity, 23–25, 27, 39–42, 44, 49, 60, 75, 83, 92, 98, 126–27, 132

Jewish Mission, 41

Jews/Judaism, 10, 17–19, 21–24, 26, 30–31, 38–41, 44, 46–50, 52–53, 55–58, 61, 64, 66, 69–72, 75–77, 81, 83–85, 89, 91–93, 95–99, 101–4, 108–9, 111–12, 120–22, 126, 129–33

John (son of Zebedee), 24, **40**

John Mark, 23–25

Josephus, 33, 70

Justification, 6, 19–20, 30, 46–47, 59, 66, 75, 78, 80, 90, 100, 112–13, 116, 118, 134

Justification, doctrine of, 45, 48, 134

Law, 1–4, 6, 13–15, 17–20, 22–26, 28–31, 39–42, **43–49, 52–75,** 77, 79–81, 83–86, 88–109, 111–12, 115–17, 120–22, 124–34

Law of Christ, **116,** 125

Life, 2, 14, 46–48, 53, 56–57, 61–62, 65, 72, 74, 81, 85, 95, 98–99, 101, 115–18, 121, 128, 130–32, 134

Lord, **120–22,** 129–30

Love, 14, 97–98, 102–4, 107–8, 111–13, 115, 118, 121, 128

Love commandment, 97, **100–104, 107,** 111–12, 115–17

Luke, 2–3, 9, 18, 20–26, 31, 35, 38–39, 77

Macedonia, 2, 26

Melchizidek, 91

Messiah. See Christ

Mission, 9–10, 26–27, 35, 40–41, 76–77, 124, 126–27, 129–31, 133–34

Moses, 28, 46, 63–64, **70–72,** 90–91, 93, 99

Onesimus, 77

Peter. See Cephas

Pharisee(s), 21–22, 26, 28, 39, 46–47, 96

Philippi, 2, 26, 41, 133

Philo of Alexandria, 58, 85, 89

Prayer, 52

Proclamation/preaching, 4, 9, 26, 29, 35, 38, 46, 49–54, 56, 58–59, 62, 65, 75–76, 86, 97–99, 102, 111–12, 125, 130–34

Promise, 2, 4, 46–48, 53, 56–58, 60–70, 72–73, 78–79, 81, 84–86, 89–93, 96–99, 101, 103–4, 107, 117, 121–22, 125, 130–34

Religion, 83, 110, 120, 124

Revelation, 12, **17–19,** 30, 38, 74, 80, 99, 117, 134

Righteousness, 6, 19, 30, **45–48,** 53, 55–61, 63, 65–66, 70, 72, 74–75, 80–81, 85, 95–98, 101, 103–4, 111, 118, 128, 130–34

Rome, 2–3, 20, 26–27, 45, 72, 120

Salvation, 12–13, 19, 128–29

Sarah, 88–92

Silas/Silvanus, 25–27, 39

Sin, 4, 48, 53, 72, 74, 81, 83, 95, 98–99, 102, 107, 112, 116, 118, 128, 131, 133

Sinai, 46, 53, 58, 70–71, 73, 84–85, 90–91, 93, 96, 116, 124

Slavery (enslavement), 39, 61, 80–81, 88, 90, 92–93, 95, 98, 102–3, 128

Son (of God), **29–31,** 35–36, 48–49, 52–53, 60, 62, 74–75, 80, 115–16, 129–31

Spirit, 1–2, 14, 25, 30, 52–53, 55, 59, 61–62, 66, 72, 75, 80–81, 96, 98–100,

102, **106–8,** 112, 115–17, 120–21,
125, 128
Stephen, 21–23
Syria, 4, 20, 23, 25–26, 35, 38, 40, 126
Tarsus, 21, 23
Testament. See Covenant
Theology, 6, 13, 19, 45, 99, 123–26, 132,
134
Thessalonica, 2, 26, 133
Timothy, 25, 27, 39
Titus, 24–27, 38–39, 44, 124
Tradition, 16–19, 28–30, 40, 45–46, 50,
52–53, 56, 60, 64, 66, 69–72, 84–85,
89–93, 97, 101–2, 104, 108–9, 111,
118, 121–22, 125, 129–33
Truth, 9, 38–39, 44, 51, 53, 86, 97, 108,
118
Vision, 17–19, 38
Will. See Covenant
Wisdom theology, 64, 133
Works of the flesh, **107–10**
Works of the law. See Law
Zion, 41